Thriving in the
COMMUNITY COLLEGE
and Beyond

A Customized Textbook for Anoka Ramsey Community College

Kendall Hunt
publishing company

ANOKA-RAMSEY
COMMUNITY COLLEGE

Brief Contents

Chapter 1

WELCOME TO ANOKA-RAMSEY COMMUNITY
COLLEGE   1

Chapter 2

COLLEGE KNOWLEDGE   29

Chapter 3

STRENGTHS AND MAKING CONNECTIONS:
FOUR STEPS TO YOUR SUCCESS   51

Chapter 4

TIME MANAGEMENT   81

Chapter 5

GOAL SETTING AND MOTIVATION   109

Chapter 6

HIGHER-LEVEL THINKING   135

Chapter 7

DIVERSITY AND THE COMMUNITY COLLEGE
EXPERIENCE   165

Chapter 8

DEEP LEARNING: STRATEGIC NOTE-TAKING,
READING, AND STUDYING   211

Chapter 9

TEST-TAKING SKILLS AND STRATEGIES   251

Contents

Preface   ix
Introduction   xvii

Chapter 1: Welcome To Anoka-Ramsey Community College   1

The Jargon of College   1
Where Do I Go?   4
Records & Registration Office   4
Academic Advising Center   4
Financial Aid Office   4
Counseling Services   5
Campus Security & Safety   5
Career Center   5
College Bookstore   5
Business Office   5
Academic Support Center   5
Math Skills Center   5
Adult Basic Education (ABE)   5
Institutional Advancement Office   6
TRIO Student Support Services (SSS)   6
Student Life & Athletics   6
Library   6
Testing Center   6
Disability Services   6
Veteran Services   6
Activate Your Anoka-Ramsey Student Technology Services!   6
Tips for Success in College   7
The Basics   7
Use Your Resources!   8
Outside the Classroom   8
Student Checklist   8
Before Classes Begin   8
Each Semester   9
Every Year   9
As Needed   9
Student Resources   10
Academic Advising   10
Academic Departments   10
Academic Support Centers   11
Math Skills Center   11
Writing Services   11
TRIO Student Support Services   11
Career Services Office   11
Counseling Services   12
Students with Disabilities   12
English Language Learners   12
Libraries   12
Office of Diversity & Multicultural Affairs   13
Testing Services   13

Veterans Services   13
Safety & Transportation   13
Technology Services   14
D2L Brightspace (D2L) Account   16
Step-by-Step Registration Process   16
Understanding the Different Course Offerings   16
How to Register Guide: 16
Online Resources at ARCC   19
D2L Brightspace   19
Activating a STAR ID: 19
STAR ID Self Service   21
To install Office 2016 on your personal device   22
How to log on to your college email account for the first time   24

Chapter 2: College Knowledge
EFFECTIVE COLLEGE BEHAVIOR IN CLASS AND ONLINE   29

Top Tips for Academic Success   31
The Importance of Time Spent on Coursework outside of Class   36
Effective Classroom Behavior: The Fundamentals   37
How to E-mail (or not) your Instructor   40
An example of what not to do: 40
An example of an appropriate e-mail: 40
Chapter Summary and Highlights   41
Learning More through the World Wide Web: Internet-Based Resources   43
References   43
Chapter 2 Exercises   45

Chapter 3: Strengths and Making Connections: Four Steps to Your Success
USING POWERFUL PRINCIPLES OF STUDENT SUCCESS AND KEY CAMPUS RESOURCES   51

What Is StrengthsQuest?   52
Four Steps to College Success   52
First Step of College Success: Active Involvement (Engagement)   53
Active Involvement in the Learning Process   53
Active Listening and Note Taking in Class   53
Active Class Participation   56
Active Reading   56
Second Step for College Success: Capitalizing on Campus Resources (Resourcefulness)   58
Academic Support Services   58
Disability Services (a.k.a. Office for Students with Special Needs)   59

College Library   59
Academic Advisement   59
Student Development Services   60
Financial Aid   61
Counseling Center   61
Third Step for College Success: Interpersonal Interaction
    and Collaboration (Social Integration)   61
    Interacting with Faculty Members   62
    Interacting with Academic Advisors   64
    Interaction with Peers (Student–Student Interaction)   64
    Collaborative Learning   66
Fourth Step for College Success: Reflection and Self-
    Awareness (Mindfulness)   68
    Self-Awareness   69
    Self-Monitoring   69
    Self-Assessment   70
Chapter Summary and Highlights   70
    A Checklist of Success Promoting Principles and
        Practices   70
Learning More through the World Wide Web: Internet-Based
    Resources   72
References   72
Chapter 3 Exercises   75

Chapter 4: Time Management

PRIORITIZING TASKS, PREVENTING PROCRASTINATION,
AND PROMOTING PRODUCTIVITY   81

The Importance of Time Management   81
Strategies for Managing Time and Tasks   83
Creating a Time-Management Plan   86
Dealing with Procrastination   92
Myths That Promote Procrastination   93
    Psychological Causes of Procrastination   93
Strategies for Preventing and Overcoming
    Procrastination   95
Chapter Summary and Highlights   98
Learning More through the World Wide
    Web: Internet-Based Resources   99
References   99
Chapter 4 Exercises   101

Chapter 5: Goal Setting and Motivation

MOVING FROM INTENTION TO ACTION   109

The Relationship between Goal Setting and Success   109
Characteristics of a Well-Designed Goal   110
Characteristics of Successful People   116
    Internal Locus of Control   116
    Self-Efficacy   117
Grit   118
Growth Mindset   122
Chapter Summary and Highlights   124
Learning More through the World Wide Web: Internet-
    Based Resources   125
References   126
Chapter 5 Exercises   128

Chapter 6: Higher-Level Thinking

MOVING BEYOND BASIC KNOWLEDGE TO CRITICAL
AND CREATIVE THINKING   135

What Is Higher-Level Thinking?   135
Defining and Describing the Major Forms of Higher-Level
    Thinking   136
    Analysis (Analytical Thinking)   137
    Synthesis (Integrative Thinking)   138
    Application (Applied Thinking)   138
    Multidimensional Thinking   139
    Balanced Thinking   140
    Critical Thinking (Evaluation)   142
    Creative Thinking   148
Using Higher-Level Thinking Skills to Improve Academic
    Performance   150
Strategies for Increasing Creativity   154
Chapter Summary and Highlights   156
Learning More through the World Wide Web: Internet-
    Based Resources   158
References   158
Chapter 6 Exercises   160

Chapter 7: Diversity and the Community College Experience

LEARNING ABOUT AND FROM HUMAN
DIFFERENCES   165

What Is Diversity?   165
What Is Racial Diversity?   167
What Is Cultural Diversity?   170
What Is an Ethnic Group?   171
The Relationship between Diversity and Humanity   172
What Is Individuality?   175
Major Forms or Types of Diversity in Today's World   175
    Ethnic and Racial Diversity   175
    Socioeconomic Diversity   178
    International Diversity   179
    Generational Diversity   179
    Sexual Diversity: LGBT, LGBTQ, LGBTQA, TBL   181
The Benefits of Experiencing Diversity   183
    Diversity Increases Self-Awareness and Self-
        Knowledge   183
    Diversity Deepens Learning   183
    Diversity Promotes Critical Thinking   184
    Diversity Stimulates Creative Thinking   184
    Diversity Enhances Career Preparation and Career
        Success   185
Overcoming Barriers to Diversity   186
    Ethnocentrism   186
    Stereotyping   187
    Prejudice   189
    Discrimination   191
Strategies for Overcoming Stereotypes and Prejudices   193
Chapter Summary and Highlights   199
Learning More through the World Wide Web:
    Internet-Based Resources   200

References   200
Chapter 7 Exercises   204

Chapter 8: Deep Learning

STRATEGIC NOTE-TAKING, READING, AND
STUDYING   211

What Is Deep Learning?   212
Stages in the Learning and Memory Process   212
Effective Lecture-Listening and Note-Taking
    Strategies   213
Pre-Lecture Strategies: What to Do *Before* Class   214
Listening and Note-Taking Strategies: What to Do *During*
    Class   215
Post-Lecture Strategies: What to Do *After* Class   217
Strategic Reading   219
    Pre-Reading Strategies: What to Do *Before* Reading   220
    Strategies to Use *During* the Reading Process   221
    Post-Reading Strategies: What to Do *After* Reading   223
Strategic Studying: Learning Deeply and Remembering
    Longer   226
    Give Studying Your Undivided Attention   226
Make Meaningful Associations   228
    Integrate Information from Lectures and Readings   229
    Distribute Study Time across Separate Study Sessions   230
    Use the "Part-to-Whole" Study Method   231
    Capitalize on the Power of Visual Learning   232
    Build Variety into the Study Process   233
    Learning Styles: Identifying Your Learning
        Preferences   234
    Learn with Emotion   237
    Learn Collaboratively   237

Self-Monitor: Reflect on What you're Learning and Assess
    Whether you're Learning it Deeply   238
Chapter Summary and Highlights   240
Learning More through the World Wide Web:
    Internet-Based Resources   241
References   241
Chapter 8 Exercises   244

Chapter 9: Test-Taking Skills and Strategies

WHAT TO DO BEFORE, DURING, AND AFTER
TESTS   251

Pre-Test Strategies: What to Do *in Advance* of Tests   252
    Recitation   252
    Creating Retrieval Cues   253
Strategies to Use *Immediately Before* a Test   254
Strategies to Use *During* Tests   257
Strategies for Answering Multiple-Choice Test
    Questions   258
Strategies for Answering Essay Questions   261
Strategies for Online Tests   264
Post-Test Strategies: What to Do *After* Receiving Your Test
    Results   265
Strategies for Reducing Test Anxiety   268
Chapter Summary and Highlights   270
Learning More through the World Wide Web: Internet-
    Based Resources   271
References   271
Chapter 9 Exercises   273

Preface

WELCOME TO OUR BOOK

Plan and Purpose of This Book

This book is designed to help you make a smooth transition to college as well as equip you with strategies for success that you can use throughout college and beyond. Its aim is to promote the academic excellence and personal development of all students—whether you're a student who is (a) transitioning to college directly from high school or from a full-time or part-time job, (b) living on or off campus, or (c) attending college on a full-time or part-time basis. Whatever your previous educational record may have been, college is a new ball game played on a different field with different rules and expectations. If you haven't been a particularly successful student in the past, this book will help you become a successful student in the future. If you have been a successful student in high school, this book will make you an even stronger student in college.

One of the book's major goals is to help you put into practice a powerful principle of human learning and personal success: *mindfulness*. When you're mindful, you're aware of *what* you're doing and *if* you're doing it in the most effective way. Mindfulness or self-awareness is the critical first step toward self-improvement and success in any aspect of your life. If you develop the habit of remaining aware of whether you're "doing college" strategically (e.g., by using the key strategies identified in this book), you will have taken a huge step toward college success.

Rather than trying to figure out how to do college on your own through random trial-and- error, this book gives you a game plan for getting it right from the start and an inside track for getting off to a fast start. Its plan is built on a solid foundation of research that equips you with a comprehensive set of well-documented strategies for doing college successfully.

Specific action strategies make up the heart of this book. You will find that these practical strategies aren't presented simply as a laundry list of what-to-do tips dispensed by authority figures who think they know what's best for you. Instead, the recommendations are accompanied by evidence-based reasons for *why* they're effective and they're organized into broader *principles* that tie the strategies together into a meaningful plan. It's not only important for you to know *what* to do, but also *why* to do it. If you understand the reason behind a suggested strategy, you're more likely to take that strategy seriously and implement it effectively.

When specific strategies are organized into general principles, they become more powerful because you're able to see how the same principle may be generalized and applied across different subjects and situations. Understanding the key principles that underlie effective strategies also empowers you to create additional strategies of your own that follow or flow from the same general principle. This promotes deeper, more powerful learning than simply collecting a bunch of tips about what you should or shouldn't do in college. We believe that you're ready and able to meet the challenge of deeper learning.

Since the strategies cited in this book are research-based, you'll find references cited regularly throughout all the chapters and a sizable reference section at the end of each chapter. Your professors will expect you to think critically and support

> More than 30 years of research has shown that mindfulness is figuratively and literally enlivening. It's the way you feel when you're feeling passionate."
>
> *—Dr. Ellen Langer, Harvard University, mindfulness researcher and author of* The Power of Mindful Learning

> Important achievements require a clear focus, all-out-effort, and a bottomless trunk full of strategies."
>
> *—Carol Dweck, Stanford professor, and author of* Mindset: The New Psychology of Success

> The man who also knows why will be his own boss. As to methods there may be a million and then some, but principles are few. The man who grasps principles can successfully select his own methods. The man who tries methods, ignoring principles, is sure to have trouble."
>
> *—Ralph Waldo Emerson, 19th-century author, poet, and philosopher*

your ideas with evidence. As authors, we should do the same and model that behavior for you.

You will find that the references cited represent a balanced blend of older, "classic" studies and more recent "cutting edge" research from a variety of fields. The time span of references cited serves to highlight the long-standing relevance of the ideas presented and their power to withstand the test of time. It also underscores the fact that the subject of success in college and beyond, like any other academic subject in the college curriculum, rests on a solid body of research and scholarship that spans multiple decades.

Preview of Content

Chapter 1

Welcome to Anoka-Ramsey Community College
Effective College Behavior In Class and Online

This chapter identifies needed information fo all students entering college for the first time.

Chapter 2

College Knowledge
Effective College Behavior In Class and Online

This chapter identifies top tips for academic success you can implement immediately, including what to do inside and outside the classroom. It also alerts you to in-class and out-of-class behavior that should be avoided in college.

Chapter 3

Strengths and Making Connections: Four Steps to College Success
Using Powerful Student-Success Principles & Key Campus Resources

This chapter focuses on the "big picture"—the most powerful principles you can implement to promote your own success and the key campus resources you can to use to help you succeed. It describes *what* these key principles and resources are, *why* they're effective, and *how* to capitalize on them.

Chapter 4

Time Management
Prioritizing Tasks, Preventing Procrastination, and Promoting Productivity

Time is a valuable personal resource—if you gain greater control of it, you gain greater control of your life. Time managed well not only enables you to get work done in a timely manner, it also enables you to set and attain personal priorities and maintain balance in your life. This chapter offers a comprehensive set of strategies for managing time, combating procrastination, and ensuring that you spend time in a way that aligns with your educational goals and priorities.

Chapter 5

Goal Setting and Motivation
Moving from Intention to Action

The path to personal success begins with goals and finding the means (succession of steps) to reach those goals. People who set specific goals are more likely to succeed

> " I could really relate to everything we talked about. It is a great class because you can use it in your other classes."

> " Everything we learned we will apply in our lives."

> " This is the only course I've ever taken that was about me."
> —*Comments made by students when evaluating their first-year experience course*

> " In high school, a lot of the work was done while in school, but in college all of your work is done on your time. You really have to organize yourself in order to get everything done."
> —*First-year student's response to a question about what was most surprising about college life*

than people who simply tell themselves they're going to try hard and do their best. This chapter lays out the key steps involved in the process of setting effective goals, identifies key self-motivational strategies for staying on track and sustaining progress toward our goals, and describes how personal qualities such as self-efficacy, grit, and growth mindset are essential for achieving goals.

Chapter 6
Higher-Level Thinking
Moving Beyond Basic Knowledge to Critical and Creative Thinking

National surveys consistently show that the primary goal of college faculty is teaching students how to think critically. This chapter will help you understand what critical thinking is and empower you to think critically and creatively. You will acquire thinking strategies that move you beyond memorization to higher levels of thought and learn ways to demonstrate higher-level thinking on college tests and assignments.

Chapter 7
Diversity and the Community College Experience
Learning about and from Human Differences

This chapter clarifies what "diversity" really means and demonstrates how experiencing diversity can deepen learning, promote critical and creative thinking, and contribute to your personal and professional development. Strategies are provided for overcoming cultural barriers and biases that block our development of rewarding relationships with diverse people and learning from others whose cultural backgrounds differ from our own. Simply stated, we learn more from people who are different from us than we do from people similar to us. There's more diversity among college students today than at any other time in history. This chapter will help you capitalize on this learning opportunity.

Chapter 8
Deep Learning
Strategic Note-Taking, Reading, and Studying

This chapter helps you apply research on human learning and the human brain to become a more effective and efficient learner. It takes you through three key stages of the learning process—from the first stage of acquiring information through lectures and readings, through the second stage of studying and retaining the information you've acquired, to the final stage of retrieving (recalling) the information you studied. The ultimate goal of this chapter is to supply you with a set of powerful strategies that makes your learning *deep* (not surface-level memorization), *durable* (long-lasting), and *retrievable* (accessible to you when you need it).

Chapter 9
Test-Taking Skills and Strategies
What to do Before, During, and After Tests

This chapter supplies you with a systematic set of strategies for improving your performance on different types of tests, including multiple-choice and essay. It identifies strategies that can be used before, during, and after tests, as well as practical tips for becoming more "test wise" and less "test anxious."

Process and Style of Presentation

As important as *what* information is contained in a book is *how* that information is presented. When writing this text, we made an intentional attempt to present information in a way that would: (a) stimulate your motivation to learn, (b) deepen your understanding of what you're learning, and (c) strengthen your retention (memory) for what you've learned.

We attempted to do this by incorporating the following principles of motivation, learning, and memory throughout the text.

- Each chapter begins with a **Preview** of the chapter's key goals and content, followed by a **Thought Starter**—a question designed to stimulate your thoughts and feelings about the upcoming material. This pre-reading exercise is designed to "warm up" or "tune up" your brain, preparing it to connect the ideas you're about to encounter in the chapter with the ideas you already have in your head. It's an instructional strategy that implements one of the most powerful principles of learning: we learn most effectively by relating what we're going to learn to what we've already learned and stored in our brain.

- Within each chapter, we periodically interrupt your reading with opportunities for *reflection*—**Think About It** questions that prompt you to pause and think about the material you've just read. These timely pauses for thought should keep you alert and mentally active throughout the reading process. They serve to intercept "attention drift" that normally takes place when the brain continually receives and processes information for an extended period, such as it does when reading (Willis, 2007). These reflections also deepen your understanding of the material because they ask you to *write* in response to your reading. Writing stimulates deeper learning and higher levels of thinking than simply underlining or highlighting sentences. We recommend keeping a record of your written responses to the textbook's reflection questions in a *learning journal*.

- **Exercises** at the *end* of each chapter ask you to reflect further on the knowledge you've acquired and transform that knowledge into informed action. We achieve *wisdom* when we move beyond simply acquiring knowledge to *applying* the knowledge—putting it into practice to help us become more wise, effective, and successful human beings (Staudinger, 2008).

  The strategic positioning of the *Thought Starter* questions at the beginning of each chapter, the *Think About It* reflections interspersed throughout the chapter, and the application *Exercises* at the end of the chapter will keep you actively involved at three key stages of the reading process: the beginning, middle, and end.

- **End-of-Chapter Reflections** ask you questions that allow you to reflect on what you learned in the chapter and how you can apply it to your success in college and life.

- Information is presented through **multiple modes of input**, which include: diagrams, pictures, cartoons, words of wisdom from famous and successful people, advice from current and former college students, and personal stories drawn from the authors' experiences. When you receive information through different formats, you process that information through multiple sensory modalities (input channels). This deepens learning by enabling your brain to lay down multiple memory tracks (traces) of the information it's taking in (Willis, 2007).

What follows is a list of the book's seven key instructional features. *As you read these features, make a quick note in the side margin about how effective you think this feature will be in terms of motivating you to read and learn from the book.*

1. Research and Scholarly Support

The book's ideas and recommendations are grounded in research and scholarship drawn from a variety of academic fields. You will find references cited regularly throughout the chapters and a sizable reference section at the end of each chapter. The sheer quantity of references cited serves as testimony to the fact that the subject matter of this book is built on a solid body of research and scholarship, just like any other academic subject studied in the college curriculum. You'll also find that the references include a balanced blend of older, "classic" scholarship and more recent "cutting edge" research.

2. Boxed Summaries

At different points in the text, you will find boxes containing summaries of top tips for success. These summaries pull together key strategies relating to the same concept and organize them in the same place physically, which will help you organize and retain them mentally.

3. Quotes

Throughout the book, quotes from successful and influential people appear in the side margins that relate to and reinforce ideas covered at that point of the chapter. You'll find quotes from famous individuals who have lived in different historical periods and who have specialized in a variety of fields, including politics, philosophy, religion, science, business, music, art, and athletics. The wide-ranging time frames, cultures, and fields of study represented by the people quoted demonstrate that their words of wisdom are timeless and universal. It's our hope that the words of these highly successful and respected individuals will inspire you to put their words in practice.

You can also learn a lot from the firsthand experiences of current and former students. Throughout the book, you'll find comments and advice from students at different stages of the college experience, including college graduates (alumni). Studies show that students can learn a great deal from their peers—especially from more experienced peers who've "been there, done that." By hearing about their success stories and stumbling blocks, you can benefit from their college experiences to improve your college experience.

4. Authors' Experiences

In each chapter, you will find at least one author's experience related to the chapter topic. We share our own experiences as college students, our professional experiences working with students as instructors and advisors, and our personal experiences in other areas of our lives. Studies show that when people hear stories shared by others, their understanding and memory for key ideas contained in the stories is deepened and strengthened (McDrury & Alterio, 2002). We share our stories for the purpose of personalizing the book and with the hope that you'll learn from our experiences—including learning from our mistakes!

> "
>
> It is hard to know how any student could truly understand whom [he or she] wants to be without thinking carefully about what career to pursue."
>
> —Derek Bok, president emeritus, Harvard University

Think About It—Journal Entry P.1

Have you received any tips or advice from friends or family about what to do, or what not to do in college?

_____

If you have, what kind of advice did you receive and who gave it to you?

_____

_____

If you haven't, why do you think none of your friends or family members have offered you any advice?

_____

_____

_____

_____

_____

5. Concept Maps (Graphic Organizers): Verbal-Visual Aids

Throughout the book, you will find ideas visually organized into diagrams, charts, and figures. When important concepts are represented in a visual-spatial format, we're more likely to retain them because two different memory traces are recorded in our brain: verbal (words) and visual (images).

6. Cartoons: Emotional-Visual Aids

You will find cartoons sprinkled throughout the text to lighten up the reading and provide you with a little entertainment. More importantly, the cartoons relate to an important concept and are also intended to strengthen your retention of that concept by reinforcing it with a visual image (drawing) and an emotional experience (humor). If the cartoon triggers at least a snicker, your body will release adrenaline—a hormone that facilitates memory formation. If it generates actual laughter, it will also stimulate your brain to release endorphins—natural, morphine-like chemicals that lower stress and elevate mood.

7. Learning More through the World Wide Web

At the end of each chapter are web-based resources containing additional information relating to the chapter's major ideas. One of the major goals of a college education is to prepare students to become independent, self-directed learners. We hope that the information presented in each chapter's topic will stimulate your interest and motivation to learn more about the topic. If it does, you can use the online resources cited at the end of the chapter to access additional information.

Think About It—Journal Entry P.2

Look back at the seven features of this book that have just been described. Which of these features do you think will be most effective for stimulating your interest in reading and learning from the book?

_____

_____

_____

_____

_____

We firmly believe that the content of this book, and the manner in which the content is delivered, will empower you not only to survive college, but to *thrive* in college and beyond. The skills and strategies found on the following pages promote success throughout life. Self-awareness, effective planning and decision making, learning deeply and remembering longer, thinking critically and creatively, managing time and money effectively, communicating and relating effectively with others, and maintaining health and wellness are more than college success skills—they are *life* success skills.

Introduction

Welcome to Community College

In the introduction to this book, you'll learn why college has the potential to be the most enriching experience of your life and one will benefit you throughout life. The first year of college is a particularly critical stage of your educational development. It's a transitional stage during which students encounter the greatest challenges, the most stress, the most academic difficulties, and the highest risk of dropping out. However, it's also the year when students experience the greatest amount of learning and personal growth. These findings highlight the power of the first-year experience, the value of first-year courses designed to promote college success, and the importance of books like this.

In the introduction, you'll find convincing evidence that new students who participate in first-year experience courses (college-success courses) are more likely to stick with college, complete their degree, and get the most out of their college experience.

Summary and Conclusion

It is our hope that the content of this book and the manner in which the content is presented will motivate and empower you to make the most of your community college experience. Don't forget that the skills and strategies discussed are relevant to life beyond college. Effective planning and decision making, learning deeply and remembering longer, thinking critically and creatively, managing time and money responsibly, communicating and relating effectively with others, and maintaining health and wellness are more than just college skills: they are life skills.

> Learning doesn't stop after college; it's a lifelong process. If you strive to apply the ideas in this book, you'll develop habits that will enable you to thrive in college and beyond.

AUTHOR'S EXPERIENCE

I've learned a lot from teaching the first-year seminar (college success course) and from writing this book. Before I taught this course, I didn't have a clear idea about the meaning, purpose, and value of a college education, or why general education was so important for achieving personal and professional success. By preparing for this course, I also learned new strategies for improving my memory and my writing, as well as for managing my time, money, and health. I continue to use these strategies in my personal and professional life. My only regret is that I didn't take a course like this when I was a college freshman. If I had, I would have been able to apply these life success skills earlier in my life.

—*Joe Cuseo*

Note

This is more than just a textbook for first-term students. It's a college success *and* life success *book; it contains principles and strategies that can promote your success in college* and *improve the quality of your life.*

Sincerely,

Joe Cuseo, Aaron Thompson, & Julie McLaughlin

References

McDrury, J., and Alterio, M. G. (2002). *Learning through Storytelling: using reflection and experience in higher education contexts*. Palmerston North: Dunmore Press.

Staudinger, U. M. (2008). A psychology of wisdom: History and recent developments. *Research in Human Development, 5*, 107–120.

Willis, J. (2007). *Brain-friendly strategies for the inclusion classroom*. Alexandria, VA: Association for Supervision and Curriculum Development.

Introduction

WHY COMMUNITY COLLEGE?

Congratulations! We applaud your decision to continue your education. Your previous enrollment in school was required, but your decision to continue your education in college is entirely *your choice*. By choosing to enter *higher education*, you've chosen to learn and think at a higher level than you did in high school. You're about to begin an exciting and challenging journey that has the potential to be the most enriching experience of your life.

Think About It—Journal Entry I.1

Why have you decided to attend college?

_____

_____

_____

What are you most *looking forward to* about college?

_____

_____

_____

_____

> Ready for takeoff, On my adventure today, As I take a seat in my chair And clear the way.
>
> Eager people around, With destinations to go, As a woman at the front says, "Please find a seat in any row."
>
> Some people are anxious, Waiting to take flight, To soar above the rest, With aspirations in sight
>
> Our first day of college, A chance to start anew, To find out who we are, And learn what is true.
>
> —Waiting to Take Flight, *a poem by Kimberly Castaneda, first-year student*

> People often ask me why I prefer to teach at a community college when I have degrees from more elite institutions. I chose to teach at a community college because it celebrates committed, passionate teachers. Teaching at a community college is the best thing that ever happened to me."
>
> —*Professor Ellen Olmstead, "It's the Community-College Life for Me,"* The Chronicle of Higher Education

The Community College Experience

You're about to join approximately 8 million (4,900,000 part-time and 3,120,000 full-time) students enrolled at more than 1,000 community colleges in the United States today. Student enrollment at community colleges has been growing faster than all other types of colleges and universities in the United States (Desrochers, Lenihan, & Wellman, 2010); the diversity of students enrolled in America's community colleges makes it the most diverse system of education in the world. (See **Box I.1** for a snapshot summary of student diversity at America's community colleges today.) According to the American Association of Community Colleges (2014), 52% of your peers are white and 48% are nonwhite; 36% of you are first in your family to attend college; 17% of you are single parents; 17% of you are non-U.S. citizens; 7% of you are veterans; and 4% of you are students with disabilities. As you will learn in Chapter 8, a diverse student body represents a golden *educational* opportunity for enhancing learning, personal development, and career preparation. The diversity found at teaching-oriented community colleges represents a unique learning environment that's tough to match at other types of colleges and universities.

Box I.1

Student Diversity in America's Community Colleges

- There are approximately 13 million students currently enrolled in approximately 1,132 community colleges in the United States; they account for almost half of all first-year college students in America today.
- More than 770,000 community college students will earn an associate degree this year, and more than 436,000 will earn a certificate.
- Most first-year community college students are employed either part- or full-time and attend college part-time.
- The average age of the American community college student is 28.
- Almost 36% of all community college students are the first in their family to attend college.
- More than 45% of community college students are members of minority racial or ethnic groups.
- Close to 6% of international students attend America's community colleges.

Source: American Association of Community Colleges (2014).

There are two other groups of students that are growing in number and adding to the student diversity found in America's community colleges:

- Veterans returning from the war in the Middle East who have been afforded the opportunity to attend college with the help of generous financial aid provided by a GI Bill passed in 2009.
- Displaced workers over the age of 20 who have lost full-time jobs due to job layoffs and company closings triggered by the current economic recession.

PERSONAL EXPERIENCE

There are some challenges us vets do face when we get out and go to college. There is that natural gap in maturity [between] the regular college student versus the veteran student. While some students come in late on a regular basis, veteran students are often early to class. Also some students talk during a lecture, while a veteran student gives the instructor the utmost attention. But these are things that are drilled into our heads being raised in the military. Things like loyalty, respect, and integrity.

—*Veteran student*

> "The scariest thing for me to have done was to get out [of the military] and not have a plan. I firmly believe that you have to plan for success. Success doesn't just happen; you have to work for it."
>
> —First-year veteran student

PERSONAL EXPERIENCE

Many of these new students [displaced workers] feel that going back to school was the best thing that they have ever done. They feel better about themselves because of the daily challenges, making contacts and developing new relationships with classmates, and the thrill of learning helps them to believe in themselves and feel successful. I hear these comments: "This is a wonderful opportunity for me." "I realized what was important to me." "I've wanted to go back to school for a long time."

—*Community College counselor*

> "I am very impressed by the displaced workers who are returning to school. While one would expect the workers to be down and depressed, most of them are viewing this as an opportunity to pursue an opportunity [and] a dream delayed."
>
> —Community college counselor

©Matej Hudovernik/Shutterstock.com

The community college has been called "America's college" (Cohen, Brawer, & Kisker, 2014) because it's an American invention. It's also referred to as "democracy's college" (Topper & Powers, 2013) because its open-door admissions policy embodies the democratic principle of equal opportunity for all people—regardless of their age, gender, ethnicity, race, religion, prior educational history, or family income. The community college system provides accessible, affordable higher education for all people who want to improve their quality of life and pursue the American dream. America's community colleges are the "Ellis Island" of higher education because they embody the American ideal of providing equal educational opportunity and a gateway to success for all people.

Think About It—Journal Entry I.2

Why have you decided to attend the college you're at now?

_____

_____

_____

Are you happy to be here? Why or why not?

_____

_____

_____

> "Community colleges are the 'unsung heroes' of the nation's education system. They may not get the credit they deserve, they may not get the same resources as other schools, but they provide a gateway to millions of Americans to good jobs and a better life."
>
> —Barack Obama, 44th president of the United States

Studies show that compared to high school graduates, students who earn a community college credential—whether it be a certificate or an associate degree—have higher rates of employment, earn higher wages (approximately $400,000 more over a course of a lifetime), and have children who are more likely to complete a college degree (Gagliardi & Hiemstra, 2013; Ganzglass, 2014; Mullin & Phillippe, 2013; Tinto, 2012). For community college students who eventually transfer to a four-year college and complete a bachelor's degree, they experience additional benefits similar to students who start their college education at four-year campuses (Pascarella & Terenzini, 2005). These benefits are summarized in **Box I.2**.

Box I.2

The Power of College: Economic and Personal Benefits of a College Education

Approximately 31% of Americans hold a four-year (bachelor's) degree (Lumina Foundation, 2015). When they are compared with people from similar social and economic backgrounds who did not continue their education beyond high school, research reveals that a college education is well worth it—in terms of both personal development and career advancement.

Summarized below are positive outcomes associated with a college education and a college degree. Their wide-ranging impact on the whole person and society at large serve as testimony to the power of the college experience.

1. Economic and Career Benefits

- Job security and stability—college graduates have lower rates of unemployment and lower risk of being laid off work
- Higher income—the gap between the earnings of high school and college graduates is large and *growing*. Individuals holding a bachelor's degree earn an average salary that's $17,500 higher than high school graduates. When these differences are calculated over a lifetime, the income of families headed by people with a bachelor's degree earn an income that's over a million dollars more than families headed by people with a high school diploma. (See Figure I.1.)

It's an irrefutable fact that college gives you a significant and persistent advantage decade after decade."

—*Mary C. Daly, vice president of the Federal Reserve Bank of San Francisco (quoted in the Los Angeles Times, April 15, 2015)*

- Better retirement and pension benefits
- Career versatility and mobility—greater ability to move out of one position into another (a college graduate has more job options)
- Career advancement—greater opportunity to move up to higher-level professional positions (in other words, a college graduate has more opportunities for job promotions)
- Career satisfaction—college graduates are more likely to be in careers that interest them and in positions they find stimulating, challenging, and personally fulfilling
- Career autonomy—college graduates have more opportunities to work independently (without supervision) and make their own on-the-job decisions
- Career prestige—college graduates are more likely to hold higher status positions, (i.e., jobs considered to be desirable and highly regarded by society)

FIGURE I.1

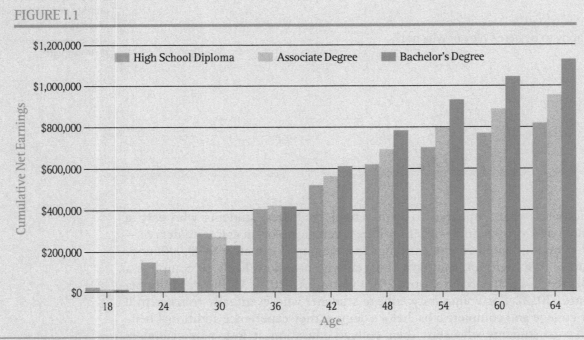

(continued)

Box I.2 *(continued)*

2. Advanced Intellectual Skills

College graduates possess:

- Greater knowledge
- More effective problem-solving skills—better ability to deal with complex and ambiguous (uncertain) problems
- Greater openness to new ideas
- More advanced levels of moral reasoning
- More effective consumer choices and decisions
- Wiser long-term investments
- Clearer sense of self-identity—greater awareness and knowledge of personal talents, interests, values, and needs
- Greater likelihood of learning continually throughout life

> Without exception, the observed changes [during college] involve greater breadth, expansion, and appreciation for the new and different . . . and the evidence for their presence is compelling."
>
> —*Ernest Pascarella and Pat Terenzini*, How College Affects Students

3. Physical Health Benefits

- Better health insurance—college graduates are more likely to have insurance coverage and have more comprehensive coverage
- Better dietary habits
- Exercise more regularly
- Have lower rates of obesity
- Live longer and healthier lives

4. Social Benefits

- Greater social self-confidence
- Better ability to understand and communicate effectively with others
- Greater popularity
- More effective leadership skills
- Higher levels of marital satisfaction

5. Emotional Benefits

- Lower levels of anxiety
- Higher levels of self-esteem
- Greater sense of self-efficacy—college graduates believe they have more influence or control over the outcomes of their lives
- Higher levels of psychological well-being
- Higher levels of life satisfaction and happiness

6. Effective Citizenship

- Greater interest in national issues—both social and political
- Greater knowledge of current events
- Higher voting participation rates
- Higher rates of participation in civic affairs and community service

7. Higher Quality of Life for Their Children

- Less likely to smoke during pregnancy
- Provide better health care for their children
- Spend more time with their children
- More likely to involve their children in stimulating educational activities that advance their cognitive (mental) development
- More likely to save money for their children to go to college
- More likely to have children who graduate from college
- More likely that their children attain higher status, higher salary careers

> My three-month-old boy is very important to me, and it is important I graduate from college so my son, as well as I, live a better life".
>
> —*First-year student's response to the question: "What is most important to you?"*

Sources: Andres & Wyn (2010); Astin (1993); Bowen (1977, 1997) ; Baum, Ma,, & Payea (2013); Carnevale, Strohl, & Melton (2011); Dee (2004); Feldman & Newcomb (1994); Hamilton (2011, 2014); Knox, Lindsay, & Kolb (1993); Lumina Foundation (2013, 2015); Pascarella & Terenzini (2005); Pew Research Center (2014); Seifert, et al. (2008); SHEEO (2012); The Hamilton Project (2014); Tomsho (2009); U.S. Bureau of Labor Statistics (2015).

Think About It—Journal Entry I.3

Glance back at the seven major benefits or positive outcomes of a college education listed in **Box I.2**. If you were to rank them in terms of their importance to you, which three would rank at the top your list? Why?

> "For the individual, having access to and successfully graduating from an institution of higher education has proved to be the path to a better job, to better health and to a better life."
>
> —*The College Board*

After college, it's probably safe to say that you will never again be a member of an organization or community with as many resources and services available to you that have been intentionally designed to promote your learning, development, and success. If you capitalize on the resources available to you, and if you utilize effective college-going strategies—such as those suggested in this book—you can create a life-changing experience for yourself that will enhance your quality of life for the remainder of your life.

The Importance of the First Year of College

Your transition into higher education represents an important life transition. Somewhat similar to an immigrant moving to a new country, you're moving into a new culture with unfamiliar expectations, regulations, customs, and language (Chaskes, 1996).

> "One of the major transitions from high school to college involves the unlearning of past attitudes, values, and behaviors and the learning of new ones. This represents a major social and psychological transition and a time when students may be more ready to change than at any other point in their college career."
>
> —*Ernest Pascarella & Patrick Terenzini*, How College Affects Students

The *first* year of college is undoubtedly the most important year of the college experience because it's a *transitional* stage. Students report the most change, the most learning, and the most development during their first year of college (Flowers, et al., 2001; HERI, 2014; Light, 2001). Other research suggests that the academic habits students develop in their first year are likely to persist throughout their remaining years of college (Schilling, 2001). When graduating seniors look back at their college experience, many of them say that their first year was the time of greatest change and the time when they made the most significant improvements in their approach to learning. Here's how one senior put it during a personal interview:

Interviewer: What have you learned about your approach to learning [in college]?

Student: I had to learn how to study. I went through high school with a 4.0 average. I didn't have to study. It was a breeze. I got to the university and there was no structure. No one took attendance to make sure I was in class. No one checked my homework. No one told me I had to do something. There were no quizzes on the readings. I did not work well with this lack of structure. It took my first year and a half to learn to deal with it. But I had to teach myself to manage my time. I had to teach myself how to study. I had to teach myself how to learn in a different environment (Chickering & Schlossberg, 1998, p. 47).

In some ways, the first-year experience in college is similar to ocean surfing or downhill skiing: It can be filled with the most exciting thrills—greatest learning and development, but also the most dangerous spills—it's the year when students experience the most stress, the most academic difficulties, and the highest college withdrawal rates (American College Testing, 2012; Bartlett, 2002; Sax, Bryant, & Gilmartin, 2004). The ultimate goal of downhill skiing and surfing is to experience the thrills, avoid the spills, and finish the run on your feet and feeling exhilarated. The same can be said for the first year of college; studies show that if students complete their first-year experience in good standing, their chances for successfully completing college increase dramatically (American College Testing, 2009).

You'll find that the research cited and the advice provided in this book point to one major conclusion: Success in college depends on you—you make it happen by what you do and how well you capitalize on the resources available to you. Don't let college happen *to* you; make it happen *for* you—take charge of your college experience and take advantage of the college resources that are at your command.

After reviewing 40 years of research on how college affects students, two distinguished researchers reached the following conclusion:

The impact of college is largely determined by individual effort and involvement in the academic, interpersonal, and extracurricular [co-curricular] offerings on a campus. Students are not passive recipients of institutional efforts to "educate" or "change" them, but rather bear major responsibility for any gains they derive from their postsecondary [college] experience (Pascarella & Terenzini, 2005, p. 602).

Compared to your previous experiences in school, college will provide you with a broader range of courses to choose from, more resources to capitalize on, and more decision-making opportunities. Your particular college experience will end up being different than any other college student because you have the freedom to actively shape and create it in a way that's uniquely your own.

Think About It—Journal Entry I.4

How did you feel on your first day of college?

_____

_____

_____

Why did you feel this way?

_____

_____

_____

_____

What students do during college counts more than who they are or where they go to college."

—*George Kuh, author,* Student Success in College

Being in this class has helped me a lot. What I learned I will apply to all my other classes."

I feel like I have so much to take away from this class and will continue to keep it with me the rest of my college career."

This course will be a hard act to follow. This is one of the most valuable classes I will ever take."

—*Comments made by students when evaluating their first-year experience course*

Importance of a First-Year Experience Course (also known as a First-Year Seminar)

If you're reading this book, you are already beginning to take charge of your college experience because you're likely to be enrolled in a course that's designed to promote your college success. Research strongly indicates that new students who participate in first-year experience courses are more likely to continue in college until they complete their degree and perform at a higher level. These positive effects have been found for:

- All types of students (under-prepared and well-prepared, minority and majority, residential and commuter, male and female),
- Students at all types of colleges (two-year and four-year, public and private),
- Students attending colleges of all sizes (small, mid-sized, and large), and
- Students attending college in all locations (urban, suburban, and rural).

(Sources: Barefoot, et al., 1998; Boudreau & Kromrey, 1994; Cuseo, 2011; Cuseo & Barefoot, 1996; Fidler & Godwin, 1994; Glass & Garrett, 1995; Grunder & Hellmich, 1996; Hunter & Linder, 2005; Porter & Swing, 2006; Shanley & Witten, 1990; Sidle & McReynolds, 1999; Starke, Harth, & Sirianni, 2001; Thomson, 1998; Tobolowsky, 2005).

There has been more research on the first-year experience course and more evidence supporting its positive impact on student success than any other course in the college curriculum. Give this course your best effort and take full advantage of what it has to offer. If you do, you'll take an important first step toward excelling in college and in life beyond college.

Enjoy the trip!

> "Being in this class has helped me a lot. What I learned I will apply to all my other classes."

> "I feel like I have so much to take away from this class and will continue to keep it with me the rest of my college career."

> "This course will be a hard act to follow. This is one of the most valuable classes I will ever take."

> —Comments made by students when evaluating their first-year experience course

Introduction Reflection

After reading the Introduction, how do you think this course will benefit you?

List and briefly describe three things you hope to learn or accomplish as a result of successfully completing this course.

References

American Association of Community Colleges. (2014). FACT SHEET. Washington, DC: Author.

American College Testing (2015). *College student retention and graduation rates from 2000 through 2015*. Retrieved from http://www.act.org/research/policymakers/pdf/retain_2015.pdf.

Andres, L., & Wyn, J. (2010). *The making of a generation: The children of the 1970s in adulthood*. Buffalo, NY: University of Toronto Press.

Astin, A. W. (1993). *What matters in college?* San Francisco: Jossey-Bass.

Barefoot, B. O., Warnock, C. L., Dickinson, M. P., Richardson, S. E., & Roberts, M. R. (Eds.). (1998). *Exploring the evidence: Vol. 2. Reporting outcomes of first-year seminars* (Monograph No. 29). Columbia: National Resource Center for the First-Year Experience and Students in Transition, University of South Carolina.

Bartlett, T. (2002). Freshman pay, mentally and physically, as they adjust to college life. *Chronicle of Higher Education, 48*, 35–37.

Baum, S., Ma, J., & Payea, K. (2013). *Education pays 2013: The benefits of higher education for individuals and society*. Washington DC: The College Board. Retrieved from http://trends.collegeboard.org/sites/default/files/education-pays-2013-full-report-022714.pdf.

Boudreau, C., & Kromrey, J. (1994). A longitudinal study of the retention and academic performance of participants in a freshman orientation course. *Journal of College Student Development, 35*, 444–449.

Bowen, H. R. (1977). *Investment in learning: The individual and social value of American higher education*. San Francisco: Jossey-Bass.

Bowen, H. R. (1997). *Investment in learning: The individual and social value of American higher education* (2nd ed.). Baltimore: Johns Hopkins Press.

Carnevale, A. P., Strohl, J., & Melton, M. (2011). *What's in worth? The economic value of college majors*. Washington DC: Center on Education and the Workforce, Georgetown University. Retrieved from http:cew.georgetown.edu/whatsitworth/

Chaskes, J. (1996). The first-year student as immigrant. *Journal of The Freshman Year Experience & Students in Transition, 8*(1), 79–91.

Chickering, A. W., & Schlossberg, N. K. (1998). Moving on: Seniors as people in transition. In J. N. Gardner, G. Van der Veer, et al. (Eds.), *The senior year experience* (pp. 37–50). San Francisco: Jossey-Bass.

Cohen, A, M., Brawer, F. B., & Kisker, C. B. (2014). *The American Community College*. San Francisco: Jossey-Bass.

Cuseo, J. B., & Barefoot, B. O. (1996). A natural marriage: The extended orientation seminar and the community college. In J. Henkin (Ed.), *The community college: Opportunity and access for America's first-year students* (pp. 59–68). Columbia: National Resource Center for the First-Year Experience and Students in Transition, University of South Carolina.

Dee, T. (2004). Are there civic returns to education? *Journal of Public Economics, 88*, 1697–1720.

Desrochers, D. M., Lenihan, C. M., & Wellman, J. V. (2010). *Trends in college spending 1998-2008: Where does the money come from? Where does it go? What does it buy?* Washington, DC: Delta Project on Postsecondary Education Costs, Productivity, and Accountability.

Feldman, K. A., & Newcomb, T. M. (1994). *The impact of College on students*. New Brunswick: Transaction Publishers.

Fidler, P., & Godwin, M. (1994). Retaining African-American students through the freshman seminar. *Journal of Developmental Education, 17*, 34–41.

Flowers, L., Osterlind, S., Pascarella, E., & Pierson, C. (2001). How much do students learn in college? Cross-sectional estimates using the College Basic Academic Subjects Examination. *Journal of Higher Education, 72*, 565–583.

Gagliardi, J. & Hiemstra, H. (2013). *College still pays*. Kentucky Postsecondary Education Policy Brief. Retrieved from http://cpe.ky.gov/NR/rdonlyres/8DE2CF1E-51A2-4C27-8C2B-41FB126252FE/0/CollegeStillPayspolicybrief.pdf.

Ganzglass, E. (2014). Scaling "stackable credentials": Implications for implementation and policy. Center for Postsecondary and Economic Success. Retrieved from http://www.clasp.org/resources-and-publications/files/2014-03-21-Stackable-Credentials-Paper-FINAL.pdf

Glass, J., & Garrett, M. (1995). Student participation in a college orientation course: Retention, and grade point average. *Community College Journal of Research and Practice, 19*, 117–132.

Grunder, P., & Hellmich, D. (1996). Academic persistence and achievement of remedial students in a community college's success program. *Community College Review, 24*, 21–33.

Hamilton, W. (2011, December 29). "College still worth it, study says." *Los Angeles Times*, p. B2.

Hamilton, W. (2014, June 25). "College still good bet, study says." *Los Angeles Times*, p. B4.

HERI (Higher Education Research Institute) (2014). *Your first college year survey 2014*. Los Angeles, CA: Cooperative Institutional Research Program, University of California-Los Angeles.

Hunter, M. A., & Linder, C. W. (2005). First-year seminars. In M. L. Upcraft, J. N. Gardner, B. O. Barefoot, et al. (Eds.), *Challenging and supporting the first-year student: A handbook for improving the first year of college* (pp. 275–291). San Francisco: Jossey-Bass.

Knox, W. E., Lindsay, P., & Kolb, M. N. (1993). Does college make a difference? Long-term changes in activities and attitudes. Westport, CT: Greenwood.

Light, R. J. (2001). *Making the most of college: Students speak their minds*. Cambridge, MA: Harvard University Press.

Lumina Foundation (2013). *A stronger nation through higher education*. Indianapolis IN: Author. Retrieved from http://www.pesc.org/library/docs/about_us/whitepapers/a-stronger-nation-2013lumina.pdf.

Lumina Foundation (2015). *A stronger nation through higher education*. Indianapolis IN: Author. Retrieved from http://www.luminafoundation.org/files/publications/A_stronger_nation_through_higher_education-2015.pdf.

Mullin, C., & Phillippe, K. (2013). *Community college contributions* (No. AACC Policy Brief 2013-01PB). American Association of Community Colleges. Retrieved from http://www.aacc.nche.edu/Publications/Briefs/Documents/2013PB_01.pdf.

Pascarella, E., & Terenzini, P. (2005). *How college affects students: A third decade of research* (Vol. 2). San Francisco: Jossey-Bass.

Pew Research Center (2014, February). *The rising cost of not going to college*. Retrieved from http://www.pewsocialtrends.org/2014/02/11/the-rising-cost-of-not-going-to-college/.

Porter, S. R., & Swing, R. L. (2006). Understanding how first-year seminars affect persistence. *Research in Higher Education, 47*(1), 89–109.

Sax, L. J., Bryant, A. N., & Gilmartin, S. K. (2004). A longitudinal investigation of emotional health among male and female first-year college students. *Journal of the First-Year Experience, 16*, 39–65.

Schilling, K. (2001, August). *Plenary address*. Presented at The Summer Institute on First-Year Assessment, Asheville, North Carolina.

Seifert, T. A., Goodman, K. M., Lindsay, N., Jorgensen, J. D., Wolniak, G. C., Pascarella, E. T., & Blaich, C. (2008). The effects of liberal arts experiences on liberal arts outcomes. *Research in Higher Education, 49*, 107–125.

Shanley, M., & Witten, C. (1990). University 101 freshman seminar course: A longitudinal study of persistence, retention, and graduation rates. *NASPA Journal, 27*, 344–352.

SHEEO (State Higher Education Executive Officers) (2012). *State higher education finance, FY 2011*. Retrieved from http://www.sheeo.org/sites/default/files/publications/SHEF_FY11.pdf.

Sidle, M., & McReynolds, J. (1999). The freshman year experience: Student retention and student success. *NASPA Journal, 36*, 288–300.

Starke, M. C., Harth, M., & Sirianni, F. (2001). Retention, bonding, and academic achievement: Success of a first-year seminar. *Journal of the First-Year Experience and Students in Transition, 13*(2), 7–35.

The Hamilton Project (2014). *Major decisions: What graduates earn over their lifetimes*. Washington, DC: Brookings Institution. Retrieved from http://www.hamiltonproject.org/papers/major_decisions_what_graduates_earn_over_their_lifetimes/

Thomson, R. (1998). University of Vermont. In B. O. Barefoot, C. L. Warnock, M. P. Dickinson, S. E. Richardson, & M. R. Roberts (Eds.). (1998). *Exploring the evidence: Vol. 2. Reporting outcomes of first-year seminars* (Monograph No. 29, pp. 77–78). Columbia: National Resource Center for the First-Year Experience and Students in Transition, University of South Carolina.

Tinto, V. (2012). *Completing college: Rethinking institutional action*. Chicago: The University of Chicago Press.

Tobolowsky, B. F. (2005). *The 2003 national survey on first-year seminars: Continuing innovations in the college curriculum* (Monograph No. 41). Columbia, SC: University of South Carolina, National Resource Center for the First-Year Experience and Students in Transition.

Tomsho, R. (2009, April 22). Study tallies education's gap on GDP. Wall Street Journal. Retrieved from http://www.wsj.com/articles/SB124040633530943487

Topper, A. M., & Powers, J. M. (2013). Democracy's college: The american community college in the 21st century: Framing the issue. *Educational Policy Analysis Archives, 21*(14), 1–12.

U.S. Bureau of Labor Statistics (2015). *Employment projections*. United States of Department of Labor. Retrieved from http://www.bls.gov/emp/ep_chart_001.htm.

CHAPTER 1

Welcome To Anoka-Ramsey Community College

The Jargon of College

Associate Degree—two types of associate majors are offered. (1) Technological and vocational specialties that are generally completed in 2 years of college study and are usually sufficient for entrance into an occupational field, and (2) college or university parallel programs that are like the first 2 years of a 4 year college curriculum often referred to as a Transfer Degree. Examples-AS Degree in Community Health, AS Degree in Business.

Associate of Arts (AA)—Awarded by a community college to students who successfully complete the prescribed program in an academic area. They are intended to provide a broad liberal arts and sciences background. The A.A. degree is traditionally designed to transfer towards a bachelor's degree.

Associate of Science (AS)—Intended to provide a liberal arts and science background and to provide the foundation for baccalaureate programs.

Associate of Applied Science (AAS)—Intended primarily to prepare people for employment.

Add/Drop Period—A period at the beginning of each semester, or at the beginning of a late start class, when students may add and drop classes without negative impact on their academic record. ARCC's drop/add deadline is the 5th day of each semester.

Adult Basic Education (ABE)—A free program to help students develop basic skills; such as reading, writing, math, work skills, English and technology.

Articulation Agreement—An agreement specifies that all or some credits from a particular degree will be accepted towards a specified four-year degree program/major of study.

Bachelor's Degree—Sometimes called baccalaureate degrees; generally require 4 to 5 years of study. The Bachelor of Arts (BA) and Bachelor of Science (BS) are the most common baccalaureates, and both include general education courses, a major and electives. The BS is more likely to be awarded in the sciences and for professional or technical fields of study. BA degrees are more often awarded in the humanities and arts. However, there are no absolute differences between the degrees, and policies concerning their award vary from college to college. (These programs generally require a minimum of 120 credits).

Blended/Hybrid—Courses in which some traditional face-to-face "seat time" has been replaced by online learning activities.

Career/Occupational Programs—Programs designed to lead directly to employment or career advancement.

Certificate—Non-degree offerings below the associate degree and are most often offered in technical and vocational fields of study. They generally lead to employment in an occupational field. Examples-Certificate in Biomedical Technician, Business Leadership, or Computer Network Security.

Credit Hour—The amount of college credit earned for the satisfactory completion of a course.

Completion Rate—The calculation of the number of credits completed divided by the number of credits attempted in a semester or over several semesters.

D2L Brightspace (D2L)—The online tool used to facilitate online learning.

Dean's List—A list of students recognized for having received high grades.

Degree Audit Reporting System (DARS)—An electronic summary of a student's academic progress toward completion of degree or program.

Drop—Discontinuing a class within the drop/add period. A drop is not recorded on students' transcripts.

Drop/Add Period—A period at the beginning of each term, or at the beginning of a late start class, when students may drop or add classes. ARCC's drop/add deadline is the 5th day of each semester.

Elective—Courses not specifically required for graduation. An elective permits students to select some courses of their choice within their program.

FAFSA (Free Application for Federal Student Aid)—This is the application a student fills out to be eligible for grants, loans, and work-study.

Full-time Student—A full-time student is enrolled for 12 or more credits in a semester.

Grade Point Average (GPA)—The total number of points per credit hour earned. Each letter grade has an equivalent point value: A = 4 points, B = 3 points, C = 2 points, D=1 point, F/NC = 0 Points. Students can calculate their GPA for each course by multiplying the number of points a grade is worth times the number of credit hours for the course.

Grant—An outright award of funds, usually based on need, which ***does not*** have to be repaid.

Hold—A hold is placed on students' academic record when an outstanding obligation, monetary or material, occurs. The hold is released when the obligation is met. When a hold is placed on a record, the person may not be allowed to register, receive transcripts, or receive other services from the college until the hold is released.

Incomplete—An incomplete (I) is a temporary grade which may be given at the instructors discretion to a student when illness, necessary absence, or other reasons beyond the control of the student prevent completion of course requirements by the end of the academic term.

Learning Community—A learning community consists of the same students taking several classes around a common theme, but with different instructors. The instructors of these classes work together to coordinate what the students will learn.

Loans—Loans are borrowed funds that **must be** repaid.

Major/Minor—A major is the main field that you want to specialize in while you are still an undergraduate at a college. A minor is a secondary field that you want to specialize in while you are working on your major.

Minnesota Transfer Curriculum (MnTC)—A collaborative effort among all two and four year public colleges and universities in Minnesota to help students transfer their coursework in general education. 40 credits are required in ten goal areas. These courses are also used in the general education portion of the AA, AS, and AAS programs.

MnSCU (Minnesota State Colleges and Universities)—Comprised of 32 public higher education institutions including 25 two-year colleges and 7 four-year universities.

My.anokaramsey.edu—This is the e-mail address that is provided for you by the college. It is the official method of notification by the college.

Office Hours—The specific hours that faculty has reserved to be in their office to assist students.

Online—Course materials are presented over the internet using the web-based software D2L. The instructors will use D2L to give assignments, answer questions, lead discussions, etc. Students should expect to interact with the instructor and their peers.

Pass/Fail—Students may enroll in certain courses on a Pass/Fail (P/F) basis. While courses in which students earn P grades receive full college credit and count towards graduation, P grades are not counted when computing a student's GPA. However, if a student elects to take a course under the P/F option and receives an F, the F grade will affect GPA. P/F grades become part of a student's permanent academic record. Students selecting the P/F option must meet the stated prerequisites for a given class, complete all course requirements, and take all examinations.

Peer Tutoring—Tutoring in which a student is assisting another student.

Professional Tutoring—Tutoring in which a college graduate is assisting a student. Typically, the tutor has a degree related to the subject being discussed.

Prerequisite—Specified conditions, requirements, or classes that must be completed before enrolling in a class. For example, Math 0250 is a prerequisite for Math 1200.

Satisfactory Academic Progress (SAP)—Students must meet or exceed a cumulative GPA of 2.0 and a cumulative completion rate of 67%. If one or both of these measures are not met for one semester, the student will be placed on academic warning. If in the following semester, these measures are still not met, the student will be placed on suspension.

Scholarships—These are monetary awards given to students in recognition of academic achievement or financial need.

Semester—A term or period of time in an academic year. There are two semesters and one or two summer sessions in most semester system schools. One semester is typically 16 weeks long.

Syllabus—A document of course requirements that instructors give to students on the first day of class. This syllabus usually contains detailed information such as learning objectives, an instructor's contact information, grading system, attendance policies, and testing and assignment dates.

Transcript—An official record of a student's college grade and academic standing.

Transfer Programs—Programs with courses leading to an Associate's degree which are generally accepted in transfer to Bachelor degree granting colleges and universities.

Withdrawal—Discontinuing a course after the drop/add period but before the withdrawal deadline. A withdrawal is recorded on the transcript as a "W". Withdrawals do not influence GPA, but do negatively impact completion rate and academic progress.

Work-Study—The federal government and the college provide funds to employ students on a part-time basis on campus. Work-study is part of a student's financial aid package.

Where Do I Go?

- Change my address?
- File a graduation application?
- Register for a course?
- Order an official transcript?
- Withdraw from a class?

Records & Registration Office:
Cambridge and Coon Rapids—763.433.1400

- Discuss changing my major?
- Talk with an academic advisor?
- Sign up for classes?
- Talk about general academic program questions?
- Find information about academic probation and suspension?
- Ask about career resources?

Academic Advising Center:
Cambridge and Coon Rapids—763.433.1230

- Get Pell Grant information?
- Apply for federal student aid?
- Learn about the Federal Loan Program?
- Ask about the work-study program?

Financial Aid Office:
Cambridge and Coon Rapids—763.433.1500

- Pay my tuition?
- Ask about creating a payment plan for my tuition?
- Pay my student fees or library fines?
- Talk with someone about personal concerns?

- Receive career counseling?
- Take a career assessment?

Counseling Services:
Cambridge—763.433.1840 • *Coon Rapids—763.433.1240*

- Search the Lost and Found?
- Report a campus safety concern?
- Get information about parking and transportation services?

Campus Security & Safety:
Cambridge and Coon Rapids—763.433.1330

- Resume and Cover Letter assistance?
- Explore job opportunities?
- What can I do with my major?

Career Center:
Cambridge and Coon Rapids –763.433.1430

- Buy books and supplies for my courses?
- Sell back my books after the semester is over?
- Buy college souvenirs, clothing, and gifts?

College Bookstore:
Cambridge—763.433.1850 • *Coon Rapids—763.433.1250*

- How do I join a club?
- Join Student Senate?
- Try out for a college athletic team?

Business Office:
Cambridge and Coon Rapids—763.433.1600

- Get information on study skills, time management, etc.?
- Meet with a peer or professional tutor?
- Find out about study groups?

Academic Support Center:
Cambridge—763.433.1990 • *Coon Rapids—63.433.1190*

- Receive tutoring in developmental math courses?

Math Skills Center:
Coon Rapids—763.433.1260

- Receive assistance with GED preparation, reading enhancement, and basic math and writing skills?

Adult Basic Education (ABE):
Cambridge and Coon Rapids—763.433.1940

- Get a foundation scholarship application?
- Apply for a foundation scholarship?

Institutional Advancement Office:
Cambridge and Coon Rapids—763.433.1130

- Find out if I am eligible for personal, one on one academic advising?

TRIO Student Support Services (SSS):
Coon Rapids—763.433.1170   •   *Cambridge—763.433-1170*

Student Life & Athletics:
Cambridge and Coon Rapids—763.433.1320

- Do online research for my classes?
- Check out a book or video for a class assignment?
- Find out what other research resources are available?

Library:
Cambridge—763.433.1950   •   *Coon Rapids—763.433.1150*

- Take the Accuplacer placement test?
- Schedule a make-up test?

Testing Center:
Cambridge—763.433.1980   •   *Coon Rapids—763.433.1180*

- Apply for accommodations for a documented disability?

Disability Services:
Cambridge and Coon Rapids—763.433.1350

- Receive help with my military benefits?
- Get academic advising?

Veteran Services:
Cambridge and Coon Rapids—763.433.1856

Activate Your Anoka-Ramsey Student Technology Services!

We hope you are excited to start at Anoka-Ramsey! As a reminder, you should do the following as soon as possible after you register for a course.

1. StarID information—this will allow you to use campus computers, sign on to the school's wireless network, and provides access to your student email, D2L Brightspace and your e-services account. You will need your StarID and the password that you used to apply. If you do not remember your StarID or password visit: https://www.anokaramsey.edu/password You will be able to look up your StarID and reset your password.
2. Activate your student email—important college information, including your financial aid award letter, is communicated to you via your school email.
   A. On the top bar of the college web site (www.anokaramsey.edu), hover over "Current Students"
   B. Select "Email" from the dropdown list.
   C. Click on "Activate your student email account (the one you created in Step 1). This will provide you with your new student email address. Please write it down for future reference.

D. Test it out: Go to mail.anokaramsey.edu. Your user id is your my.anoka ramsey.edu email address (the one you wrote down in Step C); your password is the same as your campus computer/StarID password (the one you created in Step 1). The first time you access email, you will need to choose and set your time zone (Central: US and Canada).

E. Forward your email to account that you regularly check by clicking the settings icon in the upper-right corner. Click "options" on the left column and follow on-screen instructions.

3. **Activate your D2L Brightspace**—Most classes utilize D2L Brightspace, so it is to your advantage to familiarize yourself with your "online classroom". You will not be able to enter specific D2L class sites until the FIRST day of classes; however, several weeks before the start of the term, you will be able to see which classes will be using D2L.

A. From ARCC's home page- www.anokaramsey.edu, hover over "Current Students"

B. Select "D2L Brightspace" from the menu options

C. Enter your information:
   Username: StarID
   Password: This is the same password you created in Step 1.

You can also access D2L Brightspace by visiting: https://anokaramsey.ims.mnscu.edu/

For detailed instructions, visit http://www.anokaramsey.edu/resources/Technology

For help, contact the Information Technology Helpdesk: 763-433-1510 or it- helpdesk@anokaramsey.edu.

Tips for Success in College

The Basics

- Make the Student Home page at www.AnokaRamsey.edu/resources/ your home page for quick access to student log-in areas, and timely news and resources.
- Check the academic calendars in this planner and visit www.anokaramsey.edu/calendar/ often to find important dates and deadlines, such as class drop, add and withdrawal dates, class start dates, final exam dates and more.
- Manage your time. Plan ahead to meet your deadlines. Use this organizer or one of your own.
- Be prepared and ask for help when you need it.
- Think about your course selections. Read course descriptions online and get help from an academic advisor when choosing your courses.
- Enroll in courses that interest you and expand your horizons.
- Do not miss the first class. You will meet the instructor and learn about course expectations, including attendance policy.
- Understand the course syllabus—an outline of course requirements—evaluations, expectations and due dates.
- Be on time, participate in class discussions, take detailed notes, and ask questions of your instructor and/or classmates.
- Plan study time. Commit to a schedule that includes two to three hours of study per week outside of class for every class hour.
- Do not procrastinate. It causes stress and you don't learn the material nearly as well.

- Visit the Academic Support Center (ASC) for free tutoring help.
- Be original! Do not plagiarize. It is illegal and you don't learn by doing it.
- Work hard and study hard to meet your academic goals.
- Keep track of your grades and Grade Point Average (GPA). Visit back2college. com/gpa.htm for a free grade point average calculator.
- Set goals for the day, the course, the semester, the year, your college career and your life. Write these goals down so you can refer to them often.
- Do not give up! When things get tough, ask for help and focus on your goal(s): a college degree or certificate, a more fulfilling career, better wage earning potential. Whatever your goal is, you can reach it.

Use Your Resources!

- Ask for help! Faculty and staff members are committed to your success.
- Get to know your instructors, their office locations and office hours. Instructors can help you with the subject and with college in general. They are your single greatest resource.
- See an academic advisor early and often. They can help you figure out the best paths to get to where you want to be.
- Check into alternative credits to see if your out-of-college experiences can earn credits toward a degree or certificate. Visit www.anokaramsey.edu/resources/ credit-for-prior-learning/ for details.
- Take advantage of the libraries and academic advising services at both campuses.

Outside the Classroom

- Take advantage of the many opportunities Anoka-Ramsey offers for supporting your education outside of the classroom.
- Get involved in athletics, theatre, music, art, student organizations and clubs, campus events and activities.
- Attend workshops and other learning opportunities offered throughout the year.

Student Checklist

This list will help you take the necessary steps to achieve your goals at Anoka-Ramsey Community College. If you have any questions, please call at 763-433-1100. Additional details are also available at the Student Resources page (http://www.anokaramsey.edu/resources/)

Before Classes Begin

- Pay Tuition or Set-Up a Payment Plan
- Buy Books
- Initialize Your Student Email Account
  Your student email is the official form of communication from the college.
- Have your StarID and password information available
  Admitted students are issued an eight-digit StarID that is given at time of application. The password that was created at this time, is the one that you will use to access computers, email, D2L Brightspace and your e-services account. If you do not remember your password or StarID visit anokaramsey.edu/password for assistance.

With your Star ID you can access your Student E-services account to:
- Register, add, drop, or withdraw classes
- Check holds on your record
- Pay your tuition and fees
- View or change your address
- View financial aid status/awards
- View your grades or print your transcript (academic record)
- Print a degree audit report (DARS)

- Get Your Photo ID Cards

  Photo ID cards are generally issued during Registration Planning Sessions (RPS) and are available for all students. The card is required to check out library materials and access library databases, use the fitness center, open weight room or open gym. It is also required for free entrance into some student activities, two free tickets to college productions, use of the free car-starting service at the Coon Rapids Campus, and to receive student discounts at participating local businesses. There is a $5 fee to replace lost ID cards.

  Photo IDs are taken at the Cambridge Campus Information Desk and at the Coon Rapids Campus Room SC114.

Each Semester
- **Check Your Student Email Daily**
- **Meet with Your Advisor**
- **Be Aware of Priority Registration Dates**
- **Be Aware of Tuition Due Dates**

  Failure to pay your tuition on time may result in you being dropped from a class for non-payment.
- **Check Class Add/Drop/Withdrawal Dates**
- **Check Dates for Midterms and Finals**
- **Be Aware of Satisfactory Academic Progress Standards**

  Students must maintain a cumulative grade point average of 2.0 and a cumulative completion rate of 67% to remain in good standing, continue enrollment and remain eligible for financial aid.
- **Visit Department Pages**

  Most Academic Departments at Anoka-Ramsey host their own Web pages containing important information for current students.

Every Year
- **Review Your Transcript**

  Your transcript is the official record of your academic history. Review it every year to be sure it is accurate.

As Needed
- Keep your address and phone number(s) current with the Records & Registration Office. Changes can be managed online through your e-services account.
- Visit *www.AnokaRamsey.edu/resources/forms/* to review Printable Student Forms.
- **Review Academic Catalog**

  The *Student Academic Catalog* is issued annually at *www.anokaramsey.edu/academics/academic-catalog/* to provide information about admissions, academic calendars, registration and records, costs and financial assistance, transfer policies, course descriptions, degrees and certificates, programs of study, student life activities, student policies, student services and more.

- **Apply to Graduate**
  Anoka-Ramsey Community College hosts two commencement ceremonies each spring, one for Cambridge Campus graduates and one for Coon Rapids Campus graduates.
  The deadlines for submitting your graduation application are:
  Fall Semester: July 1
  Spring Semester: November 1
  Summer Session: April 1

Student Resources

Everyone needs help at some point, and those who ask for the help they need are often the most successful. So don't hesitate. Reach out. There are services to keep you on course to success.

Academic Advising

Academic Advising is a great place to start for planning course registration and a path to your higher education goals.

An academic advisor can help you with:
- Course placement, sequencing and consultation
- Schedule and course difficulties
- Degree planning and graduation requirements
- Transfer options and course planning
- Campus service referrals
- Rehabilitative (SAP) Advising
- DARS report interpretation
- Dropping or withdrawing
- Maximum Time Frame
- Petition and appeal questions

Academic Advising offices at both campuses are located behind the Information Desks.

Academic Departments

Faculty members in most subjects have developed Academic Department Web pages as resources for students in their classes.

Visit www.anokaramsey.edu/academics/department-faculty/ to link to the academic department Web pages:

Accounting, American Sign Language, Anthropology, Art, Biomedical Technology, Biology, Business, Chinese, Chemistry, Computer and Information Sciences, Computer Networking, Economics, Engineering, English, French, Geography, German, History, Honors, Humanities, Integrative Health and Healing, Journalism, Mathematics, Music, Natural Science, Nursing, Philosophy, Physical Therapist Assistant (PTA), Physics, Political Science, Psychology, Reading and Study Skills, Sociology, Spanish, Speech, Theatre, and Wellness.

Academic Support Centers

The Academic Support Center (ASC) provides free, drop-in peer tutoring in a variety of subject areas.

The ASC supports an on-site computer lab, a collection of hand-outs on study-skills and writing tips, and study-group information. The ASC also provides tutoring support for online courses.

Math Skills Center

The Math Skills and Advising Center at the Coon Rapids Campus (Room L122) is available to help students brush up on their math skills, improve their test scores and get the assistance they need to succeed in college.

If you tested into Math 0100, 0240, or 0250 you are eligible for free academic advising and tutoring services.

Writing Services

Writing tutors can help you with writing in any subject area and at any stage in the writing process, from brainstorming to a final draft. The goal is to make you a better writer overall, not to "fix" an individual piece of writing. Tutoring services are not only for students struggling with writing. Students at any level can benefit from talking with a trained writing tutor.

TRIO Student Support Services

The Student Support Services (SSS) program serves 175 students at the Coon Rapids Campus and 140 students at the Cambridge campus. TRIO provides a positive learning environment to help ensure the academic success of its participants. Eligible participants are those who are first-generation, of moderate income, or participants with a disability.

This free service includes academic advising, career guidance, workshops, cultural activities and social events. For more information, visit *www.anokaramsey.edu/resources/trio-programs/*.

Career Services Office

Coon Rapids Campus, Room SC273; Cambridge by appointment) for students and alumni offering one-on-one assistance in creating job search strategies, resume and cover letter critiques and guidance, interviewing preparation, such as mock interviews, and a library of resources on careers and employment skills. The Career Services office also offers a spring employment skills fair. For more information or to schedule an appointment, call 763-433-1430.

Career Services offers classes, workshops, books and one-on-one assistance with making decisions related to your career planning process.

Career Services includes:
- Resume and cover letter assistance
- Job search assistance
- Exploration into careers related to chosen major

To schedule an individual counseling appointment at the Cambridge Campus, call 763-433-1840; at the Coon Rapids Campus, call 763-433-1240.

Experiential Learning, Internships and Field Experience

The Experiential Learning program engages students, faculty and staff with volunteer opportunities and service learning projects that cultivate a life-long spirit of service.

Counseling Services

Our counselors are professionally trained and certified to provide you with support and guidance in the areas of academics, career planning and personal concerns that may affect your academic success.

Counselors at Anoka-Ramsey can help with:
- personal counseling
- career counseling and assessments
- various mental health topics

Counseling also provides career assistance through the Career Development Course
- Visit www.anokaramsey.edu/resources/career-services/ for more details.

Students with Disabilities

Students with documented disabilities or other special needs, such as learning disabilities, physical challenges or health concerns, are able to request disability accommodations from Disability Services to realize their potential for academic success. Please request services in a timely manner to assure availability.

Disability Services include:
- Interpreters for hard-of-hearing or deaf students
- Textbooks on tape/CD and Braille (requires advanced request)
- Note-takers or permission to tape lectures
- Testing accommodations
- Assistive technology (Dragon Naturally Speaking voice recognition)
- Accommodations for wheelchair or other special furniture
- Referral to outside agencies for additional services
- Priority registration

English Language Learners

Anoka-Ramsey offers materials and services for English Language Learners (ELL) and for students for whom English is a Second Language (ESL). Free English for Academic Purposes (EAP) classes are also available to help build skills in college-level English, American academic writing and vocabulary. A dedicated ELL/ESL computer terminal located in the Academic Support Center (ASC) may be used to practice reading, writing, and speaking skills. In the library, students will find a videotape series profiling everyday situations faced by individuals new to the United States, as well as audiotape recorded books of fiction, classics, and language skills.

Libraries

The Cambridge Campus and the Coon Rapids Campus each have a library to provide a variety of instructional resources and services to students. Each library also has individual study spaces as well as listening and viewing areas.

The book, periodical and non-print collections in each library are coordinated with the college curriculum to provide students with the resources relevant to their courses of study.

Photo ID cards are required to check out materials, request materials from other libraries, and to access library databases.

Office of Diversity & Multicultural Affairs

The Office of Diversity and Multicultural Affairs enhances the involvement of underrepresented and underserved students to promote a campus community that embraces, celebrates and creates inclusive learning environments.

Visit www.anokaramsey.edu/campus-life/diversity-inclusion/often to learn more about diversity and multiculturalism.

Testing Services

The Testing Centers at the Cambridge Campus and the Coon Rapids Campus serve students by providing the College Board Placement Test (Accuplacer) for appropriate course placement, as well as alternative and make-up testing.

Visit www.anokaramsey.edu/resources/testing-services/ for more details.

Veterans Services

Veteran Services are available at both campuses to assist veterans, current military members, and dependents with all aspects of their state and federal benefits.

Anoka-Ramsey employs full-time Veterans Services staff to help with advising, course planning, and benefits questions. Anoka-Ramsey also houses the North Metro Regional Coordinator for the Minnesota Higher Education Veterans Programs.

Together, these resources provide for veterans' needs regarding their education, state and federal benefit referral, and military-to-civilian transition issues.

Visit www.anokaramsey.edu/resources/veterans-services/ for more information about veteran services.

Safety & Transportation

Safety and security is provided to Anoka-Ramsey students, faculty and staff on a proactive basis with an emphasis on crime prevention. Students and staff are encouraged to report safety issues and incidences to the Public Safety Office at 763-433-1330.

Cambridge Campus

General Security Services Inc. provides security at the Cambridge Campus, Monday through Thursday, 8 am to 10:30 pm; Fridays, 8 am to 4:30 pm.

The Cambridge Police Department patrols the outside grounds during the late evening hours and Friday night through the weekend and holidays.

Coon Rapids Campus

General Security Services Inc. provides security services at the Coon Rapids Campus, Monday through Friday, 8 am to 4:30 pm.

The Coon Rapids Police Department Reserves patrol the buildings and grounds and provide security escort services, Monday through Thursday, 6:30 to 10:30 pm. The Coon Rapids Police patrol outside grounds during the late evening hours and Friday night through the weekend and holidays.

Car Starting Service

The Coon Rapids Campus offers a free car-starting service to students. Students need to call the Hwy 10 Mobile Station at 763-757-6789 directly and present Student/Tech ID card for service.

Security Escort Service

A security escort service is available at each campus to walk you to and/or from your car or class Monday through Thursday evenings, 6 to 10 pm at the Cambridge Campus and 6:30 to 10:20 pm at the Coon Rapids Campus. To use the service, use the black courtesy telephone at various entrances or inquire at the Information Center. Requests for the service must be made prior to 9:45 pm at the Cambridge Campus and 10 pm at the Coon Rapids Campus.

Parking

Anoka-Ramsey students, employees and other people with a purpose or function at the college may park on college property. Numerous parking areas have been designated for accessible parking. Violators of parking rules and regulations may be ticketed by the local law enforcement agency.

Parking is prohibited on college roadways, sidewalks, landscaped areas, safety zones, loading zones, within 10 feet of intersections, adjacent to yellow curbs, and in areas where parking is expressly prohibited by signs.

People parking automobiles on property owned, leased or occupied by Anoka-Ramsey do so at their own risk. The college or the state are not responsible for loss of property, damage to automobile while parked, damage which may be incurred through the process of impounding the automobile or for any other damage or loss, sustained while on a college parking facility.

Campus Security Recommendations

- Do not loan your keys to anyone, even a classmate or a friend.
- Do not put your name or address on key rings in case they are lost or misplaced.
- Do not leave personal property (purses, briefcases, calculators, tech ID, etc.) unattended or visible in a locked car.
- Do not give personal identification information to strangers.
- Lock your car doors and do not leave your keys in the vehicle.
- Park your car in a well-lit or a secure area.
- Avoid walking alone at night and walk where there is plenty of light and traffic.
- Call for a security escort. Cambridge Campus: 763-433-1840; Coon Rapids Campus: 763-433-1240.
- Be alert to your surroundings. If you suspect you are being followed, walk fast, go in a different direction, go to the other side of the street and yell for help, and head quickly for a lighted area or a group of people.
- Report suspicious activity. Cambridge Campus: 763-433-1840; Coon Rapids Campus: 763-433-1240.
- Have your keys ready when returning to your residence or vehicle and keep your personal or valuable items concealed and close to your body.

Technology Services

Anoka-Ramsey provides technology resources to all enrolled students, faculty and staff. The college Information Technology Department takes pride in providing high-quality support and service.

For college-related technical assistance, please contact the IT Helpdesk.

Contact Information

Telephone: 763-433-1510
Email: IT.Helpdesk@AnokaRamsey.edu

Computer Lab Hours and Locations
Cambridge Campus Rm F207
Monday–Thursday: 7:30 am to 10 pm
Friday: 7:30 am to 3:30 pm
Saturday/Sunday: CLOSED

Coon Rapids Campus Rm T124
Monday–Thursday: 7:30 am to 10 pm
Friday/Saturday: 7:30 am to 3:30 pm
Sunday: CLOSED
NOTE: Hours subject to change due to observation of federal holidays.

Course Registration Account

Upon admittance to Anoka-Ramsey, each student is provided a course registration account to manage their courses, view grades, pay tuition and check financial aid status.

Provided with the acceptance letter, each student receives a unique student number and a password. The password is temporary and needs to be changed at the first login to the course registration system.

NOTE: The course registration account is separate from the college network, college email and D2L Brightspace accounts.

College Network Account

Each student is provided a college network account which provides access to college lab computers and printers, the wireless network, student-allocated network storage and student email.

For information on your StarID and password, visit *AnokaRamsey.edu/password* and follow the onscreen instructions.

For security reasons the account password is set to expire 180 days after the account initialization and every 180 days thereafter.

NOTE: The college network account is separate from the course registration and D2L Brightspace accounts.

College Email Account

After admittance to Anoka-Ramsey, each student receives an official college email account which serves as the official communication method used by college faculty and staff to contact and update students.

Students are required to monitor this account and are responsible for any communications received to this account.

Finding your college email address can be done from the "Current Students" drop-down menu located at the top of the college Home page. From the menu, select "Student Email" and click on the green button labeled "Activate." Log onto the next page using your college network account name (Student ID) and password. If successful, your email address will be displayed.

Students may check college email by visiting Outlook.com. To log into email, use your full college email address and your college network account password. At first login you will be required to set your current time zone.

D2L Brightspace (D2L) Account

D2L Brightspace is an online tool Anoka-Ramsey faculty use to facilitate online learning.

Students enrolled in online courses, hybrid courses or web-supplemented courses are granted access to course specific material, course-related discussion boards and other online resources via D2L Brightspace. Not all courses are available in D2L Brightspace.

To access your D2L Brightspace account for the first time select "D2L Brightspace (D2L)" from the Student Home page drop-down menu on the college Home page and follow the onscreen instructions located on the right-side of the pop-up box.

NOTE: The D2L Brightspace account is separate from the course registration and college network accounts.

Step-by-Step Registration Process

Understanding the Different Course Offerings

Online Section/Internet:

In an online section, course materials are presented almost exclusively over the internet. Although there may be an initial orientation meeting, the class does not meet in-person or on campus regularly, and course materials and assignments are exchanged electronically (via the internet, D2L, and e-mail).

Blended Online and Web Enhanced-Limited Seat Time:

In a blended online and web enhanced section, a significant portion of the course is delivered via the internet. The class does have scheduled "in-person" or "on campus" meeting times. Do not register for the course if you cannot attend the "in-person" meetings.

Late Start Courses:

Courses starting after the fifth day of the semester are considered "Late Start". Refunds are calculated according to the beginning date of the course; 100% refunds are available only through the day after the first scheduled day of class.

How to Register Guide:

Each semester, it is important that you see an advisor for assistance with course selection.

Step 1: Visit www.anokaramsey.edu and hover over "Admissions". Click on "Registration for Current Students".

Step 2: Click on "Register for Courses".

Step 3: Enter your StarID and password.

Step 4: Choose which campus you want to attend.

Step 5: Choose the semester, subject, delivery, and then click on "Find Courses"

Step 6: Once you have selected a course, click "Add to Cart". Adding a course to your cart does not register you for a class.

Step 7: When you have added all your classes to the cart, click on "Course Cart".

Step 8: Once in your cart, check the box next to the course(s) you want to register for and then click "Register for Checked Courses" at the bottom of the page.

Step 9: Enter your password number. If you have successfully registered for the course, you will see a green check mark next to each course on the next screen. To view your final schedule, click on "View/Modify Class Schedule" on the left-hand side of the screen.

Schedule Conflict Worksheet

Time	Monday	Tuesday	Wednesday	Thursday	Friday	Saturday
7:00 a.m.						
8:00 a.m.						
9:00 a.m.						
10:00 a.m.						
11:00 a.m.						
12:00 p.m.						
1:00 p.m.						
2:00 p.m.						
3:00 p.m.						
4:00 p.m.						
5:00 p.m.						
6:00 p.m.						
7:00 p.m.						
8:00 p.m.						
9:00 p.m.						

Schedule Worksheet

Course ID	Department	Course Number	Course Section	Course Title	Hour	Days	Credits

Who Should a Student Meet With?

COUNSELOR (MaryAnn Larios, Nancy Elk, John Hennen, Jill Harrison and Isabelle Schmidt)	CAREER CENTER COORDINATOR (Christa Hayes)	ADVISOR
Need assistance with: • Career Exploration/Counseling (undecided on a major or career) • Career Assessments • Major Fair • Personal Issues • Mental Health • Life/Work Balance • Referral for Long-Term Counseling • Academic Concerns • Probation and Suspension Issues	Need assistance with: • Career Information (web or print resources) • Resume Writing • Cover Letter Writing • Job/Internship Search Strategies • Interviewing Skills • Internship/Field Experience • Job Fairs and ARCC Job Board • Employee Relation	Need assistance with: • Choosing Classes • Registration • Degree Planning • Transfer Questions • DARS Reports • Graduation • Accuplacer Results • Dropping or Withdrawing • Maximum Time Frame

Rev. 4/16

Online Resources at ARCC

D2L Brightspace

As a student at Anoka-Ramsey Community College, you will frequently be using an online learning management system called D2L Brightspace in conjunction with your face-to-face classes. Many instructors use this system to post your grades, house content for your classes, provide online discussions pertinent to your learning, and offer you an ability to connect with your classmates and instructors outside of the classroom.

If you are new to D2L Brightspace, consider learning more about how to navigate the system by visiting the self-paced video at: https://community.brightspace.com/resources/videos

Another website with a good overview of D2L Brightspace is: https://nhcc.ims.mnscu.edu/shared/V10-3_Training/Student/D2LStudentTrainingVideos.html

For help learning how to use D2L Brightspace, go to http://www.anokatech.edu/TechnologyServices/D2L-Brightspace.aspx and click on "Learning Resources".

Activating a STAR ID:

Open up a browser and go to https://starid.mnscu.edu/
Click on "activate your STAR ID"

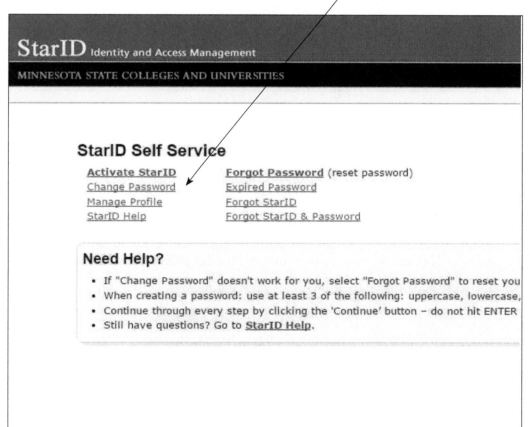

Students/Staff/Faculty must select one of the following options to verify their identity before they can activate a StarID, reset a forgotten password or retrieve a forgotten StarID.

1. Tech ID (Student ID): Student provides their Tech ID (frequently know as a Student ID), the institution that assigned the ID and their social security number. (Faculty/Staff also have a tech id)
2. Library Card Barcode: Student provides the barcode number from their PALS system library card, the institution that assigned library card and their SSN.
3. Personal Email Address: Student/Staff/Faculty enters a personal email address to request that a verification code be sent to the address.
    *   The email address entered by the student should be associated with their ISRS account and appear in their StarID profile. The student may have provided this email address when they applied to a school on-line or they may have added it to their eServices account at some other point. The email address may have also been assigned to the student's account by admissions or registration staff.
    *   The StarID system checks to see that the email address exists in the system and is assigned to a person with a StarID. If this check is OK, the system sends an email with a verification code to the email address.

- The student can then select the Verification Code option to complete the Activate StarID, Forgot Password or Forgot StarID process.

  Notes about Personal Email Address:
  - The StarID system will also send a verification code to an institution-ally managed email address. If the student is not using StarID to log into their institutionally manage email, this is okay. But if they are using StarID for their institutionally managed email, then they will not be able to retrieve the verification code and use it to complete the Activate StarID, Forgot Password or Forgot StarID process.
  - If the user receives error message, "We cannot verify the email address that you have entered", support staff should verify that the email address appears in their StarID profile. Log into https://starid.mnscu.edu/idm/ with your StarID (you need a help desk role).

4. **Verification Code:** The student can use the verification code sent the email addressed that provided using the Personal Email Address option.
   - A verification code expires 1 hours after it is generated. An attempt to use the verification code after it has expired results in an error message stating that have entered an invalid or expired verification code.
   - A verification code can be used once only. Once used, it will not be accepted again.

STAR ID Self Service

Click on Star ID Self Service when you need to change your password, etc. Passwords expire every 180 days, cannot contain any part of your name, and have to contain at least 3 of the following: upper case, lower case, numbers, special characters – such as ^&%

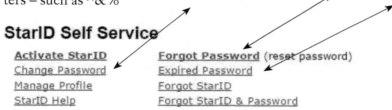

StarID Self Service

Activate StarID	**Forgot Password** (reset password)
Change Password	Expired Password
Manage Profile	Forgot StarID
StarID Help	Forgot StarID & Password

Need Help?

- If "Change Password" doesn't work for you, select "Forgot Password" to reset you
- When creating a password: use at least 3 of the following: uppercase, lowercase,
- Continue through every step by clicking the 'Continue' button – do not hit ENTER
- Still have questions? Go to **StarID Help**.

If you are having problems with your STAR ID, please contact:

Office of Information Technology
Anoka Technical College and Anoka-Ramsey Community College
(763) 433-1510
It.helpdesk@anokaramsey.edu or it.helpdesk@anokatech.edu

To install Office 2016 on your personal device

1. Log on to Outlook web access http://mail.office365.com/my.anokatech.edu or http://mail.office365.com/my.anokaramsey.edu
2. Click on the "gear" icon in the upper right hand corner and choose "Office365 Settings"

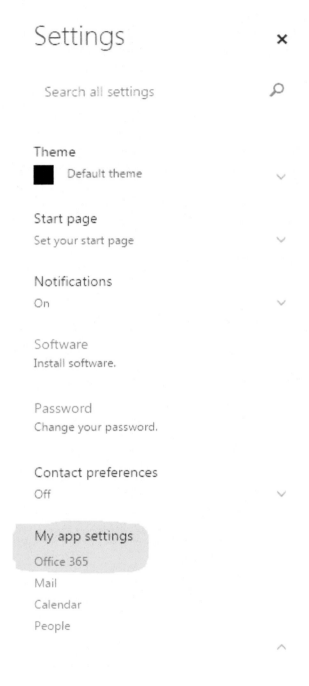

3. Click on "Software"
4. Make sure you see "Install Office 365 ProPlus with the new 2016 apps" and click Install.

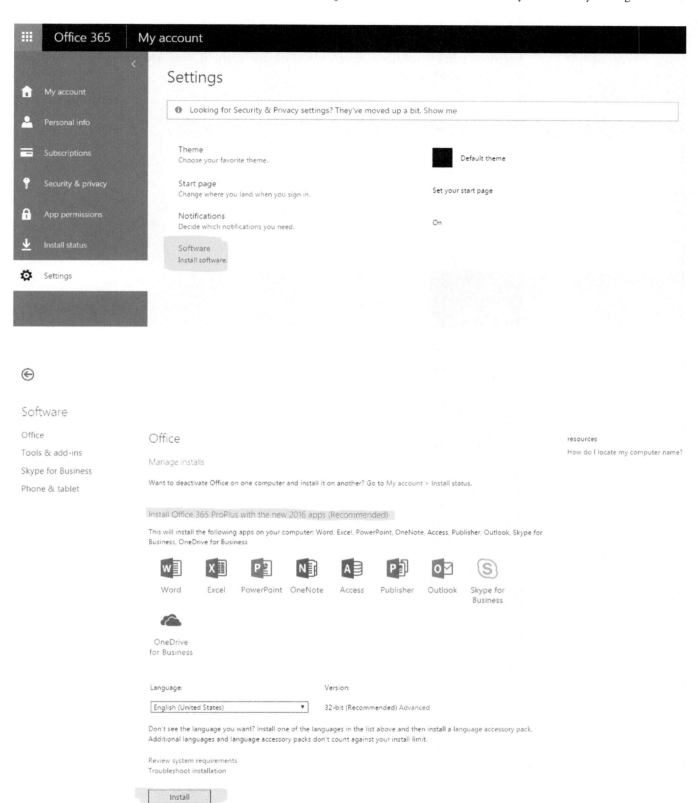

How to log on to your college email account for the first time

Logon to http://outlook.com/owa/anokatech.edu if you are an Anoka Technical College student and

Login: http://outlook.com/owa/anokaramsey.edu if you are an Anoka-Ramsey Community College student using your college email address and STAR ID password.

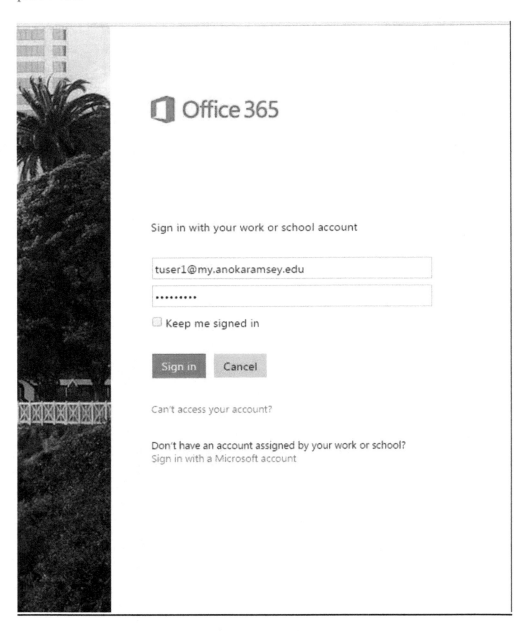

A box will come up where you choose English and time zone:

Choose Central Time US and Canada:

When you first log on it will look like the below. Click on mail

Notes

Notes

College Knowledge

EFFECTIVE COLLEGE BEHAVIOR IN CLASS AND ONLINE

This chapter identifies top tips for academic success you can implement immediately, including what to do inside and outside the classroom. It also alerts you to in-class and out-of-class behavior that should be avoided in college.

Chapter Preview

Equip you with key academic strategies for getting off to a good start in college, and increase your awareness of behaviors that reflect academic incivility and lack of academic integrity.

Learning Goal

 Think About It—Journal Entry 2.1

Thought Starter

1. In what three major ways do you think college will differ from high school? If you have been out of high school for a while and are just now returning to school, what are the biggest changes you see?

_____

_____

_____

_____

2. What three personal characteristics, qualities, or strategies do you think will be most important for college success?

_____

_____

_____

_____

_____

Box 2.1

Birds of a Different Feather: High School vs. College

High School	*College*
Your classes are mostly arranged for you.	You arrange your own schedule in consultation with your advisor. Schedules tend to look lighter than they really are.
Your time is structured by others.	You manage your own time.
You go from one class directly to another, spending six hours per day—30 hours per week—in class.	You have free time between classes; class times vary throughout the day and evening; and you spend 12–16 hours each week in class if you are a full-time student.
The school year is 36 weeks long; some classes extend over both semesters, and some do not.	The academic year may be divided into separate semesters or quarters.
Teachers monitor class attendance.	Professors may not formally monitor class attendance; you're expected to have the self-discipline to show up and get down information that's presented in class.
Teachers often write information on the board for you to put in your notes.	Professors may lecture nonstop, expecting you to identify and write down important information in your notes. Professors don't record all their key points on the board. Notes that professors write on the board are used to supplement or complement the lecture, not to summarize for the lecture.
Teachers provide you with information you missed when you were absent.	Professors expect you to get information you missed from classmates.
You are given short reading assignments that are then discussed, and often reviewed, in class.	You're assigned substantial amounts of reading and writing that may not be directly addressed in class.
You seldom need to read anything more than once and sometimes listening in class is enough.	You need to review class notes and read material regularly.
Teachers present material to help you understand the textbook.	Professors may not follow the textbook, but you may be expected to relate class sessions to textbook readings.
You may have studied outside of class for zero to two hours per week.	You need to study for at least two to three hours outside of class for each hour spent in class.
Teachers remind you of assignments and due dates.	Professors expect you to consult the course syllabus for assignments and deadlines.

Source: Southern Methodist University (2006).

College teachers don't tell you what you're supposed to do. They just expect you to do it. High school teachers tell you about five times what you're supposed to do."
—*College sophomore (Appleby, 2008)*

If you have been out of school for a while, consider what has changed in your life since high school. You probably have more and different responsibilities now (e.g., a mortgage, children, etc.). Reflect on how you will manage these responsibilities with your college work (Chapter 4 on time management will give you some strategies). You will also notice the classroom environment has changed quite a bit over the years. You will rely on technology much more to assist with your education than you did years ago. If you need help with your technology skills, see if your school offers a basic technology course or has a technology help desk. You might also want to ask some of your more tech savvy classmates for some technology tips.

Think About It—Journal Entry 2.2

Look back at the differences between high school and college listed in **Box 2.1**.

Which differences were you least aware or were most surprised to see?

Why?

Top Tips for Academic Success

1. Read the course syllabus carefully when you first receive it and refer to it throughout the term. (See **Box 2.2** for details and strategies.)

Box 2.2

Reading and Understanding a Syllabus

What's in a syllabus? A course syllabus is a document created by instructors that will probably be given to you on the first day of class. The syllabus has been called a contract between the student and the instructor. Please pay careful attention to all parts of the syllabus and make a copy to keep with you at all times. You are responsible for adhering to this contract. However, your instructor can change the syllabus as he/she deems necessary. A syllabus usually contains the following components (not necessarily in this order):

1. Course department, prefix, number, title, credit hours, semester and year, and course reference number.
2. Meeting times and location, instructor information (name, office location, office hours, contact information).
3. Catalog course description, including prerequisites and/or corequisites (courses students need to have taken before this one or at the same time); prerequisite skill sets (e.g., programming languages, familiarity with software).
4. Text(s) with dates, supplemental text(s), other required readings, and references readings (books, reserve readings, course readers, software, and supplies with information about where they can be obtained). You are expected to have these on the first day or soon after the first day.
5. Student learning outcomes and/or course objectives (this is what the instructor is telling you that he or she will work the lectures around, and you will have learning opportunities around them throughout the course). The tests, quizzes, papers, etc., are based on these objectives.
6. Skills and knowledge students will gain. These are the new items you will have learned after the course is completed. You may hear these referred to as competencies.
7. Course organization. This tells you step-by-step how this course will be taught.
8. Explanation of the topical organization of the course. This will give you an idea of the specific topics that will be covered in class.
9. Course requirements (what students will have to do in the course: assignments, exams, projects, performances, attendance, participation, etc.). Usually the nature and format of assignments and the expected length of written work, as well as due dates for assignments and dates for exams, will be explained.
10. Evaluation and grading policy: what grades are based on, especially your final grade. Always keep up on what grade you have in class and discuss how to improve it with the instructor on a regular basis.
11. Course policies and expectations: may include policies on attendance, participation, tardiness, academic integrity, missing homework, missed exams, recording classroom activities, food in class, laptop use, cell phone use, etc.
12. Other expectations such as student behavior (e.g., respectful consideration of one another's perspectives, open-mindedness, creative risk-taking).
13. Course calendar/schedule (sometimes the instructor will put "tentative" before these words, letting you know it is subject to change). However, this is a class-to-class breakdown of topics and assignments (readings, homework, project due dates).

As a college student, you are responsible for knowing the contents of the course syllabus. It is not the instructor's responsibility to go over it with you. Be sure you read and understand your syllabi for all your courses. If you have any questions, be sure to ask your instructor right away.

"My biggest recommendation: GO TO CLASS. I learned this the hard way my first semester. You'll be surprised what you pick up just by being there. I wish someone would have informed me of this before I started school."

—Advice to new students from a college sophomore (Walsh, 2005)

2. **Don't miss class.** Not surprisingly, the total amount of time you spend on learning is associated with how much you learn and how deeply you learn. This association leads to a straightforward recommendation: Attend all your classes in all your courses. It may be tempting to skip or cut classes because college professors are less likely to monitor your attendance or take roll than high school teachers. However, don't let this new freedom fool you into thinking that missing classes will not affect your course grades. Over the past 75 years, numerous studies have shown a direct relationship between class attendance and course grades—as one goes up or down, so does the other (Credé, Roch, Kieszczynka, 2010; Launius, 1997; Shimoff & Catania, 2001; Tagliacollo, Vol-

pato, & Pereira, 2010). **Figure 2.1** depicts the results of a study conducted at the City Colleges of Chicago, which shows the relationship between students' class attendance during the first five weeks of the term and their final course grades.

Note

Look at going to class like going to work. If you miss work days, it lowers your pay; if you miss classes, it lowers your grades.

3. **Adopt a seating location in class that maximizes attention and minimizes distraction.** Many years of research show that students who sit in the front and center of class tend to earn higher test scores and course grades (Benedict & Hoag, 2004; Rennels & Chaudhair, 1988; Tagliacollo, Volpato, & Pereira, 2010). These results have been found even when students are assigned seats by their instructor, so it's not just a matter of more motivated and studious students sitting in the front of the room. Instead, the better academic performance achieved by students sitting front and center stems from learning advantages associated with this seating location.

FIGURE 2.1: **Percentage of Classes Attended and Final Course Grades**

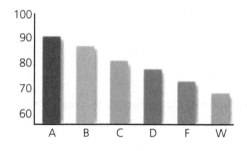

City Colleges of Chicago

Front-and-center seating benefits your academic performance by improving your vision of material written on the board or screen and your ability to hear the instructor's lectures. In additi on, sitting in the front means you don't have to peer over or around the heads of other students. This results in more direct eye contact with the instructor, which increases your focus of attention, reduces your sense of anonymity, and increases your level of involvement in class.

Lastly, sitting in the front of class can also reduce your level of anxiety about speaking in class because you will not have numerous classmates sitting in front of you turning around to look at you when you speak.

The *bottom line:* When you enter a classroom, get in the habit of heading for a seat in the front and center of class. In large classes, it's even more important to get to know your instructors—not only to improve your attention, note taking, and class participation—but also to improve your instructors' ability to remember who you are and how well you performed in class. This will work to your advantage when you ask your instructors for letters of recommendation later in your college career.

Eighty percent of success is showing up."

—Woody Allen, Oscar & Golden Globe winning film director, writer, and author

I like to sit up front so I am not distracted by others and I don't have to look around people's heads to see the chalkboard."

—First-year college student

I tend to sit at the very front of my classrooms. It helps me focus and take notes better. It also eliminates distractions."

—First-year college student

4. **Sit by people who will enable (not disable) your ability to listen and learn.** Intentionally sit near classmates who will not distract you or interfere with the quality of your note taking. The human attention span has a limited capacity; we can give all or part of our attention to whatever task we're performing. Actively listening to and taking notes on lecture information is a demanding task that demands undivided attention.

Note

When you enter class, you have a choice about where you're going to sit. Choose wisely by selecting a location that will maximize your attentiveness to the instructor and your effectiveness as a note-taker.

Think About It—Journal Entry 2.3

When you enter a classroom, where do you usually sit?

Why do you sit there? Is it a conscious choice or more like an automatic habit?

Do you think that the seat you usually choose places you in the best possible position for listening and learning in the classroom? Why or why not?

5. **Adopt a seating posture that screams attention.** Sitting upright and leaning forward increases attention because these signs of physical alertness reach the brain and stimulate mental alertness. If your body is in an alert and ready position, your mind picks up these physical cues and follows your body's lead. Baseball players get into a ready position before a pitch is delivered to ready themselves to catch batted balls; similarly, learners who assume a ready position in the classroom put themselves in a better position to catch ideas batted around in class. Studies show that when humans are mentally alert and ready to learn, a greater amount of C-kinase (a brain chemical) is released at the connection point between brain cells, which increases the likelihood that neurological (learning) connections are formed between them (Howard, 2014).

Another advantage to being attentive in class is that it sends a clear message to your instructor that you're a courteous and conscientious student. This can influence your instructor's perception and evaluation of your academic performance; if at the end of the course you're on the border between a higher and lower grade, you're more likely to get the benefit of the doubt.

6. **Be a self-aware learner.** One characteristic of successful learners is that they self-monitor (check themselves) while learning to remain aware of:

- Whether they're using effective learning strategies (e.g., if they're giving their undivided attention to what they're learning)
- Whether they're truly comprehending what they are learning (e.g., if they're understanding it at a deep level or memorizing it at a surface level)
- How they're regulating or adjusting their learning strategies to meet the demands of different academic tasks and subjects (e.g., if they're reading technical material in a science textbook, they read at a slower rate and check their understanding more frequently than when reading a novel) (Pintrich & Schunk, 2002).

You can begin to establish good self-monitoring habits by getting in the routine of periodically pausing to reflect on the strategies you're using to learn and how you "do" college. For instance, you can ask yourself the following questions:

- Am I listening attentively to what my instructor is saying in class?
- Am I comprehending what I'm reading outside of class?
- Am I effectively using campus resources designed to support my success?
- Am I interacting with campus professionals who can contribute to my current success and future development?
- Am I interacting and collaborating with peers who can support (not sabotage) my learning and development?
- Am I effectively implementing college success strategies (such as those identified in this book)?

> We learn neither by thinking nor by doing; we learn by thinking about what we are doing."
>
> —*George Stoddard, Professor Emeritus, University of Iowa*

Note

Successful students and successful people are mindful—*they watch what they're doing and remain aware of whether they're doing it effectively and to the best of their ability.*

 Think About It—Journal Entry 2.4

How would you rate your academic self-confidence at this point in your college experience? (Circle one.)

very confident   somewhat confident   somewhat unconfident   very unconfident

Why?

The Importance of Time Spent on Coursework outside of Class

In college, you will spend much less time sitting in class than you did in high school; however, you will be expected to spend much more time working on your courses outside of class. Less than 40% of beginning college students report having studied six or more hours per week during their final year in high school (Pryor, et al., 2012) and only one-third expect to spend more than 20 hours per week preparing for class in college (National Survey of Student Engagement, 2009).

Unfortunately, less than 10% of beginning college students say they will study at least two hours out of class for every hour spent in class—which is what most college faculty believe is necessary to do well in college (Kuh, 2005). This has to change if college students are to earn good grades. Just as successful athletes need to put in time and effort to improve their physical performance, successful students need to do the same to improve their academic performance. Studies repeatedly show that the more time college students spend on academic work outside of class, the higher grades they earn in their college courses (National Survey of Student Engagement, 2009). In one study of more than 25,000 college students it was found that the percentage of students receiving "A" grades was almost three times higher for students who spent 40 or more hours per week on academic work than it was for students who spent between 20 and 40 hours. For students who spent 20 or fewer hours per week on academic work, the percentage of them receiving a grade of "C" or below was almost twice as high as it was for students who spent 40 or more hours on academic work (Pace, 1990, 1995).

If you need further motivation to achieve good grades, keep in mind that higher grades earned in college translates into career success after college. Research on college graduates indicates that the higher their grades were in college, the higher is: (a) their starting salary, (b) the status (prestige) of their first job, and (c) their career mobility (ability to change jobs or move into different positions). This relationship between higher college grades and greater career advantages exists for students at all types of colleges and universities—regardless of the reputation or prestige of the institution the students attended (Pascarella & Terenzini, 1991, 2005). In other words, how well students do in college matters more to their career success than where they went to college.

> "I thought I would get a better education if the school had a really good reputation. Now, I think one's education depends on how much effort you put into it."
>
> —First-year college student

Think About It—Journal Entry 2.5

During your senior year in high school, about how many hours per week did you spend on schoolwork outside of class? What do you think you'll have to do differently in college?

When I went to college, I had to work to assist my family and to assist in paying for college. Although I was an 18-year-old, I came from a very poor family and it was part of my obligation to assist them financially, while it was more important to me to go to school and graduate so I could have a higher standard of living in comparison to my mother and father. Juggling my work life and school life quickly became a reality to which I had to adjust. Thus, I made sure I made the time to study and attend class as my first priority and worked with my employer to adjust my work hours around my classes. By placing my future above my immediate present, I was able to get my college degree and increase my earnings substantially beyond the earnings I had in college and way beyond my parents' earnings.

—*Aaron Thompson*

Effective Classroom Behavior: The Fundamentals

In college, there will be expectations regarding appropriate behavior inside and outside the classroom. These expectations will vary, depending on the type of course you're taking—traditional face-to-face, online, technology-enhanced, or hybrid. With a few exceptions (e.g., you can wear pajamas while participating in an online course at home), the following expectations apply to all college courses.

Regardless of the type of course you take, you will be expected to know basic computer skills such as how to save, download, and send documents, etc. If you have minimal computer skills refer to the Learn Free Basic Computer Skills website (http://www.gcflearnfree.org/basic-computer-skills) for helpful information.

1. **Avoid inappropriate and "uncivil" classroom behavior.** The following behaviors indicate to the instructor and to your classmates that you're an unmotivated student. In addition, they create a classroom climate that disturbs or disrupts the learning process. Be sure not to engage in any of them.
   - Coming to class late and/or leaving early
   - Walking in and out of the classroom during class
   - Talking with classmates while the instructor (or other classmates) is speaking
   - Disregarding deadlines set by your instructor
   - Using electronic devices for personal purposes
   - Acting disinterested in class (e.g., looking at the window or putting your head on your desk)
   - Doing homework during class time
   - Sleeping in class
   - Using electronic devices. (See **Box 2.3**)

BOX 2.3

Guidelines for Civil and Responsible Use of Personal Technology in the College Classroom

Behavior that interferes with the right of others to learn or teach in the classroom is referred to as *classroom incivility*. Listed below are forms of classroom incivility that involve student use of personal technology. Be sure to avoid them.

Using Cell Phones

Keeping a cell phone on in class is a clear form of classroom incivility because it can interfere with the right of others to learn. In a study of college students who heard a cell phone ringing during class and were later tested on information presented in class, they scored approximately 25% lower for information that was presented at the time a cell phone rang. This drop in performance was found

(continued)

Box 2.3 *(continued)*

even if the material was covered by the professor just prior to the cell phone ringing and if it was projected on a slide while the phone rang. The study also showed that students' attention to information presented in class is significantly reduced when classmates frantically search through handbags or pockets to find and silence a ringing (or vibrating) phone (Shelton, et al., 2009). These findings clearly suggest that cell phone use in class disrupts the learning process and the civil thing to do is:

The right to do something does not mean that doing it is right."

—*William Safire, American author, journalist, and presidential speech writer*

- Turn your cell phone off before entering class, or keep it out of the classroom altogether. (You can use *studiousapp.com* to automatically silence your phone at times of the day when you're in class.) In rare cases where you may need to leave class to respond to an emergency, ask your instructor for permission in advance.
- Don't check your cell phone during the class period by turning it off and on.

- Don't look at your cell phone at any time during a test because your instructor may suspect that you're looking up answers to test questions.

Text Messaging

Although this form of electronic communication is silent, it still can distract or disturb your classmates. It's also discourteous or disrespectful to instructors when you put head down and turn your attention away from them while they're speaking in class. The bottom line: Be sensitive to your classmates and your instructor—don't text in class!

Surfing the Web

Although this can be done without creating distracting sounds, it still can still create visual distractions. Unless you're taking class notes on it, keep your laptop closed to avoid distracting your classmates and raising your instructors' suspicion that you're a disinterested or disrespectful student.

Final Note: In addition to technological incivilities, other discourteous classroom behaviors include personal grooming, holding side conversations, and doing homework for other classes. Even if your attendance is perfect, "little things" you do in class that reflect inattention or disinterest can send a strong message to your instructors that you're an unmotivated and discourteous student.

 Think About It—Journal Entry 2.6

Have you observed any recent examples of classroom incivility that you thought were particularly distracting or discourteous? What was the uncivil behavior and what consequences did it have on others?

_____

_____

_____

_____

_____

Technology should be used sensitively and civilly not only inside the classroom, but outside the classroom as well. There are common rules of courtesy for Internet use (referred to as "netiquette") that should be used in social media. These rules are summarized in **Box 2.4**.

Box 2.4

Top 20 Rules to Follow for Appropriate Netiquette

1. The Internet is not private. What goes out on the airwaves stays on the airwaves! Do not post pictures to the Internet that you would not want your mom or younger cousin to see.
2. Avoid saying anything that could be interpreted as derogatory (e.g., no cursing).
3. Do not say harsh or mean things to someone over e-mail or text (this could be considered cyber bullying) and do not post nasty, mean, or insulting items about someone.
4. Do not respond to nasty e-mails sent to you.
5. Do not break up with a significant other via text or e-mail.
6. When you receive an e-mail that says to forward it to everyone you know, please don't.
7. Do not use ALL CAPITALS. IT IMPLIES YOU ARE SHOUTING!!!
8. When you send messages online, make sure you proofread and correct mistakes before sending.
9. Do not forward other people's e-mails without their permission.
10. Do not forward virus warnings. They are generally hoaxes.
11. Ask before you send huge attachments.
12. Keep your communications short and to the point.
13. Do not leave the subject field blank in e-mails.
14. Avoid posting personal messages to a listserv.
15. Avoid using texting language for e-mails or social media sites (use correct spellings and correct language mechanics).
16. Remember to treat others online as you would like to be treated.
17. Use the Internet in ways that do not take away from your learning, but add to it.
18. Allow an appropriate amount of time for a person to respond to a message (24–48 business hours).
19. Be sure to have an appropriate salutation (i.e., *good morning, hello*) and closing (i.e., *goodbye, see you tomorrow*, etc.) in your e-mails.
20. Avoid slang (i.e., *wha's up, yo*, etc.) and acronyms (*btw, lol*, etc.)

Also, be sure your communication with your instructor, both in and out of the classroom is appropriate, particularly when e-mailing your instructor. E-mailing and text messaging are very different forms of communication. Texting is very informal. E-mail, especially to an instructor, etc. is considered a professional form of communication. Be sure to treat it that way. First, be sure to send the e-mail from your school e-mail address. Other e-mails often go to spam or junk folders. Do not leave the subject line blank and be sure the subject pertains to your e-mail. Address your instructor appropriately. State your question or concern (be aware of your tone). Avoid all slang and close your e-mail appropriately. Appropriate response time for an e-mail is 24 business hours. Give your instructor enough time to respond to your e-mail and do not inundate their inbox with multiple e-mails about the same issue. See box below for an example of an appropriate e-mail to an instructor and one that could use some work.

How to E-mail (or not) your Instructor

An example of what not to do:

To: instructor@communitycollege.edu

From: pimpdaddy@bade-mail.com

Subject: WHATEVER!

Yo teach! Wha's up?
I know you did not give me an F on that test!!!! WTH!?!? I studied all night for that and I know I should not have failed. Tell me how you are gonna fix this cuz I gotta pass your class.

Peace!

An example of an appropriate e-mail:

To: instructor@communitycollege.edu

From: concernedstudent@communitycollege.edu

Subject: My test grade

Good morning instructor (name),
I am concerned about my grade on the last test. I got an F and I don't know what I did wrong. I studied all night for that test! Can I meet with you to discuss some strategies about how I might do better on the next test? I really want to pass this class.

Please let me know when you are available to meet. I appreciate your time.

Sincerely,

Concerned Student

It is important to pay attention to your behavior on social media (i.e. Facebook, Instagram, Twitter, etc.) as well. Once you post something on the Internet it is always out "in the cloud." Even when you delete a post, highly skilled people can find it. Coaches, potential employers, graduate schools, etc. are taking a closer look at social media profiles to aid in their decision making process. Just as you think before you speak, you should think before you post. Refrain from posting anything illegal, rude, disrespectful, or in poor taste. Also be sure to refrain from cyberbullying. People tend to be much more brave when they can hide behind a computer. Don't post anything online that you would not say in person. All of these things could affect your future in far more ways than you realize.

2. **Avoid plagiarism.** Plagiarism is a violation of academic integrity that involves intentional or unintentional use of someone else's work without acknowledging it, which gives the reader the impression that it's your own work. Listed below are common forms of plagiarism.
   - Paying someone, or paying a service, for a paper and turning it in as your own work.
   - Submitting an entire paper, or portion thereof, that was written by someone else.
   - Copying sections of someone else's work and inserting it into your own work.

- Cutting paragraphs from separate sources and pasting them into the body of your own paper.
- Paraphrasing or rewording someone else's words or ideas without citing that person as a source. (Good strategies for paraphrasing without plagiarizing may be found at: http://www.upenn.edu/academicintegrity/ai_para-phrasing.html.)
- Placing someone else's exact words in the body of your paper and not placing quotation marks around them.
- Failing to cite the source of factual information in your paper that's not common knowledge.

Good examples of different forms of plagiarism may be found at: http://www.princeton.edu/pr/pub/integrity/pages/plagiarism/

Two other things to keep in mind:
- If you include information in your paper and just list its source in your reference (works cited) section—without citing the source in the *body* of your paper—this still qualifies as plagiarism.
- Be sure only to include sources in your reference section that you actually used and cited in the body of your paper. Although including sources in your reference section that aren't cited in your paper isn't technically a form of plagiarism, it may be viewed as being deceitful because you're "padding" your reference section, giving the reader the impression that you incorporated more sources into your paper than you actually did.

> When a student violates an academic integrity policy no one wins, even if the person gets away with it. It isn't right to cheat and it is an insult to everyone who put the effort in and did the work, and it cheapens the school for everyone. I learned my lesson and have no intention of ever cheating again."
> —*First-year student's reflection on an academic integrity violation.*

> I understood what I did was morally wrong and now I have to overcome it and move on living morally and ethically. It's really amazing that integrity is in everything we do in our lives."
> —*First-year student's reflection on an academic integrity violation*

 Think About It—Journal Entry 2.7

Reflect back at the different forms of plagiarism just described. Were there any you were surprised to see, or didn't realize were plagiarism?

_____

_____

_____

_____

_____

_____

Chapter Summary and Highlights

This chapter highlighted the fact that successful students understand:

1. The differences between high school and college
2. The syllabus and class policies
3. What constitutes responsible classroom behavior
4. The dos and don'ts of technology

More specifically, this chapter suggested a number of "top tips" for getting off to a good start in college. These tips are summarized below.

Read the course syllabus. Review it carefully when you first receive it, save it, and refer to it throughout the term.

Don't miss class. Attend all your classes in all your courses. Studies repeatedly show that students who go to class earn higher grades. Look at going to class like going to work. If you miss work, you get lower pay; if you cut class, you get lower grades.

Intentionally choose a seat in class that maximizes attention and minimizes distraction. When you enter class, you have a choice about where you're going to sit. Choose wisely by selecting a location that will maximize your attentiveness to the instructor and your effectiveness as a note-taker. Many years of research show that students who sit in the front and center of class tend to earn higher exam scores and course grades.

Sit by people who will enable your ability to listen and learn. Intentionally sit near classmates who will not distract you or interfere with the quality of your note taking.

Be a self-aware learner. Successful students and success people are *mindful*—they watch what they're doing and remain aware of whether they're doing it effectively and to the best of their ability. You can be a self-aware learning by asking yourself questions such as:

- Am I listening attentively to what my instructor is saying in class?
- Am I comprehending what I'm reading outside of class?
- Am I effectively using campus resources designed to support my success?
- Am I interacting with campus professionals who can contribute to my current success and future development?
- Am I interacting and collaborating with peers who can support (not sabotage) my learning and development?
- Am I effectively implementing college success strategies (such as those identified in this book)?

Spend at least two hours on schoolwork out of class for every hour you spend in class. This is what most college faculty believe is necessary to succeed in college.

Avoid inappropriate classroom behavior, such as the following:

- Coming to class late and/or leaving early
- Walking in and out of the classroom during class
- Talking with classmates while the instructor is speaking
- Disregarding deadlines set by your instructor
- Using electronic devices for personal purposes
- Acting disinterested in class (e.g., looking at the window or putting your head on your desk)
- Doing homework during class time
- Using electronic devices in class (e.g., texting or surfing the web)

Avoid plagiarism. Plagiarism is a violation of academic integrity that involves intentional or unintentional use of someone else's work without acknowledging it, which gives the reader the impression that it's your own work. Common forms of plagiarism include:

- Paying someone, or paying a service, for a paper and turning it in as your own work.
- Submitting an entire paper, or portion thereof, that was written by someone else.
- Copying sections of someone else's work and inserting it into your own work.
- Cutting paragraphs from separate sources and pasting them into the body of your own paper.
- Paraphrasing or rewording someone else's words or ideas without citing that person as a source. (Good strategies for paraphrasing without plagiarizing may be found at: http://www.upenn.edu/academicintegrity/ai_paraphrasing.html.)
- Placing someone else's exact words in the body of your paper and not placing quotation marks around them.
- Failing to cite the source of factual information in your paper that's not common knowledge.

Learning More through the World Wide Web: Internet-Based Resources

For additional information on strategies for college success, see the following websites:

Using the College Syllabus
http://www.mycollegesuccessstory.com/academic-success-tools/course-syllabus.html

Classroom Etiquette & Civility
http://college.usatoday.com/2012/12/07/5-rules-for-college-classroom-etiquette/

Academic Integrity:
http://www.calea.org/calea-update-magazine/issue-100who-s-watching-character-and-integrity-21st-century

References

Appleby, D. C. (2008, June). *Diagnosing and treating the deadly 13th grade syndrome.* Paper presented at the Association of Psychological Science Convention, Chicago, IL.

Benedict, M. E., & Hoag, J. (2004). Seating location in large lectures: Are seating preferences or location related to course performance? *Journal of Economics Education, 35,* 215–231.

Credé, M., Roch, S. G., & Kieszczynka, U. M. (2010). Class attendance in college: A meta-analytic review of the relationship of class attendance with grades and student characteristics. *Review of Educational Research, 80*(2), 272–295.

Howard, P. J. (2014). *The owner's manual for the brain: Everyday applications of mind-brain research* (4th ed.). New York: HarperCollins.

Kuh, G. D. (2005). Student engagement in the first year of college. In M. L. Upcraft, J. N. Gardner, B. O. Barefoot, & Associates, *Challenging and supporting the first-year student: A handbook for improving the first year of college* (pp. 86–107). San Francisco: Jossey-Bass.

Launius, M. H. (1997). College student attendance: Attitudes and academic performance. *College Student Journal, 31*(1), 86–93.

National Survey of Student Engagement. (2009). *NSSE Annual Results 2009. Assessment for improvement: Tracking student engagement over time.* Bloomington, IN: Author.

Pace, C. (1990). *The undergraduates: A report of their activities.* Los Angeles: University of California, Center for the Study of Evaluation.

Pace, C. (1995, May). *From good processes to good products: Relating good practices in undergraduate education to student achievement.* Paper presented at the meeting of the Association for Institutional Research, Boston.

Pascarella, E., & Terenzini, P. (1991). *How college affects students: Findings and insights from twenty years of research.* San Francisco: Jossey-Bass.

Pascarella, E., & Terenzini, P. (2005). *How college affects students: A third decade of research* (Vol. 2). San Francisco: Jossey-Bass.

Pintrich, P. R., & Schunk, D. H. (2002). *Motivation in education: Theory, research, and applications.* Upper Saddle River, NJ: Merrill-Prentice Hall.

Pryor, J. H., De Angelo, L., Palucki-Blake, B., Hurtado, S., & Tran, S. (2012) *The American freshman: National norms fall 2011.* Los Angeles: Higher Education Research Institute, UCLA.

Rennels, M. R., & Chaudhair, R. B. (1988). Eye-contact and grade distribution. *Perceptual and Motor Skills, 67* (October), 627–632.

Shelton, J. T., Elliot, E. M., Eaves, S. D., & Exner, A. L. (2009). The distracting effects of a ringing cell phone: An investigation of the laboratory and the classroom setting. *Journal of Environmental Psychology,* (March). Retrieved from http://news-info.wustl.edu/news/page/normal/14225.html.

Shimoff, E., & Catania, C. A. (2001). Effects of recording attendance on grades in Introductory Psychology. *Teaching of Psychology, 23*(3), 19–195.

Tagliacollo, V. A., Volpato, G. L., & Pereira, A., Jr. (2010). Association of student position in classroom and school performance. *Educational Research, 1*(6), 198–201.

Walsh, K. (2005). *Suggestions from more experienced classmates.* Retrieved from http://www.uni.edu/walsh/introtips.html.

Chapter 2 Exercises

2.1 Quote Reflections

Review the sidebar quotes contained in this chapter and select two that were especially meaningful or inspirational to you.

For each quote, provide a three- to five-sentence explanation why you chose it.

2.2 Reality Bite

Crime and Punishment: Plagiarism and Its Consequences

In an article that appeared in an Ohio newspaper, titled "Plagiarism persists in classrooms," an English professor is quoted as saying: "Technology has made it easier to plagiarize because students can download papers and exchange information and papers through their computers. But technology has also made it easier to catch students who plagiarize." This professor works at a college that subscribes to a website that matches the content of students' papers with content from books and online sources. Many professors now require students to submit their papers through this website. If students are caught plagiarizing, for a first offense, they typically receive an F for the assignment or the course. A second offense can result in dismissal or expulsion from college, which has already happened to a few students.

Reflection and Discussion Questions

1. What do you suspect are their primary motives or reasons why students plagiarize from the web?

2. What would you say is a fair or just penalty for those found guilty of a first plagiarism violation? What do you think would be fair penalty for a second violation?

3. How might web-based plagiarism be minimized or prevented from happening in the first place?

2.3 Syllabus Review

Review the syllabus (course outline) for all classes you're enrolled in this term, and complete the following information for each course.

Self-Assessment Questions

1. Is the overall workload what you expected? Are your surprised by the amount of work required in any particular course(s)?

2. At this point in the term, what do you see as your most challenging or demanding course or courses? Why?

3. Do you think you can handle the total workload required by the full set of courses you're enrolled in this term?

4. What adjustments or changes do you think you'll make to your previous learning and study habits to accommodate your academic workload this term?

2.4 Is it or is it Not Plagiarism?

The following four incidents were brought to a judicial review board to determine if plagiarism had occurred and, if so, what the penalty should be. After reading each case, answer the questions listed below it.

Case 1. A student turned in an essay that included substantial material copied from a published source. The student admitted that he didn't cite the sources properly, but argued that it was because he misunderstood the directions, not because he was attempting to steal someone else's ideas.

Is this Plagiarism?

How severe is it? (Rate it on a scale from 1 = low to 5 = high)

What should the consequence or penalty be?

How could the accusation of plagiarism been avoided?

Case 2. A student turned in a paper that was identical to a paper submitted by another student for a different course.
Is this plagiarism?

How severe is it? (Rate it on a scale from 1 = low to 5 = high)

What should the consequence or penalty be?

How could the accusation of plagiarism been avoided?

Case 3. A student submitted a paper he wrote in a previous course as an extra credit paper for a current course.
Is this plagiarism?

How severe is it? (Rate it on a scale from 1 = low to 5 = high)

What should the consequence or penalty be?

How could the accusation of plagiarism been avoided?

Case 4. A student submitted a paper in an art history that contained some ideas from art critics she read about and whose ideas she agreed with. The student didn't cite the critics as sources, but claimed it wasn't plagiarism because their ideas were merely their own subjective judgments or opinions, not facts or findings; furthermore, they were opinions she agreed with.
Is this plagiarism?

How severe is it? (Rate it on a scale from 1 = low to 5 = high)

What should the consequence or penalty be?

How could the accusation of plagiarism been avoided?

2.5 Chapter 1 Reflection

List five strategies discussed in this chapter that you intend to use to achieve college success, and explain HOW you plan to put them into practice.

Notes

Notes

Strengths and Making Connections: Four Steps to Your Success

USING POWERFUL PRINCIPLES OF STUDENT SUCCESS AND KEY CAMPUS RESOURCES

This chapter focuses on the "big picture": powerful principles you can implement to promote your own success and key campus resources you can use to help you succeed. It describes what these key principles and resources are, why they're effective, and how to capitalize on them.

Chapter Preview

Alert you to the most powerful strategies and resources that you can use immediately to get off to a fast start in college and continually to achieve excellence throughout your college experience.

Learning Goal

Think About It—Journal Entry 3.1

Thought Starter

1. What excites you about starting college?

2. What concerns do you have about starting college?

What Is StrengthsQuest?

"We're not all designed to be straight A students, celebrities, world class athletes or the CEO of a major corporation. But we are designed to make the most of the skills and abilities we do possess. Perhaps the most splendid achievement of all is the continuing quest to surpass ourselves."—Dennis Waitley

StrengthsQuest is an online assessment that we use to help you identify your natural themes, or "talents". These are your ways of thinking, feeling, and behaving as a unique individual. By building on these talents with knowledge, skills, and self-understanding, you have the capacity to turn these talents into strengths. These strengths can then better prepare and assist you in your future academic, career, and personal experiences.

More than 7 million people in the world have completed this assessment to discover their personal themes, and this program is used at over 600 colleges and universities in North America. Your instructor will provide you with a code to access the online assessment at *http://www.strengthsquest.com*. The online assessment takes approximately 30–45 minutes to complete. After you complete the assessment, you will see your top five themes. You will also have unlimited access to the Strengths-Quest website, which allows you to print numerous reports on your specific themes, access the entire pdf of the StrengthsQuest textbook, and give you suggestions to improve your themes to lead you to greater academic, personal, and career success.

You should print your Strengths Insight and Action Planning Guide for class. This report is customized especially for you! These descriptions are written in relation to your other themes, so if you have the same theme as a classmate, chances are your descriptions read quite differently.

Also, please write down your username and password so you will be able to log into your account again in the future.

Username: _____

Password: _____

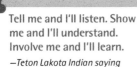

Tell me and I'll listen. Show me and I'll understand. Involve me and I'll learn.

—Teton Lakota Indian saying

Four Steps to College Success

Research points to four powerful principles of college success:

1. Active Involvement (Engagement)
2. Capitalizing on Campus Resources (Resourcefulness)
3. Interpersonal Interaction and Collaboration (Social Integration)
4. Reflection and Self-Awareness (Mindfulness)

(Sources: Astin, 1993; Kuh, et al., 2005; Light, 2001; Pascarella & Terenzini, 1991, 2005; Tinto, 1993.)

These four principles are presented in the beginning of this book because they represent the foundational basis for all success strategies discussed throughout the book.

FIGURE 3.1: **The Diamond of College Success**

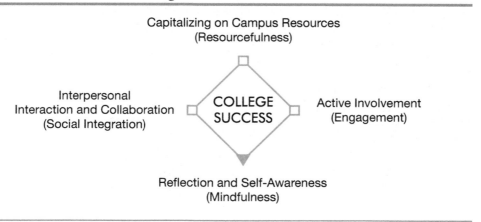

© Kendall Hunt Publishing Company

First Step of College Success: Active Involvement (Engagement)

Research indicates that active involvement may be the most powerful principle of human learning and college success (Astin, 1993; Kuh, et al., 2005). To succeed in college, you can't be a passive spectator; you need to be an active player.

Active involvement includes the following key components:

- The amount of *time* you devote to the college experience—inside and outside the classroom
- The degree of *effort or energy* (mental and physical) you invest in the learning process.

Think of something you do with intensity, passion, and commitment. If you were to approach college in the same way, you would be faithfully implementing the principle of active involvement. Here's how you can apply both key components of active involvement— time and energy—to the major learning challenges you'll face in college.

Active Involvement in the Learning Process

College success will require that you work harder (put in more time than high school) and smarter (learn more strategically and effectively). Probably the most powerful principle of effective learning is active involvement (engagement); there's simply no such thing as "passive learning." You can ensure you're actively involved in the learning process by engaging in some form of *action* on what you're learning, such as the actions listed below.

- *Writing.* For example, when reading, take notes on what you're reading rather than passively highlighting sentences.
- *Speaking.* For example, rather than studying silently, explain what you're learning to a study group partner.
- *Organizing.* For example, create an outline, diagram, or concept map that pulls together the ideas you're learning.

Active Listening and Note Taking in Class

You will find that many college professors rely heavily on the lecture method—they profess their knowledge by speaking for long stretches of time and expect students

> I never had a class before where the teacher just stands up and talks to you. He says something and you're writing it down, but then he says something else."
> —*First-year college student (Erickson, Peters, and Strommer, 2006)*

> All genuine learning is active, not passive. It is a process in which the student is the main agent, not the teacher."
> —*Mortimer Adler, American professor of philosophy and educational theorist*

to listen and take notes on the knowledge they dispense. This method of instruction places great demands on your ability to listen actively and take notes that are both accurate and complete. Research consistently shows that most test questions on college exams come from professors' lectures and students who take better class notes get better grades (Brown, 1988; Cuseo, et al., 2013; Kiewra, 2000).

The best way to apply the principle of active involvement during a class lecture is to engage in the physical action of writing notes. Writing down what your instructor is saying in class "forces" you to pay closer attention to what is being said and reinforces your retention of what was said. By taking notes, you not only hear the information (auditory memory), you also see it on paper (visual memory) and feel it in the muscles of your hand as you write it (motor memory).

Note

Your role in the college classroom is not that of a passive spectator or an absorbent sponge who sits back and soaks up information through osmosis. Instead, it's like being an aggressive detective or investigative reporter on a search-and-record mission. Your job is to actively search for information by picking your instructor's brain, picking out the instructor's key points, and recording your "pickings" in your notebook.

Box 3.1 contains a summary of top strategies for classroom listening and note taking that you can put into action right now.

Box 3.1

Top Tips for Active Listening and Note Taking in the College Classroom

One task that you'll be expected to perform during the very first week of college is taking notes in class. Studies show that professors' lecture notes are the number one source of test questions (and test answers) on college exams. You can improve the quality of your note taking and your course grades by using the following strategies.

1. Get to every class. Whether or not your instructors take roll, you're responsible for all material covered in class. Remember that a full load of college courses (12 units) only requires that you be in class about 13 hours per week. If you consider your class work to be a full-time job, any job that requires you to show up for only 13 hours a week is a pretty sweet deal; it's a deal that supplies you with much more educational freedom than you had in high school. To miss classes in college when you're required to spend so little time in class per week is an abuse of this educational freedom. It's also an abuse of the money that you, your family, and taxpaying American citizens are paying to support your college education.

2. Get to every class on time. During the first few minutes of a class session, instructors often share valuable information—such as important reminders, reviews, and previews.

3. Get organized. Bring the right equipment to class. Get a separate notebook for each class, write your name on it, date each class session, and store all class handouts in it.

4. Get in the right position.
   * The ideal place to sit in class is at the front and center of the room—where you're in the best position to hear and see what's going on.
   * The ideal posture to adopt is sitting upright and leaning forward—because your body influences your mind; if your body is in an alert and ready position, your mind is likely to follow.
   * The ideal social position to occupy in class is near motivated classmates who will not distract you, but motivate you to listen actively and take notes aggressively.

Note

These attention-focusing strategies are particularly important in large classes where you're likely to feel more anonymous, less accountable, and less engaged.

(continued)

Box 3.1 *(continued)*

5. *Get in the right frame of mind.* Come to class with the attitude that you're there to pick your instructor's brain, pick up answers to test questions, and pick up points to elevate your course grade.

6. *Get it down (in writing).* Actively look, listen, and record important points at all times in class. Pay special attention to whatever information instructors put in writing, whether it appears on the board, on a slide, or in a handout.

7. *Don't let go of your pen (or keyboard).* When in doubt, write it out (or type it out); it's better to have it and not need it than to need it and not have it.

8. *Finish strong.* During the last few minutes of class, instructors often share valuable information, such as timely reminders, reviews, and previews.

9. *Stick around.* When class ends, don't bolt out of the room; instead, hang out for a few moments and quickly review your notes (by yourself or with a classmate). This quick end-of-class review will help your brain retain the information it just received. If you detect any gaps or confusing points in your notes, try to consult with your instructor immediately after class.

For more detailed ideas and strategies on listening and note taking, see Chapter 8, **p. 213**.

Note

Most college professors don't write all important information on the board for you; instead, they expect you to listen carefully and write it down yourself.

Finish class with a rush of attention, not a rush out the door!

Think About It—Journal Entry 3.2

When you enter a classroom, where do you usually sit?

Why do you sit there? Is it a conscious choice or more like an automatic habit?

Do you think that the seat you usually choose places you in the best possible position for listening and learning in the classroom?

_____

_____

_____

Active Class Participation

You can implement the principle of active involvement in the college classroom by not only taking notes in class, but also by being an engaged participant who comes to class well prepared (e.g., having done the assigned reading), asks relevant questions, and contributes thoughtful comments during class discussions. Class participation increases your ability to stay alert and attentive in class, and it sends a clear message to your instructors that you are a motivated student who wants to learn. Class participation is also likely to account for a portion of your grade in many courses, so your attentiveness and involvement in class can have a direct, positive effect on your college grades.

Active Reading

Note-taking not only promotes active listening in class, it also promotes active reading out of class. Taking notes on what you're reading (or on information you've highlighted while reading) keeps you actively involved in the reading process because it requires more mental and physical energy than merely reading the material or passively highlighting sentences.

College professors also expect you to relate or connect what they talk about in class to the reading they've assigned. Thus, it's important to start developing good reading habits now. You can do so by using the top tips suggested in **Box 3.2**.

Box 3.2

Top Tips for Strengthening Textbook Reading Comprehension and Retention

1. **Get the textbooks required for your courses as soon as possible and get your reading assignments done on time.** Information from reading assignments ranks right behind lecture notes as a source of test questions on college exams. Many professors deliver their lectures with the expectation that you've done the assigned reading and assume you can build on that knowledge to understand their lectures. If you haven't done the reading, you'll have more difficulty following what your instructor is saying in class. Thus, by not doing the assigned reading you pay a double penalty: you miss information from the reading that's not covered in class which will likely appear on exams, and you miss understanding ideas presented in class that build on the reading.

> **"** I recommend that you read the first chapters right away because college professors get started promptly with assigning certain readings. Classes in college move very fast because, unlike high school, you do not attend class five times a week but two or three times a week."
>
> —Advice to new college students from a first-year student

2. **Read with the right equipment.**
   - Bring a writing tool (pen, pencil, or keyboard) to record important information and a storage space (notebook or computer) in which you can save and later retrieve information acquired found in your reading for later use on tests and assignments.
   - Have a dictionary nearby to quickly find the meaning of unfamiliar words that may interfere with your ability to comprehend what you're reading. Looking up definitions of unfamiliar words helps you understand what you're reading and also builds your vocabulary. A strong vocabulary will improve your reading comprehension in all college courses, as well as your performance on standardized tests, such as those required for admission to graduate and professional schools.
   - Check the back of your textbook for a glossary (list) of key terms included in the book. Each

college subject and academic discipline has its own special language, and decoding it is often the key to understanding the concepts covered in the course. The glossary that appears at the end of your textbook is more than an ancillary add-on, it's a valuable tool that you can use to improve your comprehension of course concepts. Consider making a photocopy of the glossary at the back of your textbook so you can access it easily while you're reading—without having to repeatedly stop, hold your place, and go to the back of the text to find it.

3. **Get in the right position.** Sit upright and have light coming from behind you, over the side of your body opposite your writing hand. This will reduce the distracting and fatiguing effects of glare and shadows.

4. **Get a sneak preview.** Approach the chapter by first reading its boldface headings and any chapter outline, summary, or end-of-chapter questions that may be provided. This will supply you with a mental map of the chapter's important ideas before you start your trip through it. Getting an overview of the chapter will help you keep track of its chapter's major ideas (the "big picture") and reduce your risk of getting lost in all the smaller details you encounter along the way.

5. **Finish each of your reading sessions with a short review.** Rather than using the last few minutes of a reading session to cover a few more pages, end it with a review of what you've highlighted or noted as important information. Since most forgetting takes place immediately after you stop processing (taking in) information and start doing something else, it's best to use your last minutes of reading time to "lock in" the most important information you've just read.

Note

When reading, your goal should be to discover or uncover the most important ideas, so the final step in the reading process should be to review (and lock in) the most important ideas you've discovered.

Note: For a more detailed discussion of reading comprehension and retention, see Chapter 8 (pp. 225–226).

Think About It—Journal Entry 3.3

Which of the five reading strategies listed in **Box 3.2** have you used in the past? Which of these strategies do you intend to use in the future?

> Do not be a PCP (Parking Lot→ Classroom→Parking Lot) student. The time you spend on campus will be a sound investment in your academic and professional success."
>
> —Drew Appleby, professor of psychology

> The impact of college is not simply the result of what a college does for or to a student. Rather, the impact is a result of the extent to which an individual student exploits the people, programs, facilities, opportunities, and experiences that the college makes available."
>
> —Ernest Pascarella and Patrick Terenzini, How College Affects Students

> Where I learn the material best is tutoring because they go over it and if you have questions, you can ask. They have time for you or will make time for you."
>
> —First-year college student

Second Step for College Success: Capitalizing on Campus Resources (Resourcefulness)

Successful people are *resourceful*; they seek out and take advantage of resources to help them reach their goals. Your campus is chock full of resources that have been intentionally designed to support your quest for educational and personal success. Studies show that students who utilize campus resources report higher levels of satisfaction with college and get more out of the college experience (Pascarella & Terenzini, 1991, 2005).

Note

Capitalizing on campus services is not only valuable, it's also "free"; the cost of these services has already been covered by your college tuition. By investing time and energy in campus resources, you maximize the return on your financial investment in college— you get a bigger bang for your buck.

Utilizing campus resources is a natural extension of the principle of active involvement. Successful students are *involved* students, both inside and outside the classroom. Out-of-class involvement includes involvement with campus resources. The first step toward making effective use of campus resources is becoming aware of the full range of resources available to you and what they can do for you. Listed below are key campus services that are likely to be available to you and what they can do for you.

Academic Support Services

This campus is designed to strengthen your academic performance. The individual and group tutoring provided here will help you master difficult course concepts and assignments, and the people working here are professionally trained to help you learn *how to learn*. Just as professors are experts in the subjects they teach, learning resource professionals are experts in the process of learning. They are professionals who can equip you with effective learning strategies that can be used in all courses, as well as specific strategies for dealing with the demands of certain courses and teaching styles. You're also likely to find trained peer tutors in this center who can often help you understand concepts better than more experienced professionals because they're closer to you in age and experience.

Studies show that college students who capitalize on academic support services outside the classroom achieve higher grades and are more likely to complete their college degree, particularly if they begin their involvement with these support services during their first year of college (Bailey, 2009; Cuseo, 2003). Students who seek and receive assistance from the Learning Center also show significant improvement in academic self-efficacy—that is, they develop a stronger sense of personal control over their academic performance and higher expectations for academic success (Smith, Walter, & Hoey, 1992).

Despite the powerful advantages associated with student use of academic support services, these services are typically underused by college students—especially by students who need them the most (Cuseo, 2003; Walter & Smith, 1990). Unfortunately, some college students believe that seeking academic help is admitting they're not smart, self-sufficient, or able to succeed on their own. Don't buy into this myth. In high school, students may only go to an office on campus if they're required to (e.g., if they forgot to do something or did something wrong). In college, students go to campus offices to enhance their success by taking advantage of the services and support they provide.

Note

Using academic support services doesn't mean you're helpless, need remedial repair work, or require academic life support because you're on the verge of flunking out. Instead, it's a sign that you're a motivated and resourceful student who is striving for academic excellence.

> "At colleges where I've taught, we found that the grade point average of students who used the Learning Center was higher than the college average, and honors students were more likely to use the center than other students."
>
> —Joe Cuseo, professor of psychology and lead author of this text

Disability Services (a.k.a. Office for Students with Special Needs)

If you have a physical or learning disability that's interfering with your performance in college, or you think you may have such a disability, Disability Services is the campus resource to consult for assistance and support. Programs and services typically provided by this office include:

- Assessment for learning disabilities;
- Verification of eligibility for disability support services;
- Authorization of academic accommodations for students with disabilities; and
- Specialized counseling, advising, and tutoring.

College Library

This is your campus resource for finding information and completing research assignments (e.g., term papers and group projects). Librarians are professional educators who provide instruction outside the classroom; you can learn from them just as you can learn from faculty inside the classroom. They can help you develop research skills for accessing, retrieving, and evaluating information. These are lifelong learning skills that promote your educational success at all stages of the college experience as well as your professional and personal success beyond college.

> "The next best thing to knowing something is knowing where to find it."
>
> —Dr. Samuel Johnson, English literary figure and original author of the Dictionary of the English Language (1747)

Academic Advisement

Whether or not you have an assigned academic advisor, the Academic Advising Center is your campus resource for help with course selection, educational planning, and choosing or changing a major. Some campuses have faculty advisors who are housed in their respective departments. Be sure to find out who your advisor is and where he or she is located. Studies show that students who develop clear educational and career goals are more likely to persist in college and complete their college degree (Lotkowski, Robbins, & Noeth, 2004). Research also indicates that most beginning college students need help clarifying their educational goals, deciding on a major, and identifying career options (Cuseo, 2005; Tinto, 2012). As a first-year college student, being undecided or uncertain about your educational and career goals is nothing to be embarrassed about. However, you should start thinking about your future now. Connect early and often with an academic advisor to help you clarify your educational goals and choose a field of study that best complements your interests, talents, and values.

Student Development Services

This is your campus resource for involvement in student life outside the classroom, including student clubs and organizations, recreational programs, leadership activities, and volunteer experiences. Research consistently shows that experiential learning outside the classroom contributes as much to your personal development and career success as class work (Kuh, 1995; Kuh, et al., 1994; Pascarella & Terenzini, 2005). This is one reason why most campuses no longer refer to out-of-class experiences as "*extra*curricular" activities; instead they are referred to as "*co*-curricular" experiences—which conveys the message they're equally important as classroom-based learning. Studies show that students who become actively involved in campus life are more likely to:

- Enjoy their college experience;
- Graduate from college; and
- Develop leadership skills that enhance career performance beyond college (Astin, 1993).

Note

Co-curricular experiences are also resume-building experiences, and campus professionals with whom you interact regularly while participating in co-curricular activities (e.g., director of student activities or dean of students) can be valuable resources for personal references and letters of recommendation.

Devoting some out-of-class time to co-curricular experiences should not interfere with your academic performance. Keep in mind that in college you'll be spending much less time in the classroom than you did in high school. As mentioned previously, a full load of college courses (12 units) requires that you be in class for about 13 hours per week. This can leave you with sufficient time to become involved in learning experiences on or off campus. Research indicates that students' academic performance and progress to degree completion aren't impaired if they spend 20 or fewer hours on co-curricular and part-time work experiences (Advisory Committee on Student Financial Assistance, 2008). In fact, they earn higher grades than students who don't get involved in any out-of-class activities (Pascarella, 2001; Pascarella & Terenzini, 2005).

Although co-curricular involvement is valuable, limit your involvement to no more than two or three major campus organizations at a time. Restricting the number of your out-of-class activities will not only enable you to keep up with your studies, it will be more impressive to future schools or employers because a long list of involvement in numerous activities may send the message that you're padding your resume with activities you participated in superficially (or never participated in at all).

 **Think About It—Journal Entry 3.4**

If you were to join one campus club or student organization, what would it be? How would participating in this club or organization contribute to your educational development?

_____

_____

_____

_____

_____

> Just a [long] list of club memberships is meaningless; it's a fake front. Remember that quality, not quantity, is what counts."
>
> —Lauren Pope, former director of the National Bureau for College Placement

Financial Aid

If you have questions concerning how to obtain assistance in paying for college, the staff in this office can guide you through the application process. The paperwork needed to apply for and secure financial aid can sometimes be confusing or overwhelming. Don't let the process of applying for financial aid intimidate you or prevent you from seeking financial aid because professional financial aid counselors can walk you through the process. They can also help you find:

- Part-time employment on campus through a work–study program;
- Low-interest student loans;
- Grants and scholarships.

If you have any doubt about whether you're using the most effective plan for financing your college education, make an appointment to see a professional in your Financial Aid Office right now.

Counseling Center

Here's where you can get ideas and strategies for managing college stress, gaining greater self-awareness, and reaching your full potential. Personal counselors are professionals who do more than just help students maintain mental health; they also develop students' emotional intelligence, interpersonal skills, and personal growth.

Note

Personal counseling is not just for students experiencing emotional problems. It's for all students who want to enrich the quality of their life.

Third Step for College Success: Interpersonal Interaction and Collaboration (Social Integration)

Students who become socially integrated or connected with other members of the college community are more likely to complete their first year of college and go on to complete their college degree (Pascarella & Terenzini, 2005; Tinto, 1993). (For effective ways to make interpersonal connections with key members of your college community, see **Box 3.3**.)

Box 3.3

Social Integration: Making Connections with Members of Your College Community

Listed below are top tips for making key social connections in college. Start developing these relationships right now so you can build a base of social support to help you succeed during the critical first year of college.

- Connect with a student development professional you may have met during orientation.
- Join a college club, student organization, campus committee, intramural team, or volunteer service group whose members share the same personal or career interests as you. If you can't find a club or organization you were hoping to join, consider starting it on your own. For example, if you're an English major, consider starting a Writing Club or a Book Club.
- Connect with a peer leader who has been trained to assist new students (e.g., orientation week leader, peer tutor, or peer mentor).
- Connect with classmates and team up with them to take notes, complete reading assignments, study for exams, or take classes together. Look especially to team

up with a peer who may be in more than one class with you. (For more detailed information on forming collaborative learning teams, see Chapter 8, **pp. 217–218.**)

- Connect with peers who live near you or who commute to school from the same community in which you live. If your schedules are similar, consider carpooling together.
- Connect with faculty members—particularly in a field that you're considering as a major. Visit them during office hours, converse briefly with them after class, or communicate with them via e-mail.
- Connect with an academic advisor to discuss and develop your educational plans.
- Connect with academic support professionals in your college's Learning Center for personalized academic assistance or tutoring related to any course in which you'd like to improve your performance or achieve academic excellence.
- Connect with a college librarian to get early assistance or a head start on any research
- Connect with a personal counselor or campus minister to discuss college adjustment or personal challenges you may be experiencing.

Four particular forms of interpersonal interaction have been found to promote student learning and motivation in college:

1. Student–faculty interaction,
2. Student–advisor interaction,
3. Student–mentor interaction, and
4. Student–student (peer) interaction.

Strategies for capitalizing on each of these key forms of interaction are provided below.

Interacting with Faculty Members

College success is strongly influenced by the frequency and quality of student–faculty interaction *outside the classroom*. Out-of-class contact with faculty is associated with the following positive outcomes for college students:

- Improved academic performance;
- Increased critical thinking skills;
- Greater satisfaction with the college experience;
- Increased likelihood of completing a college degree; and
- Stronger desire to pursue education beyond a four-year degree (Astin, 1993; Pascarella & Terenzini, 1991, 2005).

These positive outcomes are so powerful, strong, and widespread that we encourage you to immediately begin making connections with your professors outside of class time. Here are some of the easiest ways to do so.

1. **Seek contact with your instructors right after class.** If something covered in class captures your interest, approach your instructor to discuss it further. You could ask a quick question about something you weren't sure you understood, or have a short conversation about how the material covered in class really hit home for you or connected with something you learned in another course. Interacting briefly with instructors after class can help them get to know you as an individual and help you gain the confidence to approach them during office hours.

2. **Connect with course instructors during their office hours.** One of the most important pieces of information you'll find on a course syllabus is your instructor's office hours. College professors specifically reserve times in their weekly schedule to be available to students in their office. (Make note of them and make an earnest attempt to capitalize on them.) Try to visit the office of each of your instructors at least once, preferably early in the term, when quality time is easier to find. Don't wait until later in the term when major exams and assignments start piling up. Even if your early contact with instructors is only for a few minutes, it can be a valuable icebreaker that helps them get to know you as a person and helps you feel more comfortable interacting with them in the future.

3. **Connect with your instructors through e-mail.** Electronic communication is another effective tool for experiencing the benefits of student–faculty interaction outside the classroom, particularly if your professor's office hours conflict with your class schedule, work responsibilities, or family commitments. If you're a commuter student who doesn't live on campus, or if you're an adult student juggling family and work commitments along with your academic schedule, e-mail communication may be an especially effective and efficient way to interact with faculty. E-mail may also be a good way to initially communicate with instructors and build self-confidence to eventually seek out face-to-face interaction with them. In one national survey, almost half of college students reported that e-mail enabled them to communicate their ideas with professors on subjects they would not have discussed in person (Pew Internet & American Life Project, 2002). However, if you miss class, don't use e-mail to ask such questions as:
   - Did I miss anything important in class today?
   - Could you send me your PowerPoint slides from the class I missed?

   Also, when using e-mail to communicate with your instructors, be sure to:
   - Include your full name in the message.
   - Mention the class or course in which you're enrolled.
   - Use complete sentences, correct grammar, and avoid informal "hip" expressions (e.g., "yo," "whatup").
   - Spell check and proofread your message before sending it.
   - Include your full contact information. (If you're communicating via Facebook, watch your screen name; for example, names like "Sexsea" or "Studly" wouldn't be appropriate.)
   - Give your instructor time to reply. (Don't expect an immediate response, particularly if you send your message in the evening or on a weekend.) (See Chapter 2, **pp. 37–38,** for more netiquette guidelines.)

> [In high school] the teacher knows your name. But in college they don't know your name; they might see your face, but it means nothing to them unless you make yourself known."
> —*First-year college student*

> I wish that I would have taken advantage of professors' open-door policies when I had questions, because actually understanding what I was doing, instead of guessing, would have saved me a lot of stress and re-doing what I did wrong the first time."
> —*College sophomore (Walsh, 2005)*

Interacting with Academic Advisors

If you need some help understanding college policies and procedures, or navigating the organizational maze of course options and course requirements, an academic advisor is the person to see. Advisors also serve as key referral agents who can direct you to, and connect you with, key campus support services that best meet your educational needs and career goals.

Your academic advisor should be someone whom you feel comfortable speaking with, someone who knows your name, and someone who's familiar with your personal interests and abilities. Give advisors the opportunity to get to know you personally, and seek their input on courses, majors, and any academic difficulties you may be experiencing.

If you've been assigned a specific advisor and cannot develop a good relationship with this person, ask the director of advising or academic dean if you could make a change. Consider asking your peers or peer leaders for their recommendations.

If your college does not assign you a personal advisor, but offers advising services in an Advising Center on a drop-by or drop-in basis, you may see a different advisor each time you visit the center. If you're not comfortable working with different advisors from one visit to the next, find one you like and make that person your advisor by scheduling appointments in advance. This will enable you to consistently connect with the same advisor and develop a close, ongoing relationship with that person.

Note

Advisors can be much more than course schedulers; they can be mentors. Unlike your course instructors—who may change from term to term—your academic advisor may be the one professional on campus with whom you have regular contact and a continuous relationship throughout your college experience.

 **Think About It—Journal Entry 3.5**

Do you have a personally assigned advisor?

If yes, do you know who this person is and where he or she can be found?

If you don't have a personally assigned advisor, where will you go if you have questions about your class schedule or educational plans?

Interaction with Peers (Student–Student Interaction)

Your peers can be more than competitors or a source of negative peer pressure; they can also be collaborators, a source of positive social influence, and a resource for

FIGURE 3.2: Maslow's Theory of Self-Actualization

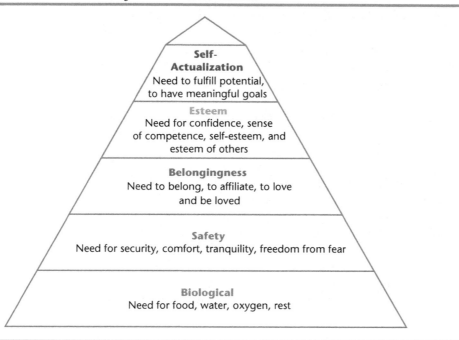

© Kendall Hunt Publishing Company

college success. Peer support is important at any stage of the college experience, but it's especially valuable during the first term of college. It's at this stage when new students have a strong need for belongingness and social acceptance because they're in the midst of a major life transition. As a new student, it may be useful to view your first-year experience through the lens of psychologist Abraham Maslow's hierarchy of human needs (see **Figure 3.2**). According to Maslow, humans only reach their full potential and achieve peak performance after their more basic emotional and social needs have been met (e.g., needs for personal safety, social acceptance, and self-esteem). Making early connections with your peers helps you meet these basic human needs, provides you with a base of social support that eases your integration into the college community, and prepares you to move up to higher levels of the need hierarchy (e.g., achieving academic excellence and reaching your educational goals).

Getting involved with campus organizations or activities is one way to connect with other students. Also, try to interact with experienced students who have spent more time at college than you. Sophomores, juniors, and seniors can be valuable social resources for a new student. In particular, seek out contact with students who have been selected and trained as peer mentors or peer leaders.

Research clearly demonstrates that college students learn as much from peers as they do from instructors and textbooks (Astin, 1993; Pascarella, 2005). One study of more than 25,000 college students revealed that when peers interact with one another while learning, they achieve higher levels of academic performance and are more likely to persist to degree completion (Astin, 1993).

Be observant—keep an eye out for peers who are successful. Start building your social support network by surrounding yourself with success-seeking and success-achieving students. Learn from them, emulate their productive habits and strategies, and use them as a social resource to promote your own success.

Surround yourself with only people who are going to lift you higher."

—*Oprah Winfrey, actress and talk-show host*

If you want to go quickly, go by yourself—if you want to go farther, go in a group."

—*African proverb*

TEAM = <u>T</u>ogether <u>E</u>veryone <u>A</u>chieves <u>M</u>ore"

—*Author unknown*

Collaborative Learning

Simply defined, collaborative learning is the process of two or more people working *interdependently* to advance each other's success—as opposed to working independently or competitively. Learning is strengthened when it takes place in a social context that involves interpersonal interaction. As scholars put it, human knowledge is "socially constructed" or built up through dialogue and an exchange of ideas; conversations with others become internalized as ideas in your mind and influence your way of thinking (Bruffee, 1993). Thus, by having frequent, intelligent conversations with others, you broaden your knowledge base, deepen your learning, and elevate the quality of your thinking.

Research from kindergarten through college shows that students who learn collaboratively in teams experience significant gains in both academic performance and interpersonal skills (Cross, Barkley, & Major, 2005; Cuseo, 1996; Gilles & Adrian, 2003; Johnson, Johnson, & Smith, 1998). In one national study that involved in-depth interviews with more than 1,600 college students, it was discovered that almost all students who struggled academically had one particular study habit in common: they always studied alone (Light, 2001).

To maximize the power of collaboration, use the following pair of guidelines to choose teammates who will enhance the quality and productivity of your learning team:

1. Observe your classmates with an eye toward identifying potentially good teammates. Look for motivated students who will actively contribute to your team's success (rather than those whom you suspect may just be hitchhikers looking for a free ride).
2. Don't team up exclusively with peers who are familiar with or similar to you in terms of their personal characteristics, backgrounds, and experiences. This familiarity can actually interfere with your team's performance by turning your learning team into a social group or gabfest that gets off track and onto topics that have nothing to do with studying (e.g., what you did last weekend or what you're planning to do next weekend). Instead, include teammates who differ from you with respect to such characteristics as: age, gender, race or ethnicity, and cultural or geographical background. Such variety brings different life experiences, styles of thinking strategies, and learning styles to your team, which enriches your team's diversity and learning capacity.

Note

Capitalize on the advantages of collaborating with peers of varied backgrounds and lifestyles. Studies show that we learn more from people who are different from us than from people similar to us (Pascarella, 2001; Thompson & Cuseo, 2014).

Keep in mind that collaborative learning can be much more than just forming study groups the night before an exam. You can team up with classmates more regularly to work on a variety of academic tasks, such as those listed below.

Note-Taking Teams. Immediately after class sessions end, take a couple of minutes to team up with other students to compare and share notes. Since listening and note-taking are demanding tasks, it's likely that a classmate will pick up an important point you missed and vice versa. By teaming up *immediately after class*, if you and your teammates find missing or confusing information, quickly consult with the instructor before leaving the room.

AUTHOR'S EXPERIENCE

During my first term in college, I was having difficulty taking complete notes in my biology course because the instructor spoke rapidly and with an unfamiliar accent. I noticed another student (Alex) sitting in the front row who was trying to take notes as best he could; however, he was experiencing the same difficulty as me. Following one particularly fast and complex lecture, we looked at each other and noticed we were both shaking our heads in frustration. We started talking about how frustrated we were and decided to join forces after every class to compare notes and identify points we missed or found confusing. First, we helped each other by comparing and sharing our notes in case one of us got something the other missed. If there were points we both missed or couldn't figure out, we went to the front of class together to consult with the instructor before he left the room. At the end of the course, Alex and I finished with the highest grades in the course.

—Joe Cuseo

Reading Teams. After completing reading assignments, team up with classmates to compare your highlighting and margin notes. See what you both identified as the most important material to be studied for upcoming exams.

Writing Teams. Students can provide each other with feedback to revise and improve their own writing. Studies show that when peers assess each other's writing, the quality of their individual writing gets better and they develop a more positive attitude about the writing process (Topping, 1998). You can form peer writing teams to help at any or all of the following stages in the writing process:

1. Topic selection and refinement: to help one another come up with a list of possible topics and subtopics to write about;
2. Pre-writing: to clarify your writing purpose and audience;
3. First draft: to improve your general writing style and tone; and
4. Final draft: to proofread, detect, and correct clerical errors before submitting your written work.

Library Research Teams. Many first-year students are unfamiliar with the process of using a college or university library to conduct academic research. Some experience "library anxiety" and avoid even stepping foot into the library, particularly if it's a large and intimidating place (Malvasi, Rudowsky, & Valencia, 2009). Forming library research teams is an effective way to develop a social support group that can make library research less intimidating by converting it from a solitary experience done alone to a collaborative venture done as a team. Working together with peers on any research task can reduce anxiety, create collective energy, and result in a final product that's superior to what could have been produced by a single person working independently.

Note

It's perfectly acceptable and ethical to team up with others to search for information and share resources. This isn't cheating or plagiarizing—as long as your final product is completed individually and what you turn into the instructor represents your own work.

> I would suggest students get to know [each] other and get together in groups to study or at least review class material. I find it is easier to ask your classmates with whom you are comfortable 'dumb' questions."
>
> *—Advice to first-year students from a college sophomore (Walsh, 2005)*

Study Teams. When seniors at Harvard University were interviewed, nearly every one of them who had participated in study groups considered the experience to be crucial to their academic progress and success (Light, 1990, 1992, 2001).

Additional research on study groups indicates that they are effective only if each member has done the required course work in advance of team meetings—for example, if all teammates attended class consistently and completed required readings (Light, 2001). To fully capitalize and maximize the power of study teams, each team member should study individually *before* studying with the group and come to the group prepared with answers and ideas to share with teammates, as well as specific questions or points of confusion about which they hope to receive help from other members of the team. This ensures that all team members are individually accountable for their own learning and equally responsible for contributing to their teammates' learning.

Note

Don't forget that team learning goes beyond late-night study groups. Students could and should form learning teams in advance of exams to help each other with other academic tasks—such as note-taking, reading, writing, and library research.

Test Review Teams. After receiving your results on course examinations (and assignments) you can collaborate with peers to review your performance as a team. When you compare your answers to the answers of other students, you're better able to identify what you did well and where you lost points. By seeing the answers of teammates who received maximum credit on certain questions, you get a clearer picture of what went wrong and what you can do next time to get it right next time.

 Think About It—Journal Entry 3.6

Think about classmates in courses you're taking this term. Would you be willing to ask any of them if they'd like to form a learning team? Why?

Fourth Step for College Success: Reflection and Self-Awareness (Mindfulness)

The final step in the learning process, whether it be learning in the classroom or learning from experience, is to step back from the process, thoughtfully review it, and connect it to what you already know. Reflection is the flip side of active involvement; both processes are necessary for learning to be complete. Active involvement ensures attention—it enables information to enter your brain—and reflection ensures consolidation—it converts that information into knowledge and remains in your brain on a long-term basis (Bligh, 2000; Roediger, Dudai, & Fitzpatrick, 2007).

Research reveals that different brain wave patterns are associated with each of these two key mental states (Bradshaw, 1995). In **Figure 3.3**, the electrical pattern on the left shows the brain waves of someone actively involved in the learning process, indicating that information is being attended to and processed by the brain.

FIGURE 3.3

High-Amplitude Brain Waves Associated with a Mental State of *Active Involvement.*

High-Frequency Brain Waves Associated with a Mental State of *Reflective Thinking.*

© Kendall Hunt Publishing Company

The electrical pattern on the right shows the brain waves of a person reflecting on information after it's been actively processed and moving that information into long-term memory. The brain wave patterns in these two different stages of the learning process indicate that deep, long-lasting learning takes place through a combination of (a) active involvement, characterized by high-amplitude "beta" brain waves; and (b) thoughtful reflection, characterized by high-frequency "alpha" brain waves (similar to someone in a meditative state).

Self-Awareness

In addition to reflecting on what you're learning, it's also important to reflect on yourself. This process is known as *introspection*—it involves turning inward to gain deeper self-awareness and understanding of who you are, what you're doing, and where you're going. Two forms of self-awareness are particularly important for success in college: (a) self-monitoring and (b) self-assessment.

Self-Monitoring

One characteristic of successful learners is that they self-monitor (check themselves) while learning to remain aware of:

* Whether they're using effective learning strategies (e.g., if they're giving their undivided attention to what they're learning);
* Whether they're truly comprehending what they are learning (e.g., if they're understanding it at a deep level or memorizing it at a surface level);
* How they're regulating or adjusting their learning strategies to meet the demands of different academic tasks and subjects (e.g., if they're reading technical material in a science textbook, they read at a slower rate and check their understanding more frequently than when reading a novel) (Pintrich & Schunk, 2002).

You can begin to establish good self-monitoring habits by getting in the routine of periodically pausing to reflect on the strategies you're using to learn and how you "do" college. For instance, you can ask yourself the following questions:

* Am I listening attentively to what my instructor is saying in class?
* Am I comprehending what I'm reading outside of class?
* Am I effectively using campus resources designed to support my success?
* Am I interacting with campus professionals who can contribute to my current success and future development?
* Am I interacting and collaborating with peers who can support (not sabotage) my learning and development?
* Am I effectively implementing college success strategies (such as those identified in this book)?

> We learn neither by thinking nor by doing; we learn by thinking about what we are doing."
>
> *—George Stoddard, Professor Emeritus, University of Iowa*

Note

Successful students and successful people are mindful—*they watch what they're doing and remain aware of whether they're doing it effectively and to the best of their ability.*

Self-Assessment

Simply defined, self-assessment is the process of reflecting on and evaluating your personal characteristics. The following are key target areas for self-assessment because they enable you to accurately identify and achieve your educational and personal goals:

"Successful students know a lot about themselves."

—Claire Weinstein and Debra Meyer, professors of educational psychology at the University of Texas

- **Personal interests.** What you like to do or enjoy doing.
- **Personal values.** What's important to you and what you care about doing.
- **Personal abilities or aptitudes.** What you do well or have the potential to do well.
- **Learning habits.** What approaches, methods, or techniques you use to learn.
- **Learning styles.** How you like or prefer to learn.
- **Personality traits.** Your temperament, emotional characteristics, and social tendencies (e.g., whether you lean toward being outgoing or reserved).

Think About It—Journal Entry 3.7

How would you rate your academic self-confidence at this point in your college experience? (Circle one.)

very confident   somewhat confident   somewhat unconfident   very unconfident

Why?

_____

_____

_____

_____

Chapter Summary and Highlights

The key ideas contained in this chapter are summarized in the following self-assessment checklist of success promoting principles and practices.

A Checklist of Success Promoting Principles and Practices

1. **Active Involvement (Engagement)**
   Inside the classroom, I will:
   - ☑ *Get to class.* I'll treat it like a job and be there on all days I'm expected to.
   - ☑ *Get involved in class.* I'll come prepared, listen actively, take notes, and participate. Outside the classroom, I will:

☑ *Read actively.* I'll take notes while I read to increase attention and retention.

☑ *Double up.* I'll spend twice as much time on academic work outside of class as I spend in class. If I'm a full-time student, I'll make it a full-time job and put in a 40-hour workweek (with occasional "overtime" as needed).

2. **Capitalizing on Campus Resources**

   I will capitalize on academic and student support services available to me, such as the:

   ☑ Academic Support Services
   ☑ College Library
   ☑ Academic Advisement
   ☑ Student Development Services
   ☑ Financial Aid
   ☑ Counseling Center

3. **Interpersonal Interaction & Collaboration (Social Integration)**

   I will interact and collaborate with the following members of my college community:

   ☑ Peers. I'll join student clubs and participate in campus organizations.
   ☑ Faculty members. I'll connect with my course instructors and other faculty members after class, in their offices, or via e-mail.
   ☑ Academic advisors. I'll see an advisor for more than course registration, and I'll find an advisor whom I can relate to and develop an ongoing relationship.

4. **Reflection & Self-Awareness (Mindfulness)**

   I will engage in:

   ☑ Reflection. I'll step back from what I'm learning, review it, and connect it to what I already.
   ☑ Self-Monitoring. I'll maintain self-awareness of how I'm learning in college and if I'm using effective strategies.
   ☑ Self-Assessment. I'll reflect on and evaluate my personal interests, talents, learning styles, and learning habits.

In short, successful students are:

- **Involved.** They *get into* it by investing time and effort in the college experience;
- **Interactive.** They *team up* for it by interacting and collaborating with others;
- **Resourceful.** They *get help* with it by capitalizing on their surrounding resources; and
- **Reflective.** They *step back* from it to think about their performance and themselves.

Think About It—Journal Entry 3.8

Identify one way in which you will put each of the following four principles of college success into practice during the next few weeks.

1. Active Involvement (Engagement)

_____

_____

_____

2.   Utilizing Campus Resources (Resourcefulness)

_____

_____

_____

3.   Interpersonal Interaction and Collaboration (Social Integration)

_____

_____

_____

4.   Reflection and Self-awareness (Mindfulness)

_____

_____

_____

_____

Learning More through the World Wide Web: Internet-Based Resources

For additional information on strategies for college success, see the following websites:

http://www.cgcc.edu/success

http://www.dartmouth.edu/~acskills/success/

www.studygs.net

References

Advisory Committee on Student Financial Assistance (2008, September). *Apply to succeed: Ensuring community college students benefit from need-based financial aid.* Washington DC: Author. Retrieved from https://www2.ed.gov/about/bdscomm/list/acsfa/applytosucceed.pdf

Astin, A. W. (1993). *What matters in college?* San Francisco: Jossey-Bass.

Bailey, G. (2009). *University of North Carolina, Greensboro application for NADE certification, tutoring program.* NADE Certification Council Archives. Searcy, AR: Harding University.

Bligh, D. A. (2000). *What's the use of lectures?* San Francisco: Jossey Bass.

Bradshaw, D. (1995). Learning theory: Harnessing the strength of a neglected resource. In D. C. A. Bradshaw (Ed.), Bringing learning to life: *The learning revolution, the economy and the individual* (pp. 79–92). London: Falmer Press.

Brown, R. D. (1988). Self-quiz on testing and grading issues. Teaching at UNL (*University of Nebraska–Lincoln*), 10(2), 1–3.

Bruffee, K. A. (1993). *Collaborative learning: Higher education, interdependence, and the authority of knowledge.* Baltimore: Johns Hopkins University Press.

Cross, K. P., Barkley, E. F., & Major, C. H. (2005). *Collaborative learning techniques: A handbook for college faculty.* San Francisco: Jossey-Bass.

Cuseo, J. B. (1996). *Cooperative learning: A pedagogy for addressing contemporary challenges and critical issues in higher education.* Stillwater, OK: New Forums Press.

Cuseo, J. B. (2003). Comprehensive academic support for students during the first year of college. In G. L. Kramer et al. (Eds.), *Student academic services: An integrated approach* (pp. 271–310). San Francisco: Jossey-Bass.

Cuseo, J. B. (2005). "Decided," "undecided," and "in transition": Implications for academic advisement, career counseling, and student retention. In R. S. Feldman (Ed.), *Improving the first year of college: Research and practice* (pp. 27–50). Mahwah, NJ: Lawrence Erlbaum.

Cuseo, J. B., & Thompson, A., Campagna, M., & Fecas, V. S. (2013). *Thriving in college & beyond: Research-based strategies for academic success and personal development* (3rd ed.). Dubuque, IA: Kendall Hunt.

Erickson, B. L., Peters, C. B., & Strommer, D. W. (2006). *Teaching first-year college students.* San Francisco: Jossey-Bass.

Gilles, R. M., & Adrian, F. (2003). *Cooperative learning: The social and intellectual outcomes of learning in groups.* London: Farmer Press.

Gordon, V. N., & Steele, G. E. (2003). Undecided first-year students: A 25-year longitudinal study. *Journal of the First-Year Experience and Students in Transition, 15*(1), 19–38.

Johnson, D., Johnson, R., & Smith, K. (1998). Cooperative learning returns to college: What evidence is there that it works? *Change, 30,* 26–35.

Kiewra, K. A. (2000). Fish giver or fishing teacher? The lure of strategy instruction. *Teaching at UNL (University of Nebraska–Lincoln), 22*(3), 1–3.

Kuh, G. D. (1995). The other curriculum: Out-of-class experiences associated with student learning and personal development. *Journal of Higher Education, 66*(2), 123–153.

Kuh, et al. (2005). Student engagement in the first year of college. In M. L. Upcraft, J. N. Gardner, B. O. Barefoot, & Associates (Eds.), *Challenging and supporting the first-year student: A handbook for improving the first year of college* (pp. 86–107). San Francisco: Jossey-Bass.

Kuh, G. D., Douglas, K. B., Lund, J. P., & Ramin-Gyurnek, J. (1994). *Student learning outside the classroom: Transcending artificial boundaries.* ASHE-ERIC Higher Education Report No. 8. Washington, DC: George Washington University, School of Education and Human Development.

Light, R. L. (1990). *The Harvard assessment seminars.* Cambridge, MA: Harvard University Press.

Light, R. L. (1992). *The Harvard assessment seminars, second report.* Cambridge, MA: Harvard University Press.

Light, R. J. (2001). *Making the most of college: Students speak their minds.* Cambridge, MA: Harvard University Press.

Lotkowski, V. A., Robbins, S. B., & Noeth, R. J. (2004). *The role of academic and non-academic factors in improving student retention.* ACT Policy Report. Retrieved from https://www.act.org/research/policymakers/pdf/college_retention.pdf.

Malvasi, M., Rudowsky, C., & Valencia, J. M. (2009). *Library Rx: Measuring and treating library anxiety, a research study.* Chicago: Association of College and Research Libraries.

Pascarella, E. T. (2001, November/December). Cognitive growth in college: Surprising and reassuring findings from the National Study of Student Learning. *Change,* pp. 21–27.

Pascarella (2005). *How College Affects Students: Ten Directions for Future Research.*

Pascarella, E., & Terenzini, P. (1991). *How college affects students: Findings and insights from twenty years of research.* San Francisco: Jossey-Bass.

Pascarella, E., & Terenzini, P. (2005). *How college affects students: A third decade of research* (Vol. 2). San Francisco: Jossey-Bass.

Pew Internet & American Life Project. (2002). *The Internet goes to college: How students are living in the future with today's technology.* Retrieved from http://www.pewinternet.org/files/old-media/Files/Reports/2002/PIP_College_Report.pdf.pdf.

Pintrich, P. R., & Schunk, D. H. (2002). *Motivation in education: Theory, research, and applications.* Upper Saddle River, NJ: Merrill-Prentice Hall.

Roediger, H. L., Dudai, Y., & Fitzpatrick, S. M. (2007). *Science of memory: concepts.* New York, NY: Oxford University Press.

Smith, J. B., Walter, T. L., & Hoey, G. (1992). Support programs and student self-efficacy: Do first-year students know when they need help? *Journal of the Freshman Year Experience, 4*(2), 41–67.

Thompson, A., & Cuseo, J. (2014). *Diversity and the college experience.* Dubuque, IA: Kendall Hunt.

Tinto, V. (1993). *Leaving college: Rethinking the causes and cures of student attrition* (2nd ed.). Chicago: University of Chicago Press.

Tinto, V. (2012). *Completing college: Rethinking institutional action.* Chicago: The University of Chicago Press.

Topping, K. (1998). Peer assessment between students in colleges and universities. *Review of Educational Research, 68*(3), 249–276.

Walsh, K. (2005). *Suggestions from more experienced classmates.* Retrieved from http://www.uni.edu/walsh/introtips.html

Walter, T. L., & Smith, J. (1990, April). *Self-assessment and academic support: Do students know they need help?* Paper presented at the annual Freshman Year Experience Conference, Austin, Texas.

Chapter 3 Exercises

3.1 Quote Reflections

Review the sidebar quotes contained in this chapter and select two that were especially meaningful or inspirational to you.

For each quote, provide a three- to five-sentence explanation why you chose it.

3.2 Reality Bite–Case Study

Alone and Disconnected: Feeling like Calling It Quits

Josephine is a first-year student in her second week of college. She doesn't feel like she's fitting in with other students on her campus. She also feels a little guilty about the time she's taking time away from family and friends, and she fears that her ties with them will be weakened or broken if she continues spending so much time at school and on schoolwork. Josephine is feeling so torn between college, her family, and her old friends that she's beginning to have second thoughts about coming back next term.

Reflection and Discussion Questions

1. What would you say to Josephine that might persuade or motivate her to stay in college?

2. What could Josephine do to get more connected with her college community and feel less disconnected from her family and hometown friends?

3. What could Josephine do for herself right now to minimize the conflict she's experiencing between her commitment to college and her commitment to family and high school friends?

4. Can you relate to Josephine's situation? If yes, in what way? If no, why not?

3.3 Creating a Master List of Resources on Your Campus

1. Construct a master list of all support services that are available to you on your campus by consulting the following sources:

   - Information published in your college catalog and student handbook
   - Information posted on your college's website
   - Information obtained by visiting with a professional in different offices or centers on your campus

2. Your final product will be a list that includes the following:

Campus Support Service	Type of Support Provided	Contact Person	Campus Location
_____	_____	_____	_____
_____	_____	_____	_____
_____	_____	_____	_____
_____	_____	_____	_____

etc.

- You can team up with other classmates to work collaboratively on this assignment. Members of your team could identify different campus resources to research and then share their findings with teammates.
- After completing this assignment, save your master list of support services for future use.

3.4 Utilizing Campus Resources

Look back at the campus resources you identified in the previous exercise, or those described on **pp. 58–60** of this chapter. Which of these resources do you plan to use this term?

Why did you identify these resources as your top priorities right now?

Ask your course instructor for recommendations about what campus resources you should consult during your first term on campus. Compare their recommendations with your selections.

3.5 Chapter 2 Reflection

WHAT do you believe is the most important principle of community college success?

WHY do you believe this is the most important one?

Explain HOW you will use this principle to assist you in being successful in college.

Notes

Notes

Time Management

PRIORITIZING TASKS, PREVENTING PROCRASTINATION, AND PROMOTING PRODUCTIVITY

Time is a valuable personal resource—if you gain greater control of it, you can greater control of your life. Time managed:

- Enables you to get work done in a timely manner,
- Enables you to attain personal priorities, and
- Maintain balance in your life.

This chapter offers a comprehensive set of strategies for managing time, combating procrastination, and ensuring that your time-spending habits are aligned with your educational goals and priorities.

Equip you with a powerful set of strategies for setting priorities, planning time, and completing tasks in a timely and productive manner.

 Think About It—Journal Entry 4.1

Complete the following sentence with the first thought that comes to your mind:

For me, time is . . .

_____

_____

_____

_____

The Importance of Time Management

For many first-year students, the beginning of college means the beginning of more independent living and self-management. Even if you've lived on your own for some time, managing time is an important skill to possess because you're likely juggling multiple responsibilities, including school, family, and work. Studies show that most first-year community college students are attending classes while working either part-time or full-time (American Association of Community Colleges, 2009).

To have any realistic chance of achieving our goals, we need an intentional and strategic plan for spending our time in a way that aligns with our goals and enables us to make steady progress toward them. Thus, setting goals, reaching goals, and managing time are interrelated skills.

Most college students struggle to at least some extent with time management, particularly first-year students who are transitioning from the lockstep schedules of high school to the more unstructured time associated with college course schedules. National surveys indicate that almost 50% of first-year college students report difficulty managing their time effectively (HERI, 2014). In college, time management skills grow in importance because students' time is less structured or controlled by school authorities or family members and more responsibility is placed on students to make their own decisions about how their time will be spent. Furthermore, the academic calendar and class scheduling patterns in college differ radically from high school. There's less "seat time" in class each week and college students are expected to do much more academic work on their courses outside of class time, which leaves them with a lot more "free time" to manage.

Simply stated, college students who have difficulty managing their time have difficulty managing college. One study compared college sophomores who had an outstanding first year (both academically and personally) with sophomores who struggled in their first year. Interviews with both groups revealed there was one key difference between them: sophomores who experienced a successful first year repeatedly brought up the topic of time during the interviews. The successful students said they had to think carefully about how they spent their time and that they needed to budget their time. In contrast, sophomores who experienced difficulty in their first year of college hardly talked about the topic of time during their interviews, even when they were specifically asked about it (Light, 2001).

Studies also indicate that people of all ages report time management to be a critical element of their life. Working adults report that setting priorities and balancing multiple responsibilities (e.g., work and family) can be a stressful juggling act (Harriott & Ferrari, 1996). For them, time management and stress management are interrelated.

These findings suggest that time management is more than just a college success skill; it's also as a life management and life success skill. When we gain greater control of our time, we gain greater control of our life. Studies show that people who manage their time well report being happier (Myers, 1993, 2000).

> "The major difference [between high school and college] is time. You have so much free time on your hands that you don't know what to do for most of the time."
>
> —First-year college student (Erickson & Strommer, Teaching College Freshmen)

> "I cannot stress enough that you need to intelligently budget your time."
>
> —Advice to new college students from a student finishing his first year in college

AUTHOR'S EXPERIENCE

I started the process of earning my doctorate a little later in life than other students. I was a married father with a preschool daughter (Sara). Since my wife left for work early in the morning, it was always my duty to get up and get Sara's day going in the right direction. In addition, I had to do the same for myself. Three days of my week were spent on campus in class or in the library. (We didn't have quick access to research on home computers then as you do now.) The other two days of the workweek and the weekend were spent on household chores, family time, and studying.

I knew that if I was to have any chance of finishing my Ph.D. in a reasonable amount of time, I had to adopt an effective schedule for managing my time. Each day of the week, I held to a strict routine. I got up in the morning, ate breakfast while reading the paper, got Sara ready for school, and got her to school. Once I returned home, I put a load of laundry in the washer, studied, wrote, and spent time concentrating on what I needed to do to be successful from 8:30 a.m. to 12:00 p.m. every day. At lunch, I had a pastrami and cheese sandwich and a soft drink while rewarding myself by watching *Perry Mason* reruns until 1:00 p.m. I then continued to study until it was time to pick up Sara from school. Each night I spent time with my wife and daughter and then prepared for the next day. I lived a life that had a preset schedule. By following that schedule, I was able to successfully complete my doctorate in a reasonable amount of time while giving my family the time they needed. (By the way, I still watch *Perry Mason* reruns.)

—*Aaron Thompson*

Strategies for Managing Time and Tasks

Effectively managing our time and our tasks involves three key processes:

1. **Analysis**—breaking down time to see how much of it we have and what we're spending it on;
2. **Itemizing**—identifying and listing the tasks that we need to complete and when we need to complete them; and
3. **Prioritizing**—ranking our tasks in terms of their importance and attacking them in order of their importance.

The following strategies can be used to implement these three processes and should help you open up more time in your schedule, enabling you to discover new ways to use your time more productively.

Think About It—Journal Entry 4.2

1. What is your greatest time waster?

2. Is there anything you can do right now to stop or eliminate it?

Become more aware of how your time is spent by breaking it into smaller units. How often have you heard someone say, "Where did all the time go?" or "I just can't seem to find the time!" One way to find out where all our time goes and find more time to get things done is by doing a *time analysis*—a detailed examination of how much total time we have and where we're spending it—including patches of wasted time when we get little done and nothing accomplished. This time analysis only has to be done for a week or two to give us a pretty good idea of where our time is going and to find better ways to use our time productively.

Identify *what* specific tasks you need to accomplish and when you need to accomplish them. When we want to remember items we need to buy at the grocery store or people we want to invite to a party, we make a list. This same list-making strategy can be used for tasks we need to complete so we don't forget about them, or forget to do them on time. One characteristic of successful people is that they are list makers; they make lists for things they want to accomplish each day (Covey, 2004).

Note

When we write out things we need to do, we're less likely to block them out and forget to do them.

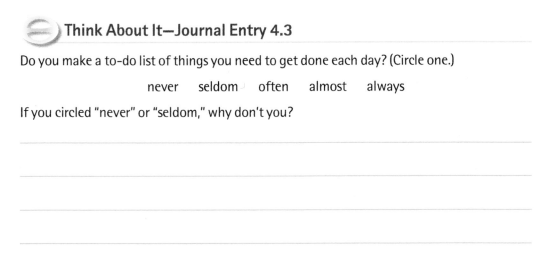

Think About It—Journal Entry 4.3

Do you make a to-do list of things you need to get done each day? (Circle one.)

never   seldom   often   almost   always

If you circled "never" or "seldom," why don't you?

_____

_____

_____

_____

Take advantage of time planning and task management tools, such as the following:

- *Small, portable planner.* You can use this device to list all your major assignments and exams for the term, along with their due dates. By pulling together all work tasks required in each of your courses and getting them in one place, it will be much easier to keep track of what you have to do and when you have to do it throughout the entire term.
- *Large, stable calendar.* In the calendar's date boxes, record your major assignments for the term. The calendar should be posted in a place you can see every day (e.g., bedroom or refrigerator). If you repeatedly see the things you have to do, you're less likely to overlook them, forget about them, or subconsciously push them out of your mind because you'd really prefer not to do them.
- *Smartphone.* These devices can be used for more than checking social networking sites and sending or receiving text messages. They can be used as a calendar tool to record due dates and set up alert functions to remind you of deadlines. Many smartphones also allow you to set up task or to-do lists and set priorities for each item entered. A variety of apps are now available for planning tasks and tracking time spent on tasks (e.g., see: http://www.rememberthemilk.com; other apps available include cozi, an organization app, and pomodoro, an app intended to boost productivity). Take advantage of cutting edge tools, but at the same time, keep in mind that planners don't plan time, people do. Effectively planning time and tasks flows from a clear vision of your goals and priorities.

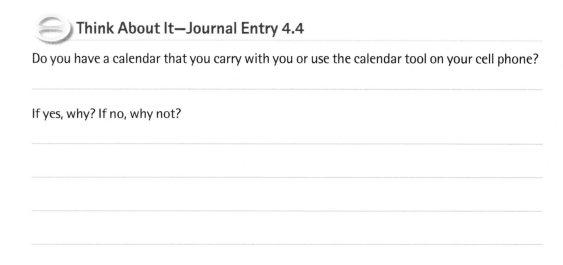

My mom ensured I got up for school on time. Once I got to school the bell would ring to let me know to move on to the next class. When I returned home, I had to do my homework and chores. My daily and weekly schedules were dictated by someone else.

When I entered college, I quickly realized that I needed to develop my own system for being organized, focused, and productive without the assistance of my mother or school authorities. Since I came from a modest background, I had to work my way through college. Juggling schedules became an art and science for me. I knew the things that I could not miss, such as work and school, and the things I could miss—TV and girls. (OK, TV, but not girls.)

After college, I spent 10 years in business—a world where I was measured by being on time and delivering a productive "bottom line." It was during this time that I discovered a scheduling book. When I became a professor, I had other mechanisms to make sure I did what I needed to do when I needed to do it. This was largely based on when my classes were offered. Other time was dedicated to working out and spending time with my family. Now, as an administrator, I have an assistant who keeps my schedule for me. She tells me where I am going, how long I should be there, and what I need to accomplish while I am there. Unless you take your parents with you or have the luxury of a personal assistant, it's important to schedule your time. Use a planner!

—Aaron Thompson

Think About It—Journal Entry 4.4

Do you have a calendar that you carry with you or use the calendar tool on your cell phone?

If yes, why? If no, why not?

Prioritize: rank tasks in order of their importance. After you itemize your work tasks by identifying and listing them, the next step is to *prioritize* them—determine the order or sequence in which they get done. Prioritizing basically involves ranking tasks in terms of their importance, with the highest priority tasks placed at the top of the list to ensure they're tackled first.

How do you decide on what tasks are to be ranked highest and tackled first? Here are two key criteria (standards of judgment) for determining your highest priority tasks:

- **Urgency.** Tasks that are closest to their deadline or due date should receive highest priority. Finishing an assignment that's due tomorrow should receive higher priority than starting an assignment that's due next month.
- **Gravity.** Tasks that carry the greatest weight (count the most) should receive highest priority. If an assignment worth 100 points and an assignment worth 10 points are due at the same time, the 100-point task should receive higher prior-

Things that matter most must never be at the mercy of things that matter least."

—Johann Wolfgang von Goethe, German poet, dramatist, and author of the epic Faust

ity. We want to be sure to invest our work time on tasks that matter most. Similar to investing money, we should invest our time on tasks that yield the greatest pay-off.

Note

Put first things first: Plan your work by identifying your most important and most urgent tasks, and work your plan by attacking these tasks first.

> "When I have lots of homework to do, I suddenly go through this urge to clean up and organize the house. I'm thinking, 'I'm not wasting my time. I'm cleaning up the house and that's something I have to do.' But all I'm really doing is avoiding school work."
>
> —College sophomore

An effective strategy for prioritizing tasks is to divide them into "A," "B," and "C" lists (Lakein, 1973; Morgenstern, 2004). The "A" list is reserved for *essential* (nonnegotiable) tasks—those that that *must* be done now. The "B" list is for *important* tasks—those that *should* be done soon. The "C" list is for *optional* tasks—those that *could* or *might* be done if there's time remaining after the more important tasks on lists A and B have been completed. Organizing tasks and time in this fashion helps you decide how to divide your labor in a way that ensures you "put first things first." You shouldn't waste time doing unimportant things to deceive yourself into thinking that you're "getting stuff done"—when, in reality, all you're doing is "keeping busy" and distracting yourself (and subtracting time) from doing the things that should be done.

AUTHOR'S EXPERIENCE

My mom is a schoolteacher, and when my sister and I were growing up she had a strict policy: when we came home from school we could have a snack, but after that we were not allowed to do anything else until our homework was finished. I remember that on days when it was really nice outside, I would beg and plead (and sometimes even argue) with my mom about going outside to play. She always won, and often I had wasted so much time arguing that I completely missed out on the opportunity to play at all. At the time I thought my mom was really mean. As I grew older (in high school and college), though, it became easy to put my homework first. My mom had taught me the importance of prioritizing and completing important things (like homework) before things that were not as important.

—*Julie McLaughlin*

Note

Developing awareness of how our time is spent is more than a brainless, clerical activity. When it's done well, it becomes an exercise in self-awareness and values clarification—how we spend our time is a true test of who we are and what we really value.

>
> "Time = Life. Therefore waste your time and waste your life, or master your time and master your life."
>
> —Alan Lakein, international expert on time management and author of the bestselling book How to Get Control of Your Time and Your Life (1973)

> "If you fail to plan, you are planning to fail."
>
> —Benjamin Franklin, renowned author, inventor, civic activist, and a founding father of the United States

Creating a Time-Management Plan

You may have heard of the old proverb, "A stitch in time saves nine." Planning your time represents the "stitch" (unit of time) that saves you nine additional stitches (units of time). Similar to successful chess players, successful time managers plan ahead and anticipate their next moves.

Don't buy into the myth that taking time to plan takes time away from getting started and getting things done. Time management experts estimate that the amount of time planning your total work actually reduces your total work time by a factor of three: for every one unit of time you spend planning, you save three units of time working (Goldsmith, 2010; Lakein, 1973). For example, 5 minutes of planning time will typically save you 15 minutes of total work time, and 10 minutes of planning time will save you 30 minutes of work time.

Planning your time saves you time because it ensures you start off in the right direction. If you have a plan of attack, you're less vulnerable to "false starts"—starting your work and then discovering you're not on the right track or not doing things in the right sequence, which forces you to retreat and start all over again.

Once you have accepted the idea that taking time to plan your time will save you time in the long run, you're ready to create a plan for effectively managing time. Listed below are specific strategies for doing so.

Be mindful of time by wearing a watch or carrying a phone that can accurately and instantly tell you the date and time. This may seem like an obvious "no-brainer", but time can't be managed if we don't know what time it is, and we can't plan a schedule if we don't know what day it is. Consider setting the time on your watch or phone slightly ahead of the actual time to help ensure that you arrive to class, work, or meetings on time. You can also equip your phone with apps to remind you of times when tasks are to be completed (e.g., *remindme.com* or *studiousapp.com*).

Carry a *small calendar, planner,* or *appointment book* at all times. This will allow you to record appointments that you may make on the run as well as enable you to jot down creative ideas or memories of things you need to do—which can sometimes pop into your mind at the most unexpected times.

Take *portable work* with you during the day that you can work at any place at any time. This will enable you to take advantage of "dead time" such as time spent sitting and waiting for appointments or transportation. Portable work allows you to resurrect dead time and transform it into productive work time. Not only is this a good time management strategy, it's a good stress management strategy because you replace the frustration and boredom associated with having no control over "wait time" with a sense of accomplishment.

Make good use of your *free time between classes* by working on assignments and studying in advance for upcoming exams. See **Box 4.1** for a summary of how you can use your out-of-class time to improve your academic performance and course grades.

Only boring people get bored."
—*Graffiti appearing in a bathroom stall at the University of Iowa, circa 1977*

Note

College professors are more likely than high school teachers to expect you to rely on your course syllabus to keep track of what you have to do and when you have to do it. Your instructors may not remind you about upcoming papers, tests, quizzes, assignments, etc.

Box 4.1

Making Productive Use of "Free Time" Outside the Classroom

Students' class schedules in college differ radically from high school. College students are often pleasantly surprised by how much "free time" they have because they're spending much less time in class. However, students are expected to spend two or more hours outside of class for every hour they spend in class. Thus, using out-of-class time strategically and productively is critical to ensuring college success.

Compared to high school, "homework" in college often doesn't involve turning in assignments on a daily or weekly basis. Academic work assigned to be done outside the college classroom may not even be collected and graded. Instead, it's often done for your own benefit to help you prepare for upcoming exams and complete written reports (e.g., assigned reading and assigned

(continued)

Box 4.1 *(continued)*

problems in math and science). Rather than formally assigning and collecting this work as homework, your professors expect that you will do this work on your own and without supervision.

> In high school we were given a homework assignment every day. Now we have a large task assigned to be done at a certain time. No one tells [us] when to start or what to do each day."
>
> —*First-year college student*

Listed in this box are strategies for working independently and in advance of college exams and assignments. By building time for each of these activities into your regular schedule, you'll make more productive use of out-of-class time, decrease your level of stress, and strengthen your academic performance.

Doing Out-of-Class Work in Advance of Exams

- **Complete reading assignments** relating to lecture topics *before* the topic is discussed in class. This will make lectures easier to understand and enable you to participate intelligently in class (e.g., by asking meaningful questions and making informed comments during class discussions).
- **Review class notes** from your last class before the next class to build a mental bridge from one class to the next. Many students don't look at their class notes until they study them right before an exam. Don't be one of those students; instead, review your notes before the next class. Rewrite any class notes that may have been sloppily written the first time. If you find notes related to the same point all over the place, reorganize them into the same section. Lastly, if you find any information gaps or confusing points in your notes, seek out the course instructor or a trusted classmate to clear them up before the next class takes place.

    By reviewing your class notes on a regular basis, you will improve your ability to understand each upcoming lecture and reduce the total time you'll need to spend studying your notes the night before an exam.
- **Review your reading notes and highlights** to improve retention of important material. If you find certain

points in your reading to be confusing, discuss them with your course instructor during office hours or with a fellow classmate outside of class.

- **Integrate class material with reading material.** Connect related information from your lecture notes and reading notes and get them in the same place (e.g., on the same index card).
- **Use a "part-to-whole" study method** whereby you study material from your class notes and assigned reading in small pieces (parts) during short, separate study sessions in advance of the exam; then make your last study session before the exam a longer review session during which you re-study all the small parts (the whole) at the same time. Don't buy into the myth that studying in advance is a waste of time because you'll forget everything you studied by test time. As will be fully explained in Chapter 8, material studied in advance of an exam remains in your brain and is still there when you later review it. Even if it doesn't immediately come back to mind when you first start reviewing it, you'll relearn it much faster than you did the first time.

Doing Out-of-Class Work in Advance of Term Papers and Research Reports

Work on large, long-range assignments due at the end of the term by breaking them into smaller, short-term tasks completed at separate times during the term. For instance, a large term paper may be broken up into the following smaller tasks and completed in separate installments.

1. Search for and decide on a topic.
2. Locate sources of information on the topic.
3. Organize information obtained from your sources into categories.
4. Develop an outline of your paper's major points and the order or sequence in which you plan to present them.
5. Construct a first draft of your paper (and, if necessary, a second or third draft).
6. Write a final draft of your paper.
7. Proofread your final draft for spelling and grammatical errors before turning it in.

Think About It—Journal Entry 4.5

Do you have time gaps between your classes this term? If you do, what have you been doing during these "free" periods between classes?

_____

_____

_____

_____

What would you say is your greatest between-class time waster?

_____

_____

_____

Do you see a need to stop or eliminate it?

_____

If yes, what could you do to convert your wasted time into productive time?

_____

_____

_____

_____

A good time management plan transforms intention into action. Once you've planned the work, the next step is to work the plan. A time management plan turns into an action plan when you: (a) preview what you intend to do, (b) review whether you actually did what you intended to do, and (c) close the gap between your intentions and actions. The action plan begins with your *daily to-do list*, bringing that list with you as the day begins, and checking off items on the list as they're completed during the day. At the end of the day, the list is reviewed to determine what got done and what still needs to be done. The uncompleted tasks then become high priorities on the following day's to-do list.

If, at the end of each day, you find many unchecked items still remaining on your daily to-do list, this probably means you're spreading yourself too thin by trying to do too many things in a single day. You may need to be more realistic about how much you can accomplish per day by shortening your daily to-do lists. Not being able to complete many of your intended daily tasks may also mean that you need to modify your time management plan by adding more work time or subtracting some non-work activities that are drawing time and attention away from your work (e.g., responding to phone calls and text messages during your planned work times). If you're consistently falling short of achieving your daily goals, honestly ask yourself if you're spending too much time on less important things (e.g., TV, video games, Facebook).

 Think About It—Journal Entry 4.6

At the end of a typical day, how often do you find that you accomplished most of the tasks you intended to accomplish? (Circle one.)

never   seldom   often   almost   always

If you circled "never" or "seldom," what strategies could you use to move the bar toward "often" or "almost always"?

_____

_____

_____

_____

Murphy's Laws:

1. Nothing is as simple as it looks.
2. Everything takes longer than it should.
3. If anything can go wrong, it will.

—Author unknown (Murphy's Laws were named after Captain Edward Murphy, a naval engineer)

"It is important to allow time for things you enjoy doing because this is what will keep you stable."

—Advice to new college students from a first-year student

A good time management plan includes reserving time for the unexpected. Always hope for the best, but prepare for the worst. Your plan should include a buffer zone or safety net that contains extra time in case you encounter unforeseen developments or unexpected emergencies. Just as you should plan to have extra funds in your account to pay for unexpected expenses (e.g., auto repair), you should plan to have extra time in your schedule for unexpected events (e.g., personal illness or family emergency).

A good time management plan contains time for work and play. Your plan shouldn't consist solely of a daunting list of work tasks you have to do; it should also include fun things you like to do. Plan time to relax, refuel, and recharge. Your overall time management plan shouldn't turn you into an obsessive-compulsive workaholic. Instead, it should represent a balanced blend of work and play, including activities that promote your mental and physical wellness—such as relaxation, recreation, and reflection. Consider following the daily "8-8-8 rule"—8 hours for sleep, 8 hours for school, and 8 hours for other activities.

If you schedule things you like to do, you're more likely do to the things you have to do. You're much more likely to faithfully execute your plan if play time is scheduled along with work time, allowing play activities to serve as a reward for completing your work tasks.

Note

An effective time management plan helps you stress less, learn more, and earn higher grades while reserving time for other things that are important to you, enabling you to attain and maintain balance in your life.

Think About It—Journal Entry 4.7

What activities do you engage in for fun or recreation?

_____

_____

_____

_____

What do you do to relax or relieve stress?

_____

_____

_____

_____

Do you build these activities into your daily or weekly schedule?

_____

_____

_____

_____

_____

A good time management plan has some flexibility. A time management plan shouldn't enslave you to a rigid work schedule. The plan should be flexible enough to allow you to occasionally bend it without breaking it. Just as work commitments and family responsibilities can crop up unexpectedly, so, too, can opportunities for fun and enjoyable activities. Your plan should allow you the freedom to modify your schedule to take advantage of these enjoyable opportunities and experiences. However, you should plan to make up the work time you lost. In other words, you can borrow or trade work time for play time, but don't "steal" it; plan to pay back the work time you borrowed by substituting it for play time that was planned for another time. If you decide not to do work you planned, the next best thing to do is re-plan when you'll do it.

Note

When you create a personal time management plan, remember it's your plan—you own it and you run it. It shouldn't run you.

Dealing with Procrastination

A major enemy of effective time management is procrastination. Procrastinators don't abide by the proverb: "Why put off till tomorrow what can be done today?" Instead, their philosophy is just the opposite: "Why do today what can be put off till tomorrow?" Adopting this philosophy promotes a perpetual pattern of postponing what needs to be done until the last possible moment, forcing the procrastinator to rush frantically to finish work on time and turn in work that's inferior or incomplete (or not turn anything in at all).

©Kendall Hunt Publishing Company.

Next time I'll start sooner!

A procrastinator's idea of planning ahead and working in advance often boils down to this scenario.

Research shows that 80% to 95% of college students procrastinate (Steel, 2007) and almost 50% report that they procrastinate consistently (Onwuegbuzie, 2000). Procrastination is such a serious issue for college students that some campuses have opened "procrastination centers" to help them (Burka & Yuen, 2008).

AUTHOR'S EXPERIENCE

During my early years in college, I was quite a procrastinator. During my sophomore year, I waited to do a major history paper until the night before it was due. Back then, I had a word processor that was little more than a typewriter; it allowed you to save your work to a floppy disk before printing. I finished writing my paper around 3:00 a.m. and hit "print," but halfway through the printing I ran out of paper. I woke up my roommate to ask if she had paper, but she didn't. So, at 3:00 a.m. I was forced to get out of my pajamas, get into my street clothes, get into my car, and drive around town to find someplace open at three in the morning that sold typing paper. By the time I found a place, got back home, printed the paper, and washed up, it was time to go to class. I could barely stay awake in any of my classes that day, and when I got my history paper back, the grade wasn't exactly that I was hoping for. I never forgot that incident. My procrastination on that paper caused me to lose sleep the night before it was due, lose attention in all my other classes on the day it was due, and lose points on the paper that I managed to do. Thereafter, I was determined not to let procrastination get the best of me.

—*Julie McLaughlin*

Myths That Promote Procrastination

To have any hope of putting a stop to procrastination, procrastinators need to let go of two popular myths or misconceptions about time and performance.

Myth 1. "I work better under pressure" (e.g., on the day or night before something is due). Procrastinators often confuse desperation with motivation. Their belief that they work better under pressure is usually a rationalization to justify the fact that they *only* work under pressure—when they have to work because they've run out of time and are under the gun of a looming deadline.

It's true that when people are under pressure, they will start working and work with frantic energy, but that doesn't mean they're working more *effectively* and producing work of better *quality*. Because procrastinators are playing "beat the clock," they focus less on doing the job well and more on beating the buzzer. This typically results in a work product that's incomplete or inferior to what could have been produced if they had begun the work process sooner.

> Haste makes waste."
> —Benjamin Franklin

Myth 2. "Studying in advance is a waste of time because you will forget it all by test time." This myth is used by procrastinators to justify putting off all studying until the night before an exam. As will be discussed in Chapter 6, studying that's distributed (spread out) over time is more effective than massed (crammed) studying all at one time. Furthermore, last minute studying before exams often involves pulling "late-nighters" or "all-nighters" that result in sleep loss. This fly-by-night strategy deprives the brain of dream sleep (a.k.a. REM sleep), which it needs to retain information and manage stress (Hobson, 1988; Voelker, 2004). Research indicates that procrastinators suffer from higher rates of stress-related physical disorders, such as insomnia, stomach problems, colds, and flu (McCance & Pychyl, 2003). Working under time pressure also increases performance pressure by leaving the procrastinators with (a) no margin of error to correct mistakes, (b) no time to seek help on their work, and (c) no chance to handle random catastrophes or setbacks that may arise at the last minute.

Psychological Causes of Procrastination

Sometimes, procrastination has deeper psychological roots. People may procrastinate for reasons that relate more to emotional issues than poor time management habits. Studies show that some people procrastinate as a psychological strategy to protect their self-esteem. Referred to as *self-handicapping* (Rhodewalt & Vohs, 2005), this strategy is used by some procrastinators, often unconsciously, to give themselves a "handicap," or disadvantage. By starting their work at the last possible moment, if their performance turns out to be less than spectacular, they can always conclude (rationalize) that it was because they were performing under a handicap—lack of time rather than lack of ability (Chu & Cho, 2005).

For example, if they receive a low grade on a test or paper, they can "save face" (self-esteem) by concluding that it was because they waited until the last minute and didn't put much time or effort into it. In other words, they had enough ability or intelligence to earn a high grade, they just didn't put in enough time. Better yet, if they happen to get a good grade—despite their last-minute, last-ditch effort—it proves just how smart they are. It shows they were able to earn a high grade, even without putting in much time at all. Thus, self-handicapping creates a fail-safe or win–win scenario that always protects the procrastinators' self-image.

> Procrastinators would rather be seen as lacking in effort than lacking in ability."
> —Joseph Ferrari, professor of psychology and procrastination researcher

Think About It—Journal Entry 4.8

Do you tend to put off work for so long that getting it done turns into an emergency or panic situation?

_____

If your answer is yes, why do you think you put yourself in this position?

_____

_____

_____

_____

If your answer is no, what motivates or enables you to avoid this scenario?

_____

_____

_____

_____

_____

_____

In addition to self-handicapping, other psychological factors have been found to contribute to procrastination, including the following:

> "Striving for excellence motivates you; striving for perfection is demoralizing."
>
> —Harriet Braiker, psychologist and best-selling author

- **Fear of failure.** The procrastinator feels better about not turning in work than turning it in and getting negative feedback (Burka & Yuen, 2008; Solomon & Rothblum, 1984);
- **Perfectionism.** The procrastinator has unrealistically high personal standards or expectations, which leads to the belief that it's better to postpone work or not do it than to risk doing it less than perfectly (Kachgal, Hansel, & Nuter, 2001);
- **Fear of success.** The procrastinator fears that doing well will show others that he has the ability to achieve success, leading others to expect him to maintain those high standards in the future (Beck, Koons, & Milgram, 2000; Ellis & Knaus, 2002);
- **Indecisiveness.** The procrastinator has difficulty making decisions, including decisions about what to do first, when to do it, or whether to do it (Anderson, 2003; Steel, 2007), so they delay doing it or don't do it at all; and
- **Thrill seeking.** The procrastinator is hooked on the adrenaline rush triggered by rushing around to get things done just before a deadline (Szalavitz, 2003).

If these psychological issues are at the root of procrastination, they must be uprooted and dealt with before the problem can be solved. This may take some time and assistance from a counseling psychologist (either on or off campus) who is professionally trained to deal with emotional issues, including those that underlie procrastination.

Think About It—Journal Entry 4.9

How often do you procrastinate? (Circle one.)

rarely   occasionally   frequently   consistently

When you do procrastinate, what's the usual cause?

Strategies for Preventing and Overcoming Procrastination

Consistently use effective time management strategies. When effective time management practices (such as those cited in this chapter) are implemented consistently, they turn into regular habits. Research indicates that procrastinators are less likely to procrastinate when they convert their intentions or vows ("I swear I'm going to start tomorrow") into concrete action plans (Gollwitzer, 1999; Gollwitzer & Sheeran, 2006). When they repeatedly practice effective time management strategies with respect to tasks they tend to procrastinate on, their bad procrastination habits gradually fade and are replaced by good time management habits (Ainslie, 1992; Baumeister, Heatherton, & Tice, 1994).

Make the start of work as inviting or appealing as possible. Starting work—getting off the starting blocks—is often the major stumbling block for procrastinators. It's common for procrastinators to experience what's known as "start-up stress"—when they're about to start a task, they start having negative feelings about it, expecting it to be difficult, stressful, or boring (Burka & Yuen, 2008).

If you have trouble starting your work, sequence your work tasks in a way that allows you to start on tasks you find more interesting or are more likely to do well. Beginning with these tasks can give you a "jump start," enabling you to overcome inertia and create momentum. You can ride this initial momentum to motivate you to attack less appealing or more daunting work tasks that come later in your work sequence, which often turn out not to be as unpleasant or time-consuming as you thought they would be. Like many events in life, anticipation of the event turns out to be worse than the event itself. In one study of college students who didn't start a project until just before its due date, it was found that they experienced anxiety and guilt while they were procrastinating, but once they began working, these negative

> We are what we repeatedly do. Excellence, then, is not an act, but a habit."
>
> —Aristotle, influential Ancient Greek philosopher

> The secret to getting ahead is getting started."
>
> —Mark Twain (Samuel Clemens), American humorist and author of the Adventures of Huckleberry Finn (1885), a.k.a. "the Great American Novel"

> Did you ever dread doing something, then it turned out to take only about 20 minutes to do?"
>
> —Conversation between two college students overheard in a coffee shop

emotions subsided and were replaced by more positive feelings of progress and accomplishment (McCance & Pychyl, 2003).

You can also reduce start-up stress by beginning your work in an environment you find pleasant and relaxing (e.g., working in your favorite coffee shop while sipping your favorite beverage). In other words, if you have trouble starting work, start it in a place you enjoy while doing something you enjoy.

Organization matters. Research indicates that disorganization is a factor that contributes to procrastination (Steel, 2007). How well you organize your workplace and manage your work materials can reduce your tendency to procrastinate. Having the right materials in the right place at the right time can make it easier to get started. Once you decide to start working, you don't want to delay acting on that decision by looking for the tools you need to work with. If you're a procrastinator, this slight delay may provide the time (and excuse) to change your mind and not start working.

Note

The less time and effort it takes to start working, the more likely the work will be started.

One simple, yet effective way to organize academic materials is to develop your own filing system. Start by filing (storing) materials from different courses in different colored folders or notebooks. This not only enables you to keep all materials related to the same course in the same place, it also gives you immediate access to them when you need them. A filing system helps get you organized, gets rid of the stress associated with having things all over the place, and reduces your risk of procrasting by reducing the time and effort it takes to get started.

Location matters. *Where* you choose to work can influence *whether* your work gets done. Research indicates that distractions promote procrastination (Steel, 2007). Thus, working in an environment that minimizes distraction and maximizes concentration will reduce the risk of procrastination.

Arrange your work environment in a way that minimizes social distractions (e.g., people nearby who are not working), and media distractions (e.g., cell phones, e-mails, text messages, music, and TV). Remove everything from your work site that's not relevant or directly related to the work you're doing.

Your concentration will also improve if you work in an environment that allows you easy access to (a) work-support materials— (e.g., class notes, textbooks, and a dictionary), and (b) social support networks (e.g., working with a group of motivated students who help you stay focused, on task, and on track toward completing your work).

> " To reduce distractions, work at a computer on campus rather than using one in your room or home."
>
> *—Advice to new college students from a student finishing her first year in college*

Think About It—Journal Entry 4.10

List your two most common sources of distraction while working. Next to each distraction, identify a strategy you might use to reduce or eliminate it.

Source of Distraction   *Strategy for Reducing this Distraction*

1. _____

2.

_____

_____

_____

If you have difficulty maintaining or sustaining commitment to your work until it's finished, schedule easier and more interesting work tasks *in the middle or toward the end* of your planned work time. Some procrastinators have difficulty starting work, others have trouble continuing and completing the work they've started (Lay & Silverman, 1996). As previously mentioned, if you have trouble starting work, it might be best for you to start with tasks you find most interesting or easiest. In contrast, if you tend to experience procrastination by not completing your work once you've started, it might be better to schedule tasks of greater interest and ease at later points during your work session. Doing so can restore or revive your interest and energy. Tackling enjoyable and easier tasks last can also provide you with an incentive or reward for completing your less enjoyable and more difficult tasks first.

> 'm very good at starting things but often have trouble keeping a sustained effort."
> —First-year college student

If you're close to completing a task, don't stop until you complete it. Just do it! Completing a task that's almost done allows you to build on the momentum you've already generated. In contrast, postponing work on a task that's near completion means that you have to overcome inertia and regenerate momentum all over again. As the old saying goes, "There's no time like the present."

> Just do it."
> —Commercial slogan of Nike, athletic equipment company named after the Greek goddess of victory

Furthermore, finishing a task gives you a sense of *closure*—the feeling of personal accomplishment and self-satisfaction that comes from knowing you've "closed the deal." Checking off a completed task can motivate you to keep going and complete the unfinished tasks ahead of you.

Divide large work tasks into smaller, bite-sized pieces. Work becomes less overwhelming and stressful when it's handled in small chunks or segments. You can conquer procrastination for large tasks by using a "divide and conquer" strategy: divide the large task into smaller, more manageable subtasks, then tackle and complete these subtasks one at a time.

Don't underestimate the power of short work sessions. They're often more effective than longer sessions because it's easier to maintain concentration and momentum for shorter periods of time. By dividing work into short sessions, you can take quick jabs at a tall task, poke holes in it, and shrink its overall size with each successive jab. This reduces the pressure of having to deliver one, big knockout punch right before the final bell (deadline date).

> To eat an elephant, first cut it into small pieces."
> —Author unknown

AUTHOR'S EXPERIENCE

The two biggest projects I've had to complete in my life were writing my doctoral thesis and writing this book. The strategy that enabled me to complete both of these large tasks was to set short-term deadlines for myself (e.g., complete five to ten pages each week). I psyched myself into thinking that these little, self-imposed due dates were really drop-dead deadlines that I had to meet. This strategy allowed me to divide one monstrous chore into a series of smaller, more manageable mini-tasks. It was like taking a huge, indigestible meal and breaking it into small, bite-sized pieces that could be easily ingested and gradually digested over time.

—*Joe Cuseo*

> I long to accomplish some great and noble task, but it is my chief duty to accomplish small tasks as if they were great and noble."
>
> —*Helen Keller, seeing- and hearing-impaired author and activist for the rights of women and the handicapped*

Chapter Summary and Highlights

Effective goal-setting gets you going, but effective time management gets things done. To manage time effectively, we need to

- *Analyze* it. Break down time and become aware of how we spend it;
- *Itemize* it. Identify the tasks we need to accomplish and their due dates; and
- *Prioritize* it. Tackle our tasks in order of their importance.

Developing a comprehensive time management plan for academic work involves long-, mid-, and short-range steps that involve:

- Planning the total term (long-range step);
- Planning your week (mid-range step); and
- Planning your day (short-range step).

A good time management plan includes the following features:

- It transforms intention to action.
- It includes time to take care of unexpected developments.
- It contains time for work and play.
- It gives you the flexibility to accommodate unforeseen opportunities.

The enemy of effective time management is procrastination. Overcoming it involves letting go of two major myths:

- Better work is produced "under pressure"—on the day or night before it's due.
- Studying in advance is a waste of time—because you'll forget it all by test time.

Effective strategies for beating the procrastination habit include the following:

- Organize your work materials to make it easy and convenient for you to start working.
- Organize your work place or space so that you work in a location that minimizes distractions and temptations not to work.
- Intentionally arrange your work schedule so that you are working on more enjoyable or stimulating tasks at times when you're less vulnerable to procrastination.
- If you're close to finishing a task, finish it, because it's often harder to restart a task than to complete one that's already been started.
- Divide large tasks into smaller, more manageable units and tackle them in separate work sessions.

Mastering the skill of managing time is critical for success in college and beyond. Time is one of our most powerful personal resources; the better we manage it, the more likely we are to achieve our goals and gain control of our life.

> Doesn't thou love life? Then do not squander time, for that is the stuff life is made of."
>
> —*Benjamin Franklin, 18th-century inventor, newspaper writer, and cosigner of the Declaration of Independence*

Learning More through the World Wide Web: Internet-Based Resources

For additional information on managing time, and preventing procrastination, see the following websites:

Time-Management Strategies for All Students:
www.studygs.net/timman.htm

www.pennstatelearning.psu.edu/resources/study-tips/time-mgt

Time-Management Strategies for Adult Students:
www.essortment.com/lifestyle/timemanagement_sjmu.htm

Beating Procrastination:
www.mindtools.com/pages/article/newHTE_96.htm

http://success.oregonstate.edu/learning-corner/time-management/managing-procrastination

References

Ainslie, G. (1992. Specious reward: A behavioral theory of impulsiveness and impulse control. *Psychological Bulletin*, *82*, 463–496.

American Association of Community Colleges 2009 Fact Sheet. (2009). Retrieved from http://www.aacc.nche.edu/About/Documents/factsheet2009.pdf.

Anderson, C. J. (2003). The psychology of doing nothing: Forms of decision avoidance result from reason and emotion. *Psychological Bulletin*, *129*, 139–167.

Baumeister, R. F., Heatherton, T. F., & Tice, D. M. (1994). *Losing control: How and why people fail at self-regulation*. San Diego, CA: Academic Press.

Beck, B. L., Koons, S. R. & Milgram, D. L. (2000). Correlates and consequences of behavioural procrastination: The effects of academic procrastination, self-consciousness, self-esteem and self-handicapping [Special issue], *Journal of Social Behaviour & Personality*, *15*(5) (2000), pp. 3–13Burka, J. B., & Yuen, L. M. (2008). *Procrastination: Why you do it, what to do about it now*. Cambridge, MA: De Capo Press.

Chu, A. H. C., & Cho, J. N. (2005). Rethinking procrastination: Positive effects of "active" procrastination behavior on attitudes and performance. *The Journal of Social Psychology*, *145*(3), 245–264.

Covey, S. R. (2004). *Seven habits of highly effective people* (3rd ed.). New York: Fireside.

Ellis, A., & Knaus, W. J. (2002). *Overcoming procrastination* (Rev. ed.). New York: New American Library.

Goldsmith, E. B. (2010). *Resource management for individuals and families*. (4th ed.). Upper Saddle River, NJ: Prentice Hall.

Gollwitzer, P. M. (1999). Implementation intentions: Strong effects of simple plans. *American Psychologist*, *54*(7), 493–503.

Gollwitzer, P. M., & Sheeran, P. (2006). Implementation intentions and goal achievement: A meta-analysis of effects and processes. *Advances in Experimental Social Psychology*, *38*, 69–119.

Harriot, J. & Ferrari, J. R. (1996). Prevalence of procrastination among samples of adults. *Psychological Reports*, *78* (1996), pp. 611–616.

HERI (Higher Education Research Institute) (2014). *Your first college year survey 2014*. Los Angeles, CA: Cooperative Institutional Research Program, University of California-Los Angeles.

Hobson, J. A. (1988). *The dreaming brain*. New York: Basic Books.

Kachgal, M. M., Hansen, L. S., & Nutter, K. T. (2001). Academic procrastination prevention/intervention: Strategies and recommendations. *Journal of Developmental Education*, *25*(1), 2–12.

Lakein, A. (1973). *How to get control of your time and your life*. New York: New American Library.

Lay, C. H., & Silverman, S. (1996). Trait procrastination, time management, and dilatory behavior. *Personality & Individual Differences*, *21*, 61–67.

Light, R. J. (2001). *Making the most of college: Students speak their minds*. Cambridge, MA: Harvard University Press.

McCance, N., & Pychyl, T. A. (2003, August). *From task avoidance to action: An experience sampling study of undergraduate students' thoughts, feelings and coping strategies in relation to academic procrastination*. Paper presented at the Third Annual Conference for Counseling Procrastinators in the Academic Context, University of Ohio, Columbus.

Morgenstern, J. (2004). *Time management from the inside out: The foolproof system for taking control of your schedule—and your life* (2nd ed.). New York: Henry Holt & Co.

Myers, D. G. (1993). *The pursuit of happiness: Who is happy—and why?* New York: Morrow.

Myers, D. G. (2000). *The American paradox: Spiritual hunger in an age of plenty*. New Haven, CT: Yale University Press.

Onwuegbuzie, A. J. (2000). Academic procrastinators and perfectionistic tendencies among graduate students. *Journal of Social Behavior and Personality, 15*, 103–109

Rhodewalt, F., & Vohs, K. D. (2005). Defensive strategies, motivation, and the self. In A. Elliot & C. Dweck (Eds.), *Handbook of competence and motivation* (pp. 548–565). New York: Guilford Press.

Solomon, L. J., & Rothblum, E. D. (1984). Academic procrastination: Frequency and cognitive-behavioral correlates. *Journal of Counseling Psychology, 31*(4), 503–509.

Steel, P. (2007). The nature of procrastination: A meta-analytic and theoretical review of quintessential self-regulatory failure. *Psychological Bulletin, 133*(1), 65–94.

Szalavitz, M. (2003, July/August). Tapping potential: Stand and deliver. *Psychology Today*, 50–54.

Voelker, R. (2004). Stress, sleep loss, and substance abuse create potent recipe for college depression. *Journal of the American Medical Association, 291*, 2177–2179.

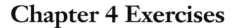

Chapter 4 Exercises

4.1 Quote Reflections

Review the sidebar quotes contained in this chapter and select two that were especially meaningful or inspirational to you.

For each quote, provide a three- to five-sentence explanation why you chose it.

4.2 Reality Bite

You have a paper due tomorrow for your 10:00 a.m. class. You stay up late writing the paper, and then your friends call and ask you to go out. The paper is finished, and you decide you can print it off when you get to school tomorrow. You have a great time with your friends and oversleep, waking at 9:45 a.m. You go straight to the computer lab and experience difficulties printing off your paper. You find a lab technician to help you, but it takes him 40 minutes to retrieve the paper. You run into class (45 minutes late) and give the paper to your instructor, who informs you that she will take the paper for late credit because the class policy states that any papers handed in after the beginning of class are considered late.

1. Who is primarily responsible for this paper being late? Why?

2. How could the situation have been avoided or handled differently?

4.3 Term at a Glance

Review the syllabus (course outline) for each course you're enrolled in this term, and complete the following information for each:

Term _____Year _____

Course ↓	Professor ↓	Exams ↓	Projects & Papers ↓	Other Assignments ↓	Attendance Policy ↓	Late & Makeup Assignment Policy ↓

1. Is the overall workload what you expected? Are you surprised by the amount of work required in any particular course or courses?

2. At this point in the term, what do you see as your most challenging or demanding course or courses? Why?

3. Do you think you can handle the total workload required for the full set of courses you're enrolled in this term?

4. What adjustments or changes could you make to your personal schedule that would make it easier to accommodate your academic workload this term?

4.4 Developing a Task Management Plan for Your First Term in College

1. Review the *course syllabus (course outline)* for each class you are enrolled in this term and highlight all major exams, tests, quizzes, assignments, and papers and the dates on which they are due.

2. Obtain a *large calendar* for the academic term (available at your campus bookstore or learning center) and record all the highlighted information for your exams and assignments for all your courses in the calendar boxes that represent their due dates. To fit this information within the calendar boxes, use creative abbreviations to represent different tasks, such as RA for reading assignment, E for exam, and TP for term paper. When you're done, you'll have a detailed chart or map of deadline dates and a master schedule for the entire term. There are several online calendars that can assist in managing your schedule (e.g., http://www.cozi.com/family-calendar.htm and http://pomodorotechnique.com/).

3. Activate the calendar and task lists functions on your PDA or smartphone. Enter your schedule, important dates, deadlines, and set alert reminders. By carrying your PDA or cell phone with your regularly, you will always have this information at your fingertips.

Reflections

1. Is your overall workload what you expected? Are your surprised by the amount of work time you will need to devote to your courses?

2. At this point in the term, what course is demanding the greatest amount of out-of-class work time? Have you been able to put in this time?

3. What adjustments or changes (if any) could you make to your personal schedule this term to create more time to handle your academic workload?

4.5 Time Analysis Inventory

1. Go to the following website: *pennstatelearning.psu.edu/resources/study-tips/time-mgt* Click on the link for the "time-management exercise."

2. Complete the time management exercise at this site. The exercise asks you to estimate the hours per day or week that you engage in various activities (e.g., sleeping, employment, and commuting). When you enter the amount of time devoted to each activity, this website will automatically compute the total number of remaining hours you have available in the week for academic work.

3. After completing your entries, answer the following questions (or provide your best estimate).

    a) How many hours per week do you have available for academic work?

    b) Do you have two hours available for academic work outside of class for each hour you spend in class? If you don't, what activities could be eliminated or reduced to create more time for academic work outside of class?

4.6 Developing a Time Management Plan for Your First Term in College

Keep in mind the task management plan you developed in Exercise 4.3, use the following *Week-at-a-Glance Grid* to map out your typical or average week for this term. Start by recording what you usually do on these days, including the times you're in class, when you work, and when you relax or recreate. You can use abbreviations (e.g., CT for class time, HW for homework, J for job, and R&R for rest and relaxation). List the abbreviations you created at the bottom of the page so that your instructor can follow them.

> "The amount of free time you have in college is much more than in high school. Always have a weekly study schedule to go by. Otherwise, time slips away and you will not be able to account for it."
>
> —Advice to new college students from a first-year student (Rhoads, 2005)

If you're a *full-time* student, plan for 25 *hours* in your week for homework (HW). (If you're a *part-time* student, find 2 *hours* you could devote to homework *for every hour* you're in class—i.e., if you're in class 9 hours per week, find 18 hours of homework time).

These homework hours could take place at any time during the week, including weekends. If you combine 25 hours per week of out-of-class school work with the amount of time you spend in class each week, you'll end up with a 40-hour academic workweek—comparable to a full-time job—which is how college should be viewed.

Week-at-a-Glance Grid

	Sunday	Monday	Tuesday	Wednesday	Thursday	Friday	Saturday
7:00 a.m.							
8:00 a.m.							
9:00 a.m.							
10:00 a.m.							
11:00 a.m.							
12:00 p.m.							
1:00 p.m.							
2:00 p.m.							
3:00 p.m.							
4:00 p.m.							
5:00 p.m.							
6:00 p.m.							
7:00 p.m.							
8:00 p.m.							
9:00 p.m.							
10:00 p.m.							
11:00 p.m.							

Reflections:

1. How likely are you to put this time management plan into practice? Circle one: Definitely Probably Unlikely
2. What would *promote or encourage* you to put this plan into practice?
3. What would *prevent or discourage* you from putting this plan into practice?
4. How do you think other students would answer the above three questions?

4.7 Ranking Priorities

Look at the tasks below and decide if they are A, B, or C priorities:

_____ Going for a run

_____ Writing a paper that is due tomorrow

_____ Paying your electric bill that is due next week

_____ Checking out what your friends are doing on Facebook

_____ Getting your haircut

_____ Making an appointment with your academic advisor to register for classes

_____ Playing your favorite video game

_____ Making it to your doctor's appointment

_____ Helping your sister plan her wedding

_____ Picking up your child's prescription from the pharmacy

_____ Studying for your final exams

_____ Calling your cousin to catch up on family gossip

_____ Making reservations for your vacation

_____ Going to see the hot new movie that has come out

_____ Getting your oil changed in your car

_____ Getting your car washed

4.8 Reality Bite

Procrastination: The Vicious Cycle

Delayla has a major paper due at the end of the term. It's now past midterm and she still hasn't started to work on it. She keeps telling herself, "I should have started sooner," but she continues to postpone her work and is becoming increasingly anxious and guilty. To relieve her growing anxiety and guilt, Delayla starts doing other tasks instead, such as cleaning her room and returning e-mails. This makes her feel a little better because these tasks keep her busy, take her mind off the term paper, and give her the feeling that at least she's getting something accomplished. Time continues to pass; the deadline for the paper grows dangerously close. Delayla now finds herself in the position of having lots of work to do and little time in which to do it.

Adapted from *Procrastination: Why You Do It, and What to do about It* (Burka & Yuen, 2008)

Reflection and Discussion Questions

1. What do you expect Delayla will do at this point? Why?

2. What grade do you think she'll end up receiving on her paper?

3. Other than simply starting sooner, what else could Delayla (and other procrastinators like her) do to break the cycle of procrastination?

4. Can you relate to this student's predicament, or do you know other students who often find themselves in this predicament?

4.9 Time Management PEPS Reflection

Look back at your PEPS Learning Style Inventory Report and answer the following questions.

1. Is your time of day preference late day, early day, or did you have no preference? Knowing this, when is the best time of day for you to take classes? To study?

2. How can you make your time of day preference part of your time management plan?

Chapter 4 Reflection

Looking back on suggestions from this chapter, what are three things you can do start managing your time better?

1.

2.

3.

Explain how you are going to make this happen.

Notes

Notes

Goal Setting and Motivation

MOVING FROM INTENTION TO ACTION

The path to success begins with goals and finding the means (succession of steps) to reach those goals. People who set specific goals are more likely to experience success than people who simply tell themselves they're going to try hard and do their best. This chapter lays out the key steps involved in the process of setting effective goals, identifies key self-motivational strategies for staying on track and sustaining progress toward goals, and describes how personal qualities such as self-efficacy, grit, and growth mindset are essential for achieving goals.

Help you set meaningful goals and maintain motivation to achieve your goals.

Think About It—Journal Entry 5.1

Complete the following sentence:

For me, success is . . .

_____

_____

_____

_____

Chapter Preview

"What keeps me going is goals."
—*Muhammad Ali, philanthropist, social activist, and Hall of Fame boxer crowned "" by* Sports Illustrated

Learning Goal

Thought Starter

"Stopping a long pattern of bad decision-making and setting positive, productive priorities and goals."
—*College sophomore's answer to the question: "What does being successful mean to you?"*

The Relationship between Goal Setting and Success

Achieving success begins with setting goals. Research shows that people who set goals and develop plans to reach them are more likely to reach them (Halvorson, 2010), and successful people set goals on a regular basis (Locke & Latham, 1990). In fact, the word *success* derives from the Latin root *successus*—meaning "to follow or come after"—as in the word *successive*. Thus, by definition, success involves a sequence of actions that leads to a desired outcome; the process starts with identifying an end (goal) and then finding a means (sequence of steps) to reach that goal.

Motivation begins with dreams and great intentions that get turned into realistic goals. Depending on the length of time it takes to reach them and the order in

"The tragedy of life doesn't lie in not reaching your goal. The tragedy of life lies in having no goal to reach."
—*Benjamin Mays, minister, scholar, activist, president of Morehouse College*

which they are to be achieved, goals may be classified into three general categories: long-range, mid-range, and short-range. Short-range goals need to be completed before a mid-range goal can be reached, and mid-range goals must be reached before a long-range goal can be achieved. For example, if your long-range goal is a successful career that requires a college degree, your mid-range goal is completing all the coursework required for a degree that will allow you entry into that career. To reach your mid-range goal of a college degree, you need to start by successfully completing the courses you're taking this term (your short-range goal).

This goal-setting process is called *means-end analysis*; it involves working backward from your long-range goal (the end) and identifying what mid-range and short-range subgoals (the means) must be reached in order to achieve your long-range goal (Brooks, 2009; Newell & Simon, 1959). Engaging in this process doesn't mean you're locking yourself into a premature plan that will restrict your flexibility or options. It's just a process that (a) gets you to think about where you want to go, (b) provides some sense of direction about how to get there, and (c) starts moving you in the right direction.

> "You've got to be careful if you don't know where you're going because you might not get there."
>
> —Yogi Berra, Hall of Fame baseball player

Characteristics of a Well-Designed Goal

Studies show that people who set specific, well-designed goals are more likely to succeed than are people who simply tell themselves they're going to try hard and do their very best (Halvorson, 2010; Latham & Locke, 2007). The acronym "SMART" is a well-known mnemonic device (memory strategy) for recalling all the key components of a well-designed goal (Doran, 1981; Meyer, 2003). **Box 5.1** describes the different components of a SMART goal.

Box 5.1

The *SMART* Method of Goal Setting

A *SMART* goal is one that's:

Specific—it states precisely what the goal is, targets exactly what needs to be done to achieve it, and provides a clear picture of what successfully reaching the goal looks like.

Example: By spending 25 hours per week on my coursework outside of class and by using the effective learning strategies (such as those recommended in this book), I'll achieve at least a 3.0 grade point average this term. (Note that this is a much more specific goal than saying, "I'm really going to work hard this term.")

Meaningful (and **M**easurable)—the goal really matters to you (not someone else) and the progress you're making toward the goal can be clearly measured (tracked).

> "Dreams can be fulfilled only when they've been *defined*."
>
> —Ernest Boyer, former United States Commissioner of Education

Example: Achieving at least a 3.0 grade point average this term is important to me because it will enable me to get into the field I'd like to major in. I'll measure my progress toward this goal by calculating the grade I'm earning in each of my courses this semester at regular intervals throughout the term.

Note: At *www.futureme.org* you can set up a program to send future e-mails to yourself that remind you to check and reflect on whether you're making steady progress toward the goals you set.

Actionable (i.e., **A**ction-Oriented)—the actions or behaviors that will be taken to reach your goal are clearly specified.

Example: I will achieve at least a 3.0 grade point average this term by (a) attending all classes, (b) taking detailed notes in all my classes, (c) completing all reading assignments before their due dates, and (d) avoiding cramming by studying in advance for all my major exams.

Realistic—there is a good chance of reaching the goal, given the time, effort, and skills needed to get there.

(continued)

Box 5.1 *(continued)*

Example: Achieving a 3.0 grade point average this term is a realistic goal because my course load is manageable, I will be working no more than 15 hours per week at my part-time job, and I'll be able to get help from campus support services for any academic skills or strategies that need to be strengthened.

Time-framed—the goal has a deadline plus a timeline or timetable that includes short-range (daily), mid-range (weekly), and long-range (monthly steps).

Example: To achieve at least a 3.0 grade point average this term, first I'll acquire all the information I need to learn by taking complete notes in my classes and complete all reading assignments (short-range step). Second, I'll learn the information I've acquired from my notes and readings, break it into parts and study the parts in separate sessions in advance of major exams (mid-range

step). Third, on the day before exams, I'll review all the information I previously studied in parts so I avoid cramming and get a good night's sleep (long-range step).

Note: The SMART process can be used to set goals in any area of your life or dimension of personal development, such as:

- self-management (e.g., time management and money management goals),
- physical development (e.g., health and fitness goals),
- social development (e.g., relationship goals),
- emotional development (e.g., stress management or anger management goals),
- intellectual development (e.g., learning and critical thinking goals),
- career development (e.g., career exploration and preparation goals),

Think About It—Journal Entry 5.2

If you were to set a SMART goal for some aspect of your life right now, what would it be and why would you set it?

_____

_____

_____

_____

In addition to the effective goal-setting properties associated with the SMART method, research reveals that the following goal-setting features characterize people who set and reach important goals.

1. Effective goal-setters set *improvement (get-better) goals* that emphasize progress and growth, rather than perfection (be-good) goals. Studies show that when people pursue get-better goals, they pursue them with greater interest and intensity, and they are more likely to enjoy the process (Halvorson, 2010). This is likely because get-better goals give us a sense of accomplishment about how far we've come—even when we still have a long way to go.

2. Effective goal-setters focus on outcomes they have *influence or control over*, not on outcomes that are beyond their control. For example, a controllable goal for

> "Nothing ever comes that is worth having, except as a result of hard work."
>
> —Booker T. Washington, born-in-slavery Black educator, author, and advisor to Republican presidents

an aspiring actress would be to improve her acting skills and opportunities, rather than to become a famous movie star—which will depend on factors that are beyond her control.

3. Effective goal-setters set goals that are *challenging and effortful*. Goals worth achieving require that we stretch ourselves and break a sweat; they require endurance, persistence, and resiliency. Studies of successful people in all occupations indicate that when they set goals that are attainable but also *challenging*, they pursue those goals more strategically, with more intensity, and with greater commitment (Latham & Locke, 2007; Locke & Latham, 2002). There's another advantage of setting challenging goals: Achieving them supplies us with a stronger sense of accomplishment, satisfaction, and self-esteem.

4. Effective goal-setters anticipate *obstacles* they may encounter along the path to their goal and have a plan in place for dealing with them. Successful people often imagine what things will be like if they don't reach their goals, which drives them to anticipate problems and setbacks before they arise (Gilbert, 2006; Harris, Griffin, & Murray, 2008). They're optimistic about succeeding, but they're not blind optimists; they realize the road will be tough and they have a realistic plan in place for dealing with the rough spots (Oettingen, 2000; Oettingen & Stephens, 2009). Thus a well-designed goal should not only include specific information about how the goal will be achieved, but also specific plans to handle anticipated impediments along the way—for example, identifying what resources and social support networks may be used to keep you on track and moving forward.

Capitalize on resources that can help you stay on track and moving toward your goal. Research indicates that success in college involves a combination of what students do for themselves (personal responsibility) and how they to capitalize on resources available to them (Pascarella & Terenzini, 1991, 2005). Successful people are resourceful; they seek out and take advantage of resources to help them reach their goals. Use your campus (and community) resources to help you achieve your long-range goals (e.g., academic advising and career counseling).

Don't forget that your peers can serve as a resource to help you reach your goals. Much has been said about the dangers of "peer pressure," but much less attention has been paid to the benefits of "peer power." The power of social support groups for helping people achieve personal goals is well documented by research in different fields (Brissette, Cohen, & Seeman, 2000; Ewell, 1997). There's also a long historical trail of research pointing to the power of peers for promoting the development and success of college students (Astin, 1993; Feldman & Newcomb, 1994; Pascarella & Terenzini, 2005). Be sure to ask yourself: Who can help me stick to my plan and complete the steps needed to reach my goal? You can harness the power of social support by surrounding yourself with peers who are committed to successfully achieve their educational goals and by avoiding "toxic" people who are likely to poison your plans or dampen your dreams.

Find motivated peers with whom you can make mutually supportive "pacts" to help one another reach your respective goals. These mutual support pacts may be viewed as "social contracts" signed by "co-witnesses" who help them stay on track and moving toward their long-range goals. Studies show that making a commitment to a goal in the presence of others increases our commitment to that goal because our successful pursuit of it is viewed not only through our own eyes, but through the eyes of others as well (Hollenbeck, Williams, & Klein, 1989; Locke, 2000).

> "Accomplishing something hard to do. Not something that has just been handed to me."
>
> *—First-year student's response to the question: "What does being successful mean to you?"*

> "Develop an inner circle of close associations in which the mutual attraction is not sharing problems or needs. The mutual attraction should be values and goals."
>
> *—Denis Waitley, former mental trainer for U.S. Olympic athletes and author of* Seeds of Greatness

Think About It—Journal Entry 5.3

What *obstacles* or *impediments* do you anticipate may interfere with your goal of succeeding in college and completing your college degree?

_____

_____

_____

_____

What *campus resources* do you think would be most helpful for dealing with your anticipated obstacles?

_____

_____

_____

_____

What *social support networks* (family members, friends, or mentors) do you think could help you overcome your anticipated obstacles?

_____

_____

_____

_____

Strategies for Maintaining Motivation and Progress toward Your Goals

The word *motivation* derives from the Latin *movere*, meaning "to move." Success comes to those who overcome inertia—they start moving toward their goal; then they maintain momentum until their goal is reached. Goal-setting only creates the potential for success; it takes motivation to turn this potential into reality by converting intention into action. We can have the best designed goals and know the way to succeed, but if we don't have the *will* to succeed, there's no way we will succeed. Studies show that goal-setting is just the first step in the process; it must be accompanied by a strong commitment to achieve the goal that has been set (Locke, 2000; Locke & Latham, 1990).

Reaching challenging goals requires that you maintain motivation and sustain effort over an extended period of time. Listed below are strategies for doing so.

> "You can lead a horse to water, but you can't make him drink."
> —*Author unknown*

Put your goals in writing and make them visible. Written goals can serve almost like a written contract that holds you accountable for following through on your commitments.

By placing written goals where you can't help but see them on a daily basis (e.g., your laptop, refrigerator, and bathroom mirror), you're less likely to "lose sight" of them and more likely to continue pursuing them. What's kept in sight is kept in mind.

Note

The next best thing to doing something you intend to do is to write down your intention to do it.

Keep your eye on the prize. Visualize reaching your long-range goals; picture it by creating vivid mental images of your future success. For example, if your goal is to achieve a college degree, visualize a crowd of cheering family, friends, and faculty at your graduation. (You could even add musical accompaniment to your visualization by playing a motivational song in your head—e.g., "We are the Champions" by Queen.) Imagine cherishing this proud memory for the rest of your life and being in a career your college degree enabled you to enter. Picture a typical workday going something like this: You wake up on a Monday morning and are excited about the upcoming workweek. When you're at work, time seems to fly by; before you know it, the day is over. When you go home after work and reflect on your day, you feel great about what you did and how well you did it.

In addition to visualizing the positive consequences of achieving your goal, you can also motivate yourself by visualizing the negative consequences of not achieving it—as illustrated by the following experience.

AUTHOR'S EXPERIENCE

My father, who spent 50 years working in the coal mines of eastern Kentucky, always had a simple, motivating statement for me to gain more education than he had. He would always say, "Son, I did not have the chance to go to school, so I have to write my name with an X and work in the coal mines. You have the opportunity to get an education and you do not have to break your back in those mines." What my father was telling me was that education would give me options in life that he did not have and that I should take advantage of those options by going to college. My dad's lack of education supplied me with drive and dedication to pursue education. My experience suggests that when you are developing your goals and motivating yourself to achieve them, it may be as important to know what you don't want as it is to know what you do want.

—*Aaron Thompson*

"Whether you think you can or you can't, you're right."

—Henry Ford, founder of Ford Motor Co. and one of the richest people of his generation.

Visualize completing the steps leading to your goal. For visualization to be really effective, you need to visualize not just the success itself (the end goal), but also the steps you'll take along the way. "Just picturing yourself crossing the finish line doesn't actually help you get there—but visualizing how you run the race (the strategies you will use, the choices you will make, the obstacles you will face) not only will give you greater confidence, but also leave you better prepared for the task ahead" (Halvorson, 2010, p. 208).

Thus, reaching a long-term goal requires focusing on the prize—your dream and *why* it's important to you; this "big picture" view provides the inspiration. At the same time, however, you have to focus on the little things—*what* it will take to get there—the nitty-gritty of due dates, to-do lists, and day-to-day tasks. This is the perspiration that transforms inspiration into action, enabling you to plug away and stay on track until your goal is achieved.

It could be said that successfully achieving a long-term goal requires two lenses, each of which provides you with a different focus point: (a) a wide-angle lens that gives you a big picture view of a future that's far ahead of you (your ultimate goal), and (b) a narrow-angle lens that allows you to focus intently on the here and now—on the steps that lie immediately ahead of you. Alternating between these two perspectives allows you to view your small, short-term chores and challenges (e.g., completing an assignment that's due next week) in light of the larger, long-range picture (e.g., college graduation and a successful future).

> "You've got to think about 'big things' while you're doing small things, so that all the small things go in the right direction."
>
> —Alvin Toffler, American futurologist and author who predicted the future effects of technology on our society

AUTHOR'S EXPERIENCE

I once helped coach a youth soccer team (five to six year olds) and noticed that many of the less successful players tended to make one of either two mistakes when they tried to advance the ball toward the goal. Some spent too much time looking down, focusing on the ball at their feet, trying to be sure that they didn't lose control of it. By not occasionally lifting their head and looking ahead, they often missed open territory, open teammates, or an open goal. Other unsuccessful players made the opposite mistake: They spent too much time with their heads up, trying to see where they were headed. By not periodically glancing down at the ball in front of them, they often lost control of it, moved ahead without it, or sometimes stumbled over it and fell flat on their face. In contrast, the more successful players had developed the habit of shifting their focus between looking down to maintain control of the ball immediately in front of them and lifting their eyes to see where they were headed.

The more I thought about how these successful soccer players alternated their perspective between looking at the ball right in front of them and looking at the goal farther ahead, it struck me that this was a metaphor for success in life. Successful people alternate between long-range and short-range perspectives; they don't lose sight of how executing the tasks immediately in front of them connect with the ultimate goal further ahead of them.

—*Joe Cuseo*

Note

Keep pursuit of your future dreams and completion of your current tasks in dual focus. Integrating these two perspectives provides you with the inspiration to set goals and the determination to reach them.

Keep a record of your progress. Research indicates that the mere act of monitoring and recording progress toward your goals increases your motivation to continue pursuing them (Locke & Latham, 2005; Matsui, Okada, & Inoshita, 1983). Keeping a regular record of your personal progress increases motivation by providing you with frequent *feedback* about whether you're on track and positive *reinforcement* for staying on track (Bandura & Cervone, 1983; Schunk, 1995).

Mark down your accomplishments in red on a calendar, or keep a journal of the short- and mid-range goals you've reached. These markings serve as benchmarks, supplying you with concrete evidence and a visible reminder of your progress. You can also mark your progress on a chart or graph, or list your achievements in a resume or portfolio. Place these displays of progress where you can see them on a daily basis and use them as a source of motivation to keep striving toward your ultimate goal (Halvorson, 2010).

> "Writing my resume was a real ego booster—I've actually done stuff!"
>
> —College student (quoted in Brooks, 2009)

This practice of ongoing (daily) assessment of our personal progress toward goal completion is a simple, yet powerful form of self-reflection that's associated with success. Research on successful people reveals that they reflect regularly on their daily progress to ensure they're on track and progressing steadily toward their goals (Covey, 1990).

Reward yourself for reaching milestones on the path toward your goal. Reaching a long-range goal is clearly rewarding because it marks the end of the trip and arrival at your desired destination. However, reaching short- and mid-range goals are not as self-rewarding because they're merely the means to the end. Thus, you need to make intentional attempts to reward yourself for climbing these smaller, yet essential stepping stones on the path to the mountain peak.

The behaviors needed to persist and persevere through all the intermediate steps needed to reach a long-range goal is more likely to take place if these behaviors are followed by reward (positive reinforcement). The process of setting small goals, moving steadily toward them, and rewarding yourself for reaching them is a simple, yet powerful self-motivational strategy. It helps you maintain momentum over an extended period of time, which is exactly what's required to reach a long-range goal. When you achieve short- and mid-range goals, check them off as milestones and reward yourself for reaching them (e.g., celebrate successful completion of midterms or finals by treating yourself to something you really enjoy).

> "Whoever wants to reach a distant goal must take many small steps."
>
> —*Helmut Schmidt, former chancellor of West Germany*

 Think About It—Journal Entry 5.4

For you, what would be effective rewards for making progress toward your goals and serve as motivators to keep you going?

_____

_____

_____

_____

Characteristics of Successful People

Achieving success involves effective use of goal-setting and motivational strategies, but it takes something more. Ultimately, success emerges from the inside out; it flows from personal qualities and attributes found within a person. Studies of successful people who achieve their goals reveal they possess the following personal characteristics. Keep these characteristics in mind as you set and pursue your goals.

Internal Locus of Control

> "If you do not find it within yourself, where will you go to get it?"
>
> —*Zen saying (Zen is a branch of Buddhism that emphasizes seeing deeply into the nature of things and ongoing self-awareness)*

Successful people have what psychologists call an "internal locus of control"; they believe that the locus (location or source) of control for events in their life is *internal*—"inside" them and within their control—rather than *external*—outside them and beyond their control. They believe that success is influenced more by attitude, effort, commitment, and preparation than by inherited ability, inborn intelligence, luck, chance, or fate (Carlson, et al., 2009; Jernigan, 2004; Rotter, 1966).

Research shows that individuals with a strong internal locus of control display the following positive qualities:

1. Greater independence and self-direction (Van Overwalle, Mervielde, & De Schuyer, 1995),

2. More accurate self-assessment of strengths and weaknesses (Hashaw, Hammond, & Rogers, 1990), and

3. Higher levels of learning and achievement (Wilhite, 1990).

Self-Efficacy

An internal locus of control contributes to the development of another positive trait that psychologists refer to as *self-efficacy*—the belief that you have power to produce a positive effect on the *outcomes* of your life (Bandura, 1994). People with low self-efficacy tend to feel helpless, powerless, and passive; they think (and allow) things to happen to them rather than taking charge and making things happen for them. College students with a strong sense of self-efficacy believe they're in control of their educational success and can shape their future, regardless of their past experience or current circumstances.

People with a strong sense of self-efficacy initiate action and exert effort. They believe success is something that's earned and the harder they work at it, the more likely they'll get it. If they encounter setbacks or bad breaks along the way, they don't give up or give in; they persevere and push on (Bandura, 1986, 1997).

Students with a strong sense of *academic self-efficacy* have been found to:

1. Put considerable effort into their studies;
2. Use active learning strategies;
3. Capitalize on campus resources; and
4. Persist in the face of obstacles (Multon, Brown, & Lent, 1991; Zimmeman, 1995, 2000).

Students with a strong sense of self-efficacy also possess a strong sense of personal responsibility. As the breakdown of the word "responsible" implies, they are "response" "able"—they believe they're able to respond to personal challenges, including academic challenges.

> I'm a great believer in luck, and I find the harder I work the more I have of it."
>
> —*Thomas Jefferson, third president of the United States*

Think About It—Journal Entry 5.5

In what area or areas of your life do you feel that you've been able to exert the most control and achieve the most positive results?

_____

_____

_____

_____

In what area(s) do you wish you had more control and were achieving better results?

_____

_____

_____

_____

What strategies have you used in the area of your life where you've been able to exert the most personal control and achieve the most positive outcomes?

Could you apply any of these same strategies to those areas in which you need to gain more control? How?

"Grit is perseverance and passion for long-term goals. Sticking with your future day in, day out, not just for the week, not just for the month, but for years and working really hard to make that future a reality."

—Angela Duckworth, psychologist, University of Pennsylvania

"How smart you are will influence the extent to which you experience something as difficult (for example, how hard a math problem is), but it says nothing about how you will deal with difficulty when it happens. It says nothing about whether you will be persistent and determined or feel overwhelmed and helpless."

—Heidi Grant Halvorson, social psychologist, and author of Succeed: How We Can Reach Your Goals

"The harder you fall, the higher you bounce."

—Chinese proverb

Grit

When you expend significant effort, energy, and sacrifice over a sustained period of time to achieve a goal, you're demonstrating grit (Stoltz, 2014). People with grit have been found to possess the following qualities (Duckworth, et al., 2007).

Persistence. They hang in there and persevere effort until they reach their goals. When the going gets tough, they don't give up—they step it up. They have the fortitude to persist in the face of frustration and adversity.

Tenacity. They pursue their goals with relentless determination. If they encounter something along the way that's hard to do, they work harder to do it.

Resilience. They bounce back from setbacks and keep striving to reach their goals. They adopt the mindset that they'll bounce back from setbacks and turn them into comebacks. How you react mentally and emotionally to a setback affects what action you take in response to it. For instance, you can react to a poor test grade by knocking yourself down with self-putdowns ("I'm a loser") or by building yourself back up with positive self-talk ("I'm going to learn from my mistakes on this test and rebound with a stronger performance on the next one").

As you can see in **Figure 5.1**, information passes through the emotional center of the human brain (lower, shaded area) before reaching the center responsible for rational thinking and future planning (upper area). As a result, when we encounter setbacks, our initial (and subconscious) tendency is to react emotionally and defensively. To counteract this tendency, we need to slow down, calm down, and make a conscious attempt to respond rationally to setbacks—thinking about how we can overcome them, learn from them, and make use of them to continue progressing toward our goal.

FIGURE 5.1: The Brain's Emotional Filter

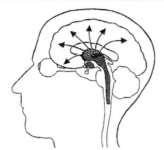

Information entering the human brain is first processed emotionally (lower shaded area)
before reaching higher areas of rational thinking and future planning.

It's noteworthy that the word *problem* derives from the Greek root *proballein*, meaning "to throw forward." This suggests that a problem is an opportunity to move ahead. You can take this approach to problems by rewording or rephrasing the problem you're experiencing in terms of a positive goal statement. (For example, "I'm flunking math" can be reframed as: "My goal is to get a grade of C or better on the next test to pull my overall course grade into passing territory.")

Similarly, the root of the word *failure* is *fallere*—meaning to "trip or fall." Thus, failing at something doesn't mean we've been defeated, it just means we've stumbled and taken a temporary spill. Success can still be achieved after a fall if we don't give up, but get up and get back to taking the next step needed to reach our goal. By viewing poor academic performances and other setbacks (particularly those occurring early in your college experience) not as failures but as learning opportunities, you put yourself in a position to bounce back and transform your setbacks into comebacks. Here are some notable people who did so:

- Louis Pasteur, famous bacteriologist, failed his admission test to the University of Paris;
- Albert Einstein, Nobel Prize–winning physicist, failed math in elementary school;
- Thomas Edison, prolific inventor, once expelled from school as "uneducable";
- Johnny Unitas, Hall of Fame football player, cut twice from professional football teams early in his career;
- Michael Jordan, Hall of fame basketball player, cut from his high school team as a sophomore.

Note

Don't let early setbacks bring you down emotionally or motivationally. Reflect on them, learn from them, and make sure they don't happen again.

> What happens is not as important as how you react to what happens."
> —*Thaddeus Golas*, Lazy Man's Guide to Enlightenment

> When written in Chinese, the word 'crisis' is composed of two characters. One represents danger, and the other represents opportunity."
> —*John F. Kennedy*, 35th president of the United States

Think About It—Journal Entry 5.6

What would you say is the biggest setback or obstacle you've overcome in your life thus far?

How did you overcome it? (What enabled you to get past it, or what did you do to prevent it from stopping you?)

> "Self-discipline is the ability to make yourself do the thing you have to do, when it ought be done, whether you like it or not."
>
> —Thomas Henry Huxley, 19th-century English biologist

Self-Discipline. People with grit have the *self-control*—they keep their actions aligned with their goal, staying on course and moving in the right direction—despite distractions and temptations (Halvorson, 2010). They resist the impulse to pursue instant gratification and do what they feel like doing instead of what needs to be done to reach their goal. They're able to sacrifice immediate, short-sighted needs and desires to do what has to be done to get where they want to be in the long run.

The ability to delay short-term (and short-sighted) gratification is distinctive human characteristic that sets us apart from other animals. As can be seen in **Figure 5.2**, the upper front part of the human brain, which is responsible for long-range planning and impulse control, is much larger in humans than chimpanzees—one of the most intelligent of all nonhuman animals.

Setting long-range goals is important but having the self-discipline to reach them is another matter. Each day, whether we're aware of it or not, we're tempted to make choices and decisions that interfere with our ability to reach our goals. We need to remain mindful about whether these choices are moving us in the direction of our goals or taking us off course.

FIGURE 5.2: **Where Thoughts, Emotions, and Drives are Experienced in the Brain**

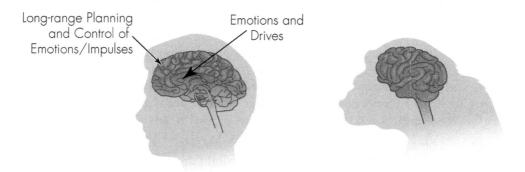

Long-range Planning and Control of Emotions/Impulses

Emotions and Drives

The part of the brain responsible for long-range planning and controlling emotions and impulses is much larger in humans than in other animals, including the highly intelligent chimpanzee.

©Kendall Hunt Publishing Company.

AUTHOR'S EXPERIENCE

When I entered college in the mid-1970s, I was a first-generation student from an extremely impoverished background. Not only did I have to work to support my education, I also needed to assist my family financially. I stocked grocery store shelves at night during the week and waited tables at a local country club on the weekends. Managing my time, school, work, and life required a lot of self-discipline. However, I always understood that my goal was to graduate from college and all of my other commitments supported that goal. One of my greatest achievements in life was to keep my mind and body focused on the ultimate prize of getting a college education. That achievement has paid off for me many times over the course of my life.

—Aaron Thompson

Note

Doing what you have *to do now allows you to do what you* want *to do later. Sacrifices made for a short time can bring benefits that last a lifetime.*

 Think About It—Journal Entry 5.7

Think about something in your life that you sacrificed for and persisted at for the longest period of time before getting there. What is it? Do you see ways in which you could apply the same approach to achieving your goals in college? Explain.

Growth Mindset

A *mindset* is a powerful belief. People with a *growth mindset* believe that intelligence and other positive qualities can be grown or developed. People with a *fixed mindset* believe just the opposite: they think that intelligence and personal characteristics are deep-seated traits that are set and unlikely to change (Dweck, 2006).

Listed below are opposing pairs of traits—one representing a fixed mindset (FM) and the other representing a growth mindset (GM). As you read through them, honestly assess whether you lean more toward a fixed or growth mindset by circling either FM or GM for each pair of traits.

I try to get better at what I do. (GM)
I try to show others (including myself) how good I am. (FM)

I try to validate myself by proving how smart or talented I am. (FM)
I validate myself by stretching myself to become smarter and more talented. (GM)

I believe that if I cannot learn to do something easily, I'm not smart. (FM)
I believe that I can learn to do something well even if it doesn't come easily at first. (GM)

I evaluate my performance by comparing it to the performance of others. (FM)
I evaluate my performance by comparing it to my past performances. (GM)

I believe I have a certain amount of intelligence and not much can be done to change it. (FM)
I believe that the amount of intelligence I start with isn't the amount I'll end up with. (GM)

I think that intelligence and personal qualities are inherited and hard to change. (FM)
I think that intelligence and personal qualities are learned and changeable. (GM)

I think success is a matter of having ability. (FM)
I think success is a matter of getting ability. (GM)

I focus on demonstrating my skills to others. (FM)
I focus on developing my skills. (GM)

I focus on proving myself (as being good or smart). (FM)
I focus on improving myself (by getting better). (GM)

I feel smart when I complete tasks quickly and without mistakes. (FM)
I feel smart when I work on something for awhile before figuring it out. (GM)

I avoid seeking constructive criticism from others because it will expose my weaknesses. (FM)
I seek out constructive criticism from others to improve myself. (GM)

I feel threatened by the success of others. (FM)
I feel I can be inspired by and learn from the success of others. (GM)

I tend to peak early and don't continually progress to higher levels of achievement. (FM)
I tend to keep progressing toward increasingly higher levels of achievement. (GM)

I think success should be effortless. (FM)
I think success should be effortful. (GM)

I view challenges as threatening because they may prove I'm not smart. (FM)
I view challenges as opportunities to develop new skills. (GM)

> "
> If you believe you can develop yourself, then you're open to accurate information about your current abilities, even if it's unflattering."
>
> —*Carol Dweck*, Growth Mindset: The New Psychology of Success

I believe effort creates talent. (GM)
I believe effort is for those who can't make it on talent. (FM)

I focus on self-improvement—about becoming the best I can be. (GM)
I focus on self-validation—about proving I'm already good. (FM)

I look at grades as labels that judge or measure my intelligence. (FM)
I look at grades as a source of feedback for improving my performance. (GM)

 Think About It—Journal Entry 5.8

Look back at the above pairs of statements and compare the total number of fixed mindset (FM) and growth mindset (GM) statements you circled.

Do your totals suggest that, in general, you lean more toward a growth or fixed mindset?

Do you see any patterns in your responses that suggest you're more likely to hold a growth mindset for certain characteristics or situations and a fixed mindset for others?

> "No matter what your ability is, effort is what ignites that ability and turns it into accomplishment."
> —Carol Dweck, Stanford psychologist and author of Mindset

> SUCCESS is peace of mind which is a direct result of self-satisfaction in knowing you made the effort to become the best that you are capable of becoming."
> —John Wooden, college basketball coach and author of the Pyramid of Success

Numerous studies show that a growth mindset is strongly associated with goal achievement and personal success (Dweck, 2006). In one study, the mindset of pre-med students taking a difficult chemistry course was measured at the start of the semester and their performance was tracked throughout the term. Students with a growth mindset consistently earned higher grades in the course. Even when students with a growth mindset did poorly on a particular test, they improved on the next one. In contrast, the performance of students with a fixed mindset showed no pattern of improvement from one exam to the next (Dweck, 2006).

In another study, students with a growth mindset (who believed their goal in college courses was to improve their grade as the course progressed) were compared to students with a fixed mindset (who believed their goal was to prove how smart they were). Students with a growth mindset achieved higher overall course grades and did so because they improved with each exam. They didn't have higher grades on the first exam, but began earning higher grades on later exams. The opposite pattern was true for fixed mindset students—their performance actually remained the same or declined over time—particularly if their first exam score was low (Halvorson, 2010).

It's been found that students can have different mindsets for different subjects and situations. Some students may have a fixed mindset for learning math, but a growth mindset for learning other subjects. However, the most important thing to remember about mindsets is that, although they're powerful, they're just beliefs held in our mind. Thus, mindsets can be changed from fixed to growth for any subject or situation. By so doing, we increase the likelihood of achieving our goals and reaching our full potential (Dweck, 2006).

> "When we change the way we look at things, the things we look at change."
>
> *—Max Planck, Nobel Prize–winning physicist*

Chapter Summary and Highlights

A key to success is challenging ourselves to set ambitious, yet realistic goals. Studies consistently show that goal-setting is a more effective self-motivational strategy than simply telling ourselves to "try hard" or "do our best." Achieving success begins with setting goals and successful people set goals on a regular basis.

The acronym "SMART" is a popular mnemonic device (memory strategy) for recalling all the key components of a well-designed goal. A ***SMART*** goal is one that is:

*S*pecific—it states precisely what the goal is and what you will do to achieve it.

*M*eaningful (and *M*easurable)—it's a goal that really matters to you and your progress toward reaching it can be steadily measured or tracked.

*A*ctionable (or *A*ction-Oriented)—it identifies concrete actions and specific behaviors you'll engage in to reach the goal.

*R*ealistic—the goal is attainable and you're aware of the amount of time, effort, and skill it will take to attain it, as well as obstacles you'll need to overcome along the way.

*T*ime-framed—the goal has a deadline and a timeline that includes a sequence of short-range, mid-range, and long-range steps.

In addition to the effective goal-setting properties associated with the SMART method, research reveals that the following goal-setting features characterize people who set and reach important goals.

1. Effective goal-setters set *improvement (get-better) goals* that emphasize progress and growth, rather than perfection (be-good) goals.
2. Effective goal-setters focus on what outcomes can *influence or control*, not on outcomes that are beyond their control.
3. Effective goal-setters set goals that are *challenging and effortful*.
4. Effective goal-setters anticipate *obstacles* they may encounter along the path to their goal and have a plan in place for dealing with them.

Setting goals ignites motivation, but maintaining motivation after it's been ignited requires use of effective self-motivational strategies. You can maintain your motivation by using such strategies as:

- Visualizing reaching your long-range goals;
- Putting your goals in writing;
- Creating a visual map of your goals;

- Keeping a record of your progress toward your goals;
- Rewarding yourself for milestones you reach along the path to your goals;
- Converting setbacks into comebacks by learning from mistakes and maintaining positive expectations.

Studies of successful people who achieve their goals reveal they possess the following personal characteristics.

Internal Locus of Control. They believe that the locus (location or source) of control for events in their life is *internal*—"inside" them and within their control—rather than *external*—outside them and beyond their control.

Self-Efficacy. They believe they have power to produce a positive effect on the *outcomes* of their lives. They believe success is something that's earned and the harder they work at it, the more likely they'll get it.

Grit. They expend significant effort, energy, and sacrifice over an extended period of time to achieve their goals. People with grit have been found to possess the following qualities:

- *Persistence*—when the going gets tough, they don't give up, they step it up; they have the fortitude to persist in the face of frustration and adversity.
- *Tenacity*—they pursue their goals with relentless determination; if they encounter something along the way that's hard to do, they work harder to do it.
- Resilience—they bounce back from setbacks and turn them into comebacks.
- *Self-Discipline*—they have *self-control*—they resist the impulse to pursue instant gratification and do what they feel like doing instead of what should be done to reach their goal; they're able to sacrifice immediate, short-sighted needs and desires to do what has to be done to get where they want to be in the long run.

Growth Mindset. They believe that intelligence and other positive qualities can be grown or developed. In contrast, people with a "fixed mindset" believe that intelligence and personal characteristics are deep-seated traits that are set and unlikely to change.

Note

Achieving success isn't a short sprint; it's a long-distance run that takes patience and perseverance. Goal-setting is the key that gets us off the starting blocks and motivation is the fuel that keeps us going until we cross the finish line.

Learning More through the World Wide Web: Internet-Based Resources

For additional information on goal-setting and motivation, see the following websites.

Goal Setting:
https://www.mindtools.com/page6.html

Self-Motivational Strategies:
www.selfmotivationstrategies.com

Self-Efficacy:
www.psychologytoday.com/blog/flourish/201002/
if-you-think-you-can-t-think-again-the-sway-self-efficacy

Grit & Resilience:
https://undergrad.stanford.edu/resilience

Growth Mindset:
www.ted.com/talks/carol_dweck_the_power_of_believing_that_you_can_
improve?language=en

References

Astin, A. W. (1993). *What matters in college?* San Francisco: Jossey-Bass.

Bandura, A. (1986). *Social foundations of thought and action: A social cognitive theory.* Englewood Cliffs, NJ: Prentice Hall.

Bandura, A. (1994). Self-efficacy. In V. S. Ramachaudran (Ed.), *Encyclopedia of human behavior* (Vol. 4, pp. 71–81). New York: Academic Press.

Bandura, A. (1997). *Self-efficacy: The exercise of control.* New York: Freeman.

Bandura, A., & Cervone, D. (1983). Self-evaluative and self-efficacy mechanisms governing the motivational effects of goal systems. *Journal of Personality and Social Psychology, 45*(5), 1017–1028.

Brissette, I., Cohen, S., & Seeman, T. E. (2000). Measuring social integration and social networks. In S. Cohen, L. G. Underwood, & B. H. Gottlieb (Eds.), *Social support measurement and intervention* (pp. 53–85). New York: Oxford University Press.

Brooks, K. (2009). *You majored in what? Mapping your path from chaos to career.* NY: Penguin.

Carlson, N. R., Miller, H., Heth, C. D., Donahoe, J. W., & Martin, G. N. (2009). *Psychology: The science of behaviour* (7th ed.). Toronto, ON: Pearson Education Canada.

Covey, S. R. (1990). Seven habits of highly effective people (2nd ed.). New York: Fireside.

Doran, G. T. (1981). "There's a S.M.A.R.T. Way to Write Management's Goals and Objectives", Management Review, Vol. 70, Issue 11, pp. 35–36.

Duckworth, A. L., Peterson, C., Matthews, M. D., & Kelly, D. R. (2007). Grit: Perseverance and passion for long-term goals. *Journal of Personality and Social Psychology, 92*(6), 1087–1101.

Dweck, C. S. (2006). *Mindset: The new psychology of success.* New York: Random House.

Ewell, P. T. (1997). Organizing for learning. *AAHE Bulletin, 50*(4), 3–6.

Feldman, K. A., & Newcomb, T. M. (1994). *The impact of college on students.* New Brunswick, NJ: Transaction Publishers. (Original work published 1969).

Gilbert, P. T. (2006). *Stumbling on happiness.* New York: Alfred A. Knopf.

Halvorson, H. G. (2010). *Succeed: How we can reach our goals.* New York: Plume.

Harris, P., Griffin, D., & Murray, S. (2008). Testing the limits of optimistic bias: Event and person moderators in a multilevel framework. *Journal of Personality and Social Psychology, 95,* 1225–1237.

Hashaw, R. M., Hammond, C. J., & Rogers, P. H. (1990). Academic locus of control and the collegiate experience. *Research & Teaching in Developmental Education, 7*(1), 45–54.

Hollenbeck, J. R., Williams, C. R., & Klein, H. J. (1989). An empirical examination of the antecedents of commitment to difficult goals. *Journal of Applied Psychology, 74*(1), 18–23.

Jernigan, C. G. (2004). What do students expect to learn? The role of learner expectancies, beliefs, and attributions for success and failure in student motivation. *Current Issues in Education* [On-line], 7(4). Retrieved January 16, 2012, from cie.asu.edu/ojs/index.php/cieatasu/article/download/824/250

Latham, G., & Locke, E. (2007). New developments in and directions for goal-setting research. *European Psychologists, 12,* 290–300.

Locke, E. A. (2000). Motivation, cognition, and action: An analysis of studies of task goals and knowledge. *Applied Psychology: An International Review, 49,* 408–429.

Locke, E. A., & Latham, G. P. (1990). *A theory of goal setting and task performance.* Englewood Cliffs, NJ: Prentice Hall.

Locke, E. A., & Latham, G. P. (2002). Building a practically useful theory of goal setting and task motivation. *American Psychologist, 57,* 705–717.

Locke, E. A., & Latham, G. P. (2005). Goal setting theory: Theory building by induction. In K.G. Smith & M.A. Mitt (Eds.), *Great minds in management: The process of theory development.* New York: Oxford.

Matsui, T., Okada, A., & Inoshita, O. (1983). Mechanism of feedback affecting task performance. *Organizational Behavior and Human Performance, 31,* 114–122.

Meyer, P. J. (2003). "What would you do if you knew you couldn't fail? Creating S.M.A.R.T. Goals". *In Attitude Is Everything: If You Want to Succeed Above and Beyond.* Meyer Resource Group, Incorporated.

Multon, K. D., Brown, S. D., & Lent, R. W. (1991). Relation of self-efficacy beliefs to academic outcomes: A meta-analytic investigation. *Journal of Counseling Psychology, 38*(1), 30–38.

Newell, A., & Simon, H. A. (1959). *The simulation of human thought.* Santa Monica, CA: Rand Corporation.

Oettingen, G. (2000). Expectancy effects on behavior depend on self-regulatory thought. *Social Cognition, 14,* 101–129.

Oettingen, G., & Stephens, E. (2009). Mental contrasting future and reality: A motivationally intelligent self-regulatory strategy. In G. Moskowitz & H. Grant (eds.), *The psychology of goals.* New York: Guilford.

Pascarella, E., & Terenzini, P. (1991). *How college affects students: Findings and insights from twenty years of research.* San Francisco: Jossey-Bass.

Pascarella, E., & Terenzini, P. (2005). *How college affects students: A third decade of research* (Vol. 2). San Francisco: Jossey-Bass.

Rotter, J. (1966). Generalized expectancies for internal versus external controls of reinforcement. *Psychological Monographs: General and Applied, 80*(609), 1–28.

Schunk, D. H. (1995). Self-efficacy and education and instruction. In J. E. Maddux (Ed.), *Self- efficacy, adaptation, and adjustment: Theory, research, and application* (pp. 281–303). New York: Plenum Press.

Snyder, C. R. (1995). Conceptualizing, measuring, and nurturing hope. *Journal of Counseling and Development, 73* (January/February), 355–360.

Stoltz, P. G. (2014). *Grit: The new science of what it takes to persevere, flourish, succeed.* San Luis Obispo: Climb Strong Press.

Van Overwalle, F. I., Mervielde, I., & De Schuyer, J. (1995). Structural modeling of the relationships between attributional dimensions, emotions, and performance of college freshmen. *Cognition and Emotion, 9*(1), 59–85.

Wilhite, S. (1990). Self-efficacy, locus of control, self-assessment of memory ability, and student activities as predictors of college course achievement. *Journal of Educational Psychology, 82*(4), 696–700.

Zimmerman, B. J. (1995). Self-efficacy and educational development. In A. Bandura (Ed.), *Self-efficacy in changing societies.* New York: Cambridge University Press.

Zimmerman, B. J. (2000). Self-efficacy: An essential motive to learn. *Contemporary Educational Psychology 25,* 82–91.

Chapter 5 Exercises

5.1 Quote Reflections

Review the sidebar quotes contained in this chapter and select two that were especially meaningful or inspirational to you.

For each quote, write a three- to five-sentence explanation why you chose it.

5.2 Reality Bite

Goals and Motivation

Lorraine has decided to go to her local community college to become an RN. She knows that nurses make good money and it is easy to get a job in the profession right now. All she really cares about is having a good job and making money. She did not realize the classes would be difficult and she has a hard time getting through them since she really is not that interested in them. She started her clinicals and HATED what she was being asked to do. She was not prepared for all the bodily fluids she would see in one day. Lorraine decides nursing is not for her and is angry that no one told her she would hate it this much! She has to find a different major now that will still make a lot of money, but she is angry that she wasted more than a year of her life as well as the money she has spent on her education.

1. Why do you think Lorraine is really unhappy with the events that have unfolded during the past year?

2. What could Lorraine have done differently to avoid this situation?

3. What goals would you suggest Lorraine set for herself?

Lorraine is clearly motivated by money; is that what is going to make her happy? Why or why not?

5.3 Clarifying Your Goals

- Take a moment to answer the following questions as honestly as possible:
- What are my highest priorities?
- What competing needs and priorities do I need to keep in check?
- How will I maintain balance across different aspects of my life?
- What am I willing and able to give up in order to achieve my educational and personal goals?
- How can I maintain motivation on a day-to-day basis?
- Who can I collaborate with to reach my goals and what will that collaboration involve?

5.4 Setting a SMART Goal to Reduce the Gap between Your Ideal Future and Your Current Reality

Think of an aspect of your life where there's a significant gap between what you'd like it to be (the ideal) and where you are (the reality).

Use the following form to identify a goal you could pursue to reduce this gap.

Goal: _____

What specific *actions* will be taken?

When will these actions be taken?

What *obstacles or roadblocks* do you anticipate?

What *resources* could you use to overcome your anticipated obstacles or roadblocks?

How will you *measure your progress*?

How will you know when you *reached or achieved* your goal?

5.5 Converting Setbacks into Comebacks: Transforming Pessimism into Optimism through Positive Self-Talk

In Hamlet, Shakespeare wrote: "There is nothing good or bad, but thinking makes it so." His point was that experiences have the potential to be positive or negative, depending on how people interpret them and react to them.

Listed below is a series of statements representing negative, motivation-destroying interpretations and reactions to a situation or experience:

a) "I'm just not good at this."

b) "There's nothing I can do about it."

c) "Nothing is going to change."

d) "This always happens to me."

e) "Everybody is going to think I'm a loser."

For each of the preceding statements, replace the negative statement with a statement that represents a more positive, self-motivating interpretation or reaction.

5.6 Self-Assessment of Hope

Studies of people who have changed their lives in productive ways indicate they exhibit "high hope" by engaging in certain behaviors that enable them to find the will and the way to reach their personal goals (Snyder, 1995). A sample of hopeful behaviors is listed below. Assess yourself on these behaviors, using the following scale:

1 = Never
2 = Rarely
3 = Frequently
4 = Almost Always

Behavior Exhibited by People Possessing High Levels of Hope

____ When I think of goals, I think of challenges, rather than setbacks and failures.

____ I seek out stories about how other people have succeeded to inspire me and give me new ideas on how to be successful.

____ I find role models I can emulate and who can advise, guide, or mentor me.

____ I tell my friends about my goals and seek their support to help me reach my goals.

____ I use positive self-talk to help me succeed.

____ I think that mistakes I make along the way to my goals are usually the result of using a wrong strategy or making a poor decision, rather than lack of talent or ability on my part.

____ When I struggle, I remember past successes and things I did that worked.

____ I reward myself when reaching smaller, short-term goals I accomplish along the way to larger, long-term goals.

Adapted from: Snyder, C. R. (1995). Conceptualizing, measuring, and nurturing hope. *Journal of Counseling and Development*, 73 (January/February), 355–360.

Self-Assessment Reflections

For any item you rated "1" or "2," explain:

(a) *Why* you "rarely" or "never" engage in the practice;

(b) *If* you intend to engage in the practice more frequently in the future;

(c) *How likely* is it that you'll engage in the practice more frequently in the future;

(d) *When do* you plan to begin engaging in the practice.

5.7 Chapter 3 Reflection

What is the one thing that motivates you the most in college?

HOW and WHY does this motivate you?

What is the one obstacle that gets in the way of your success?

How can you use your motivation to overcome your obstacle(s)?

Notes

Notes

Higher-Level Thinking

MOVING BEYOND BASIC KNOWLEDGE TO CRITICAL AND CREATIVE THINKING

National surveys consistently show that the primary goal of college faculty is teaching students how to think critically. This chapter will help you understand what critical thinking is and empower you to think in this way. You will be provided with thinking strategies that move you beyond memorization to higher levels of thinking and learn how to demonstrate higher-level thinking on college exams and assignments.

Chapter Preview

Equip you with higher-level thinking skills for achieving excellence in college and beyond.

Learning Goal

Thought Starter

 Think About It—Journal Entry 6.1

To me, critical thinking is . . .

_____

_____

_____

_____

(At a later point in this chapter, we'll ask you to flashback to the response you made here.)

What Is Higher-Level Thinking?

Contestants on TV quiz shows like *Jeopardy* are asked questions that call for knowledge of facts: Who? What? When? or Where? If game show contestants were asked higher-level thinking questions, they'd be responding to questions such as: "Why?" "How?" "What if?" Higher-level thinking (a.k.a. higher-order thinking) refers to a more advanced level of thought than that used to acquire factual knowledge. It involves reflecting on knowledge and taking it to a higher level—evaluating its validity, integrating it with something else you've learned, or creating new ideas. As its name implies, higher-level thinking involves raising the bar and jacking up your thinking to a level that goes beyond merely remembering, reproducing, or regurgitating factual information.

> "To me, thinking at a higher level means to think and analyze something beyond the obvious and find the deeper meaning."
>
> —First-year college student

The number one educational goal of college professors is to help students think at a higher or more advanced level. In national surveys of college professors teaching freshman-level through senior-level courses in various academic fields, more than 95% of faculty report that the most important goal of a college education is to develop students' ability to think critically (Gardiner, 2005; Milton, 1982). Similarly, college professors teaching introductory courses for freshmen and sophomores report that the primary educational purpose of their courses is to develop students' critical thinking skills (Higher Education Research Institute, 2009; Stark, et al., 1990). Simply stated, professors are more concerned with teaching you *how* to think than teaching you *what* to think (i.e., what facts to remember).

Compared to high school, college courses focus less on memorizing information and more on thinking about issues, concepts, and principles (Conley, 2005). Remembering information in college may get you a grade of "C," demonstrating comprehension of that information may get you a "B," and going beyond comprehension to demonstrate higher-level thinking will earn you an "A." This is not to say that acquiring knowledge and basic comprehension are unimportant; they provide the stepping stones needed to climb to higher levels of thinking—as illustrated in **Figure 6.1**.

"What is the hardest task in the world? To think."

—*Ralph Waldo Emerson, celebrated 19th-century American essayist and lecturer*

FIGURE 6.1: **The Relationship between Knowledge, Comprehension, and Higher-Level Thinking**

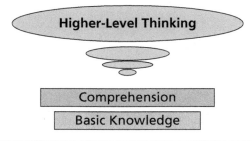

©Kendall Hunt Publishing Company.

Note

College professors expect students to do more than just retain or reproduce information; they want you to demonstrate higher levels of thinking with respect to what you learned (e.g., analyze it, evaluate it, apply it, or integrate it with other concepts you've learned).

Studies show that memory for factual information acquired in college fades quickly with the passage of time. However, higher-level thinking is a *skill* (like learning to ride a bike) that's retained on a long-term basis and used for an entire lifetime (Pascarella & Terenzini, 1991, 2005).

Note

The focus of higher-level thinking is not just to answer questions but also to question answers.

Defining and Describing the Major Forms of Higher-Level Thinking

When your college professors ask you to "think critically," they're usually asking you to use one or more of the eight forms of thinking listed in **Box 6.1**. As you read the descriptions of each form of thinking, note whether you've heard of it before.

Box 6.1

Seven Major Forms of Higher-Level Thinking

1. Analysis (Analytical Thinking). **Breaking down information to identify its essential parts and underlying elements.**
2. Synthesis (Integrative Thinking). **Building up ideas by connecting them to form a larger whole or more comprehensive system.**

3. Application (Applied Thinking). **Putting thinking into practice to solve problems and resolve issues.**
4. Multidimensional Thinking. **Viewing issues from a variety of vantage points to gain a more complete or comprehensive perspective.**
5. Balanced Thinking. **Carefully considering arguments for and against a particular position or viewpoint.**
6. Critical Thinking (Evaluation). **Judging the quality of arguments, conclusions, and thought processes—including all forms of thinking on this list.**
7. Creative Thinking. **Generating ideas that are unique, original, or distinctively different.**

> In college . . . you will be expected to get inside what you are learning to apply it, make comparisons and connections, draw implications, and use ideas."
>
> —*Robert Shoenberg, author,* Why Do I Have to Take This Course?

 Think About It—Journal Entry 6.2

Look back at the seven forms of thinking described in **Box 6.1.** Which of these forms of thinking have you used on high school exams or assignments?

_____

_____

_____

_____

_____

Analysis (Analytical Thinking)

The mental process of analysis is similar to the physical process of peeling an onion. When you analyze something, you take it apart and pick out its key parts, main points, or underlying elements. For example, if you were to analyze a chapter in this book, you would do more than cover its content; you would try to uncover or discover its main ideas by detecting its essential points and distinguishing them from background information or incidental details.

In an art course, you would use analytical thinking to identify the underlying elements or separate components of a painting or sculpture (e.g., its structure, texture, tone, and form). In the natural and social sciences, you would use analysis to identify underlying reasons or causes for natural (physical) phenomena and social events—known as "causal analysis." For instance, a causal analysis of the September 11, 2001, attack on the United States would involve identifying the key factors that led to the attack or the underlying reasons why the attack took place.

> In physics, you have to be analytical and break it [the problem] down into its parts."
>
> —*Physics student (quoted in Donald, 2002)*

 **Think About It—Journal Entry 6.3**

A TV commercial for a particular brand of liquor (which shall remain nameless) once showed a young man getting out of his car in front of a house where a party is going on. The driver gets out of his car, takes out a knife, slashes his tires, and goes inside to join the party. Using the higher-level thinking skill of analysis, what would you say are the underlying or embedded messages in this commercial?

_____

_____

_____

_____

_____

_____

Synthesis (Integrative Thinking)

When you engage in *synthesis*, you're using a thought process that's basically the opposite of analysis. Instead of breaking down or taking apart ideas, you piece them together to form an integrated whole—like piecing together parts of a puzzle. Connecting ideas learned in different courses is a form of synthesis, such as integrating ethical concepts learned in a philosophy course with marketing concepts learned in a business course to develop a comprehensive set of ethical guidelines for marketing and advertising products.

Although synthesis and analysis are seemingly opposite thought processes, they complement one another. Analysis enables you to disassemble information into its key parts; synthesis allows you to reassemble those parts into a new whole. For instance, when writing this book, we analyzed published material in many fields (e.g., psychology, history, philosophy, and biology) to detect pieces of information in these different fields that were most relevant to promoting the success of college students. We then synthesized or reassembled these parts to create a new whole—the textbook you're now reading.

Note

Synthesis is not just a summary of ideas produced by someone else, it's a thought process that integrates isolated pieces of information to generate a comprehensive product of your own.

Application (Applied Thinking)

When you learn something deeply, you transform information into knowledge; when you translate knowledge into practice, you engage in a higher-level thinking process known as *application*. It's a powerful form of higher-level thinking that allows you to transfer your knowledge to real-life situations and put it to use for practical purposes. For instance, you're engaging in application if you use the knowledge you've acquired about human relations to become more assertive, or when you take knowledge acquired in an accounting course to help manage your personal finances.

Always be on the lookout for ways to take action on the knowledge you've acquired by applying it to your personal life experiences and current events or issues. When you use your knowledge for the practical purpose of doing something good, such as bettering yourself or others, you not only demonstrate application, you also demonstrate *wisdom* (Staudinger, 2008).

Multidimensional Thinking

When you view yourself and the world around you from different perspectives or vantage points to gain a comprehensive perspective, you're engaging in *multidimensional thinking*. For instance, multidimensional thinkers are able to think from the following four key perspectives and see how each of them influences, and is influenced by, the issue they're examining.

1. Perspective of Person (Self): How does this issue affect individuals on a personal basis?
2. Perspective of Place: What impact does this issue have on people living in different parts of the country or world?
3. Perspective of Time: How will future generations of people be affected by this issue?
4. Perspective of Culture: How is this issue likely to be interpreted or experienced by groups of people who share different social customs and traditions? (the perspective of culture)

Important issues don't exist in isolation but as parts of a complex, interconnected system that involves interplay of multiple factors and perspectives. For example, global warming (climate change) is an issue that involves the gradual thickening and trapping of more heat in the earth's atmosphere as a result of a buildup in gases generated by the burning fossil fuels for industrial purposes (Intergovernmental Council on Climate Change, 2013). The consensus among today's scientists is that this buildup of human-made pollution is causing temperatures to rise (and sometimes fall) around the world, resulting in more extreme weather conditions and more frequent natural disasters—such as droughts, wildfires, hurricanes, and dust storms (Joint Science Academic Statement, 2005; National Resource Defense Council, 2005, 2012). As depicted in **Box 6.2**, understanding and addressing this issue requires understanding interrelationships among the multiple perspectives of person, place, time, and culture,

"As gold which he cannot spend will make no man rich, so knowledge which he cannot apply will make no man wise."

—Dr. Samuel Johnson, famous English literary figure and original author of the Dictionary of the English Language (1747)

"To me, thinking at a higher level is when you approach a question or topic thoughtfully, when you fully explore every aspect of that topic from all angles."

—First-year college student

Box 6.2

Understanding Climate Change from Four Key Perspectives

Person

Climate change involves humans at a personal level because individual efforts to conserve energy in our homes and our willingness to purchase energy-efficient products can play a major role in resolving this issue.

Place

Climate change is an international phenomenon that extends beyond the boundaries of any one country; it affects all countries in the world and its solution requires the joint effort of different nations around the world to reduce their level of carbon emissions.

Time

If the current trend toward higher global warming isn't addressed soon, it could seriously threaten the lives of future generations inhabiting the planet.

Culture

Industries in technologically and industrially advanced cultures are primarily responsible for contributing to the problem of climate change, yet its potentially adverse effects will be greater for less technologically advanced cultures because they lack the resources to respond to it (Joint Science Academies' Statement, 2005). Industrially advanced cultures will need to use their advanced resources and technology to devise alternative methods for generating energy in ways that reduce the risk of global warming for all cultures.

 Think About It—Journal Entry 6.4

Think of a current national or international problem (other than climate change) whose solution requires multiple perspective taking or systems thinking.

_____

_____

_____

_____

_____

Balanced Thinking

When we seek out and carefully consider arguments *for* and *against* a particular position, we're engaging in balanced thinking. The process of finding supporting evidence or reasons for a position is referred to as *adduction*—when you adduce, you identify reasons *for* a position; the process of finding evidence or reasons that contradicts a position is called *refutation*—when you refute, you provide a rebuttal *against* a particular position.

Balanced thinking involves both adduction and refutation. Each position's stronger arguments are acknowledged, and its weaker ones are refuted (Fairbairn & Winch, 1996). The goal of a balanced thinker is not to stack up evidence for one position or the other but to be an impartial judge looking at supporting and opposing evidence for both sides of an issue, and striving to draw a conclusion that's neither biased nor one-sided. When you consider the strengths and weaknesses of opposing arguments at the same time, it reduces the likelihood that you'll fall prey to an overly simplistic form of thinking typical of many first-year students—known as *dualistic* thinking—seeking the "truth" in the form of clear-cut, black-or-white answers or solutions to complex issues—where one position or theory is "right" and the others "wrong" (Perry, 1970, 1999).

Don't be surprised and frustrated if you find scholars disagreeing about what particular positions or theories are more accurate or account for most of the "truth" in their field. This is a healthy thought process known as *dialectic* or *dialogic* thinking (deriving from the root "dialogue" or "conversation"). It's a productive form of intellectual dialogue (Paul & Elder, 2014) that acknowledges different sides of a complex issue and results in a more balanced, integrated understanding of it. In a study of leaders who excel in the field of business, it was discovered that one of their distinguishing qualities was their capacity for "integrative thinking"—the ability to hold opposing or conflicting ideas in their head and use that tension to create a new and superior idea—much like how humans use their opposable thumbs to excel at manual tasks (Martin, 2007).

Keep in mind that your first step in the process of solving problems and seeking truth shouldn't be to immediately jump in and take an either-or (for-or-against) position. Instead, take a balanced thinking approach by looking at arguments for and against each position, acknowledge the strengths and weaknesses of both sides of the argument, and seek to integrate the best points of both arguments.

Lastly, balanced thinking involves more than just totaling the number of arguments for and against a position; it also involves *weighing* the strength of each argument. Arguments can vary in terms of their degree of importance or level of support. When weighing arguments, ask yourself, "What is the quality and quantity of evidence supporting it?" Consider whether the evidence is:

1. **Definitive**—so strong or compelling that a definite conclusion should be reached;
2. **Suggestive**—strong enough to suggest that a tentative or possible conclusion may be reached; or
3. **Inconclusive**—too weak to reach any conclusion.

When making class presentations and writing papers or reports, be mindful of how much weight should be assigned to different arguments and explain how their weight has been factored into your conclusion.

In some cases, after reviewing both supporting and contradictory evidence for opposing positions, balanced thinking may lead you to suspend judgment and withhold drawing a conclusion that favors one position over another. A balanced thinker may occasionally reach the following conclusion: "The evidence doesn't strongly favor one position over the other" or "More information is needed before I can make a final judgment or reach a firm conclusion." These aren't wishy-washy answers; they're legitimate conclusions to reach after all the evidence has been carefully considered. In fact, it's better to hold an undecided but informed viewpoint based on balanced thinking than to hold definite opinions that are uninformed, biased, or based on emotion—such as those often expressed by people on radio talk shows.

If you find that the more you learn, the more complicated things seem to become, this is good news. It means you're moving from simplistic to complex thinking that's more multidimensional and balanced.

> "The test of a first-rate intelligence is the ability to hold two opposed ideas in mind at the same time and still retain the ability to function."
>
> —F. Scott Fitzgerald, regarded as one of the greatest American writers of the 20th century

> "[Successful] business leaders have the capacity to hold two diametrically opposing ideas in their heads. And then, without panicking or settling for one alternative or the other, they're able to produce a synthesis that is superior to either opposing idea."
>
> —Roger Martin, dean of the Rotman School of Management, University of Toronto

> "For years I really didn't know what I believed. I always seemed to stand in the no man's land between opposing arguments, yearning to be won over by one side or the other but finding instead degrees of merit in both. But in time I came to accept, even embrace, what I called "my confusion" and to recognize it as a friend and ally, with no apologies needed."
>
> —"In Praise of the 'Wobblies,'" by Ted Gup, journalist, who has written for Time Magazine, National Geographic, and The New York Times

Think About It—Journal Entry 6.5

Consider the following positions:

1. Course requirements should be eliminated; college students should be allowed to choose the classes they want to take for their degree.

2. Course grades should be eliminated; college students should take classes on a pass–fail basis.

Using balanced thinking, identify one or more arguments *for* and *against* each of these positions?

> The more you know, the less sure you are."
>
> —*Voltaire, French historian, philosopher, and advocate for civil liberty*

Note

Balanced thinking enables you to become a more complex and comprehensive thinker capable of viewing issues from opposing sides and multiple perspectives.

Critical Thinking (Evaluation)

When we *evaluate* or *judge* the quality of an argument or work product, we're engaging in a form of higher-level thinking known as *critical thinking*. It's a skill highly valued by professors teaching students at all stages in the college experience and all subjects in the college curriculum (Higher Education Research Institute, 2009; Stark, et al., 1990). By working on developing your critical thinking skills as a first-year student, you will significantly improve you academic performance throughout your college experience.

> Critical thinking is an evaluative thought process that requires deep thinking."
>
> —*First-year college student*

Many students misinterpret critical thinking to mean "being critical"—criticizing something or somebody. Although critical thinking does involving making an evaluation or judgment, the evaluation can be either positive or negative. For instance, a movie critic can give a good (thumbs up) or bad (thumbs down) review of a film.

Critical thinking is used for many purposes beyond critiquing films, art, or music. It's a skill that enables you to "read between the lines" and cut through the fog or smog of ideas and arguments—including your own. Whether the evaluation is positive or negative (or some combination thereof), critical thinking involves backing up your evaluation with specific, well-informed reasons or evidence that support the critique. Failure to do so makes the criticism unfounded—that is, lacking any foundation or basis of support.

You can start developing the mental habit of critical thinking by using the following criteria as standards for evaluating ideas or arguments:

1. **Validity (Truthfulness).** Is it true or accurate?
2. **Morality (Ethics).** Is it fair or just?
3. **Beauty (Aesthetics).** Does it have artistic merit or value?
4. **Practicality (Usefulness).** Can it be put to use for practical or beneficial purposes?
5. **Priority (Order of Importance or Effectiveness).** Is it better than other ideas and alternative courses of action?

Think About It—Journal Entry 6.6

Flash back to **Journal Entry 6.1** on **p. 135.** How does your response compare with the definition of critical thinking just provided?

How are they similar?

_____

_____

_____

_____

_____

How do they differ?

_____

_____

_____

_____

_____

_____

Critical Thinking and Inferential Reasoning

When we make arguments or arrive at conclusions, we use a mental process called *inferential reasoning*. We start with a premise (a statement or observation) and use it to infer (step to) a conclusion. Two major ways in which we use inferential reasoning to make arguments and reach conclusions are: (a) through logical reasoning, and/or (b) citing empirical (observable) evidence.

1. *Logical Reasoning.* Reaching a conclusion by showing that it logically follows from or is logically consistent with an established premise. In other words, if statement "A" is true, it can be concluded that statement "B" is also true.

For example:

Statement A.   The constitution guarantees all U.S. citizens the right to vote. (Premise)

Statement B.   Women and people of color are citizens of the U.S.; therefore, they should have the right to vote. (Conclusion)

2. *Empirical (observable) evidence.* Reaching a conclusion by showing that it is supported with statistical data or scientific research findings. In other words, based on evidence "A," it can be concluded that "B" is true.

For example:

Statement A.   There is statistical evidence that a much higher percentage of people who smoke experience cancer and heart disease. (Premise)

Statement B.   Based on this statistical evidence, smoking is a major health risk. (Conclusion)

Although using logic and empirical evidence are different routes to conclusions, they can be combined to support the same conclusion. For instance, in this book, we use both logical arguments and empirical evidence (research and statistics) to support our conclusions and recommendations. Similarly, advocates for lowering the legal drinking age to 18 have used the following forms of logical reasoning and empirical evidence to support their position:

(a) Logical reasoning: 18-year-olds in the United States are considered to be legal adults with respect to such rights and responsibilities as voting, serving on juries, joining the military, and being held responsible for committing crimes; therefore, 18-year-olds should have the right to drink.

(b) Empirical evidence: In other countries where drinking is allowed at age 18, statistics show that they have fewer binge-drinking and drunk-driving problems than the United States.

Think About It—Journal Entry 6.7

Can you think of arguments *against* lowering the drinking age to 18 that are based on logical reasoning and empirical evidence?

_____

_____

_____

_____

_____

Drawing inferences based on logic and empirical evidence are the primary thought processes that humans use to reach conclusions about themselves and the world around them. Inferential reasoning is also the form of thinking you will use to make arguments and reach conclusions in your college courses. You'll often be required to take positions and support your conclusions with sound reasoning and solid evidence. Adopt the mindset that you're a courtroom lawyer and be ready to prove your case with logical arguments and empirical evidence (exhibit A, exhibit B, etc.).

Logical Fallacies: Inferential Reasoning Errors

Unfortunately, errors can be made in the inferential reasoning process, which are commonly referred to as *logical fallacies*. Listed below is a summary of the major types of logical fallacies. Be mindful of them in your thinking and when evaluating the thinking of others. As you read the following reasoning errors, briefly note in the margin whether you've ever witnessed it or committed it.

* **Non sequitur.** Drawing a conclusion that doesn't follow from or connect with the premise—the initial statement or observation. (*Non sequitur* derives from Latin, which literally means, "it does not follow.") Example: There was a bloody glove found at the murder scene and it doesn't fit the defendant, therefore the defendant must be innocent.

* **Selective Perception.** Seeing only examples and instances that support one's position while overlooking or ignoring those that contradict it. Example: Believers of astrology who only notice and point out people whose personalities happen to fit their astrological sign, but overlook those who don't.

* **Dogmatism.** Stubbornly clinging to a personal point of view unsupported by evidence while remaining closed-minded (nonreceptive) to other viewpoints better supported by evidence. Example: Arguing that adopting a national health system is a form of socialism that cannot work in a capitalistic economy, while ignoring the fact that there are many other nations in the world that have both a national health care system and a capitalistic economy.

* **Double Standard.** Having two sets of judgment standards—a higher standard for judging others and a lower standard for judging oneself. Example: Critically evaluating and challenging the opinions of others, but not our own.

* **Wishful Thinking.** Thinking something is true not because of logic or evidence, but because the person *wants* it to be true. Example: A teenage girl who believes she will not become pregnant, even though she and her boyfriend are having sex without any form of contraception.

* **Hasty Generalization.** Reaching a conclusion prematurely on the basis of a limited number of instances or experiences. Example: Concluding that people belonging to a racial or ethnic group are all "that way" on the basis of personal experiences with only one or two individuals.

* **Jumping to a Conclusion.** Making a leap of logic to a conclusion that's based on a single reason or factor while ignoring other possible reasons or contributing factors. Example: A shy person immediately concludes that a person who doesn't make eye contact with her doesn't like her, without considering the possibility that the lack of eye contact may be due to the fact that the other person was distracted or shy himself.

* **False Cause and Effect (a.k.a. Correlational Error).** Concluding that if two things co-occur at about the same time or in close sequence, one must *cause* the other. Example: The old belief that sexual activity causes acne because when children become teenagers, they are more sexually active and also are more likely to develop acne.

* **False Analogy.** Concluding that because two things are alike in one respect, they must be alike in another respect. This is the classic error of "comparing

A very bad (and all too common) way to misread a newspaper: To see whatever supports your point of view as fact, and anything that contradicts your point of view as bias."

—Daniel Okrent, first public editor of The New York Times

Facts do not cease to exist because they are ignored."

—Aldous Huxley, English writer and author of Brave New World.

Belief can be produced in practically unlimited quantity and intensity, without observation or reasoning, and even in defiance of both by the simple desire to believe."

—George Bernard Shaw, Irish playwright and Nobel Prize winner for literature

apples and oranges"—they're both alike in that they are fruits but they're not alike in other ways. Example: People who argue that government is a form of business, therefore it should be run like a business or run by a businessman. While it's true that government and business are societal institutions that have some similarities (e.g., budgets and payrolls), government is not a profit-making enterprise and it has purposes that are not fiscal in nature.

- **Glittering Generality.** Making a positive, general statement that isn't supported by specific details or evidence. Example: A letter of recommendation that describes the recommended person as a "wonderful person" with a "great personality," but provides little or no evidence to back up the claim.

- **Straw Man Argument.** Distorting an opponent's argument position and then attacking it. Example: Attacking an opposing political candidate for restricting civil liberties when, in fact, the opponent only supported a ban on concealed weapons.

- **Ad Hominem Argument.** Attacking the person, not the person's argument. (Literally translated, *ad hominem* means "to the man") Example: discounting a young person's argument by saying: "you're too young and inexperienced to know what you're talking about," or discounting an older person's argument by stating: "you're too old-school to understand this issue."

- **Red Herring.** Bringing up an irrelevant issue that disguises or distracts attention from the real issue being discussed or debated. (The term "red herring" derives from an old practice of dragging a herring—a strong-smelling fish—across a trail to distract the scent of pursuing dogs.) Example: People who responded to criticism of former President Richard Nixon's involvement in the Watergate scandal by arguing, "He was a good president who accomplished many great things while he was in office." (Nixon's effectiveness as a president is an irrelevant issue or a red herring; the real issue being discussed is Nixon's behavior in the Watergate scandal.)

- **Smoke Screen.** Intentionally disguising or camouflaging the truth by providing confusing or misleading explanations. Example: A politician who opposes gun control legislation by arguing that it's a violation of the constitutional right to bear arms, when in reality, the reason for his position is that he's receiving financial support from gun manufacturing companies.

- **Slippery Slope.** Using fear tactics to argue that not accepting a position will result in a "domino effect"—bad things will happen one after another—like a series of falling dominoes. Example: Arguing that "if America allows communism to happen anywhere, it will eventually happen everywhere."

- **Rhetorical Deception.** Using deceptive language to conclude that something is true without actually providing reasons or evidence. Example: Using glib words such as: "*Clearly* this is . . ." "It's *obvious* that . . ." or "Any *reasonable* person can see . . . ", without explaining why it's so "clear," "obvious," or "reasonable."

- **Circular Reasoning (a.k.a. "Begging the Question").** Drawing a conclusion by merely rewording or restating one's position without providing any supporting reasons or evidence, thus leaving the original question unanswered. This logical fallacy basically offers a conclusion that's simply a circular restatement of the premise—it's true because it's true. Example: Concluding that "stem cell research isn't ethical because it's morally wrong."

- **Appealing to Authority or Prestige.** Believing that if an authority figure or celebrity says it's true, it must be true. Example: Buying product X simply because a famous actor or athlete endorses it. Or, concluding that a course of action should be taken simply because the president says so.

- **Appealing to Tradition or Familiarity.** Concluding that if something has been considered to be true for a long time, or has always been done in a certain way, it must be true or must be the best way to do it. Example: "Throughout history, marriage has been a relationship between a man and a woman; therefore, gay marriage should be illegal."
- **Appealing to Popularity or the Majority (a.k.a. Jumping on the Bandwagon).** Believing that if an idea is popular or held by the majority of people, it must be true. Example: "So many people believe in psychics, it must be true; they can't all be wrong."
- **Appealing to Emotion.** Believing in something based on the emotional intensity of our reaction to an argument, rather than the quality of reasoning or evidence used to support the argument. Example: "If I feel strongly about something, it must be true" or believing that I should "always trust my feelings" and "just follow my heart."

Political talk shows have become shouting matches designed to push emotional hot buttons and drive us further apart. We desperately need to exchange ideas with one another rationally and courteously."

—David Boren, president, University of Oklahoma and longest-serving chairman of the U.S. Senate Intelligence Committee

 Think About It—Journal Entry 6.8

Glance back at the reasoning errors just discussed. Identify the two most common errors you've witnessed or experienced.

_____

_____

_____

What were the situations in which these errors took place?

_____

_____

_____

_____

Why do you think they took place?

_____

_____

_____

_____

_____

When I teach classes or give workshops, I often challenge students or participants to debate me on either politics or religion. I ask them to choose a political party affiliation, a religion or a branch of religion for their debate topic, or their stance on a social issue for which there are political or religious viewpoints. The ground rules are as follows: They choose the topic for debate; they can only use facts to support their argument, rebuttal, or both, and they must respond in a rational manner—without letting emotions drive their answers.

When I conduct this exercise, I usually discover that the topics people feel most strongly about are often those they haven't critically evaluated. For instance, people say they are Democrat, Republican, independent, and so on, and argue from this position; however, few of them have taken the time to critically examine whether their stated affiliation is actually consistent with their personal viewpoints. They almost always answer "no" to the following questions: "Have you read the core document (e.g., party platform) that outlines the party stance?" and "Have you engaged in self-examination of your party affiliation through reasoned discussions with others who say they have the same or a different political affiliation?"

—*Aaron Thompson*

> Too often we enjoy the comfort of opinion without the discomfort of thought."
>
> *—John F. Kennedy, 35th U.S. president*

> The principle mark of genius is not perfection but originality, the opening of new frontiers."
>
> *—Arthur Koestler, Hungarian novelist and philosopher*

> The blues are the roots. Everything else are the fruits."
>
> *—Willie Dixon, blues songwriter; commenting on how all forms of contemporary American music contain elements of blues music, which originated among African American slaves*

> Imagination should give wings to our thoughts, but imagination must be checked and documented by the factual results of the experiment."
>
> *—Louis Pasteur, French microbiologist, chemist, and founder of pasteurization (a method for preventing milk and wine from going sour)*

> Creativity isn't 'crazytivity'."
>
> *—Edward De Bono, internationally known authority on creative thinking*

Creative Thinking

Creative thinking leads you to ask the question: "Why not?" (e.g., "Why not do it a different way?"). When you generate something new or different—an original idea, strategy, or work product—you're thinking creatively.

The process of creative thinking may be viewed as an extension or higher form of synthesis. Like synthesis, separate ideas are integrated, but they're combined in a way that results in something distinctively different (Anderson & Krathwohl, 2001). For instance, the musical genre of hard rock was created by combining elements of blues and rock and roll, and folk rock was born when Bob Dylan combined musical elements of acoustic blues and amplified rock (Shelton, et al., 2003). Robert Kearns (subject of the film, "Flash of Genius") combined preexisting mechanical parts to create the intermittent windshield wiper (Seabrook, 2008).

Keep in mind that creative thinking is not restricted to the arts, it can occur in all subject areas—even in fields that seek precision and definite answers. In math, creative thinking involves using new approaches or strategies for arriving at a correct solution to a problem. In science, creativity takes place when a scientist first uses imaginative thinking to create a hypothesis or logical hunch ("What might happen if . . . ?") and then conducts an experiment to test out whether the hypothesis turns out to be true.

It could be said that thinking critically involves looking "inside the box" to evaluate the quality of its content. Thinking creatively involves looking "outside the box" to imagine other packages containing different content. Creative and critical thinking are two of the most important forms of higher-level thinking and they can work together in a cyclical and complementary fashion. Creative thinking is used to ask new questions and generate new ideas; critical thinking is used to evaluate or critique the ideas we generate (Paul & Elder, 2004). For an idea to be truly creative, it must not just be different or unusual, it must also be effective or significant (Runco, 2004; Sternberg, 2001). If our critique of what we've created reveals that it lacks quality or is ineffective, we shift back to creative thinking to generate something new and improved.

Or, the starting points for the cyclical process of creative and critical thinking may be reversed, whereby we begin by using critical thinking to evaluate an old idea or approach. If our evaluation indicates that it's not very good, we turn on the creative thinking process to come up with a quality of the new idea or different approach; then we turn back to critical thinking to evaluate the quality of the new idea we created.

Brainstorming is a problem-solving process that illustrates how creative and critical thinking work hand-in-hand. The steps or stages involved in the process of brainstorming are summarized in **Box 6.3**.

Box 6.3

The Process of Brainstorming

1. Generate as many ideas as you can, jotting them down rapidly without stopping to evaluate their validity or practicality. Studies show that worrying about whether an idea is correct often blocks creativity (Basadur, Runco, & Vega, 2000). So, at this stage of the process, just let your imagination run wild; don't be concerned about whether the idea you generate is impractical, unrealistic, or outrageous.
2. Review the ideas you generated and use them as a springboard to trigger additional ideas, or combine them into larger ideas.
3. After you run out of ideas, critically evaluate the list of ideas you've generated and eliminate those that you think are least effective.
4. From the remaining list of ideas, choose the best idea or best combination of ideas.

Note that the first two steps in the brainstorming process involve *divergent thinking*—a form of creative thinking that allows you to go off in different directions and generate diverse ideas. In contrast, the last two steps in the process involve *convergent thinking*—a form of critical thinking in which you converge (focus in) and narrow down the ideas, evaluating each of them for their effectiveness.

As this multistage process suggests, creativity doesn't just happen suddenly or effortlessly (the so-called "stroke of genius"); instead, it takes sustained mental effort (De Bono, 2007; Paul & Elder, 2004). Although creative thinking may occasionally involve spontaneous or intuitive leaps, it typically involves careful reflection and evaluation of whether any of those leaps actually land you on a good idea.

AUTHOR'S EXPERIENCE

I was once working with a friend to come up with ideas for a grant proposal. We started out by sitting at his kitchen table, exchanging ideas while sipping coffee; then we both got up and began to pace back and forth, walking all around the room while bouncing different ideas off each other. Whenever a new idea was thrown out, one of us would jot it down (whoever was pacing closer to the kitchen table at the moment).

After we ran out of ideas, we shifted gears, slowed down, and sat down at the table together to critique the ideas we generated during our "binge-thinking" episode. After some debate, we finally settled on an idea that we judged to be the best of all the ideas we produced, and we used this idea for the grant proposal—which, ultimately, was awarded to us.

> Creativity is allowing oneself to make mistakes; art is knowing which ones to keep."
>
> –Scott Adams, creator of the Dilbert comic strip and author of The Dilbert Principle

Although I wasn't fully aware of it at the time, the stimulating thought process my friend and I were engaging in was called brainstorming: first we engaged in creative thinking—our fast-paced, idea-production stage—followed by critical thinking—our slower-paced, idea-evaluation stage.

—*Joe Cuseo*

Note

Creative thinking is about generating new answers and solutions. Critical thinking is about evaluating the quality of answers and solutions we generate.

Think About It—Journal Entry 6.9

Do you consider yourself to be a creative thinker? Why?

_____

_____

_____

_____

What could you do to improve your ability to think creatively?

_____

_____

_____

_____

_____

Using Higher-Level Thinking Skills to Improve Academic Performance

Thus far, this chapter has focused primarily on helping you get a clear idea of what higher-level thinking is and what its major forms are. The remainder of the chapter focuses on helping you develop habits of higher-level thinking that can be applied to improve your performance in college and beyond.

Connect ideas you acquire in class with related ideas found in your assigned reading. When you discover information in your reading that relates to something you've learned about in class (or vice versa), make a note of it in the margin of your textbook or your class notebook. By integrating knowledge you've obtained from these two major sources, you're engaging in the higher-level thinking skill of synthesis, which you can then demonstrate on exams and assignments to improve your course grades.

When listening to lectures and completing reading assignments, pay attention not only to the content being covered but also the thought process used to cover the content. Periodically ask yourself what form of higher-level thinking your instructors are using during class presentations and authors are using when you're reading their writing. The more conscious you are of the type of higher-level thinking skills you're being exposed to, the more likely you are to develop those thinking skills yourself and demonstrate them on exams and assignments.

Periodically pause to reflect on your own thinking process. When working on different academic tasks, ask yourself what type of thinking you're doing (e.g., analysis, synthesis, or evaluation). Thinking about and becoming aware of how you're thinking while you're thinking is a mental process called _metacognition_ (Flavell, 1979; Hartman, 2001). It's a mental habit that's associated with higher-level thinking and improved problem-solving skills (Halpern, 2013; Resnick, 1986).

Asking yourself higher-level thinking questions during lectures should prevent you from asking questions like this one.

Develop habits of higher-level thinking by asking yourself higher-level thinking questions. One simple yet powerful way to help you reflect on your thinking is through self-questioning. Since thinking often involves talking to ourselves silently (or aloud), if we ask ourselves high-quality, thought-provoking questions, you can train your mind to think at a higher level. A good question can launch you on a quest or voyage to answer it by using higher-level thinking skills. Getting in the habit of asking yourself higher-level thinking questions while learning will increase the likelihood you'll display higher levels of thinking during class discussions, as well as on course exams and assignments.

> If you do not ask the right questions, you do not get the right answers."
>
> —Edward Hodnett, British poet

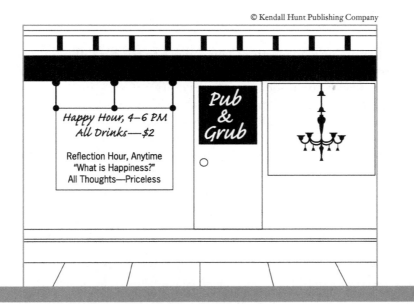

© Kendall Hunt Publishing Company

Happy Hour, 4–6 P.M.
All Drinks—$2

Reflection Hour, Anytime
"What is Happiness?"
All Thoughts—Priceless

Pub
&
Grub

 Think About It—Journal Entry 6.10

Critically evaluate the common practice of bars selling alcoholic drinks at reduced prices that's depicted in the preceding cartoon by answering the following questions:

1. What are the assumptions or implications of calling this practice "happy hour"?

2.   What are arguments for and against this practice?

_____

_____

_____

_____

_____

Box 6.4 contains key questions you can use to trigger different forms of higher-level thinking. The questions are constructed as incomplete sentences so you can fill in the blank with any topic or concept you're studying in any course you may be taking. Research indicates that when students get in the habit of using question stems such as these, they develop and demonstrate higher levels of thinking in college courses (King, 1990, 1995, 2002). As you read the questions under each of the seven forms of higher-level thinking in the following box, think about how they may be applied to material you're learning in courses this term.

Box 6.4

Self-Questioning Strategies to Trigger Different Forms of Higher-Level Thinking

1.   ANALYSIS (ANALYTICAL THINKING)—breaking down information into its essential elements or parts.

Trigger Questions:
- What are the main ideas contained in _____?
- What are the important aspects of _____?
- What are the key issues raised by _____?
- What are the major purposes of _____?
- What hidden assumptions are embedded in _____?
- What are the reasons behind _____?

2.   SYNTHESIS (INTEGRATIVE THINKING)—integrating separate pieces of information to form a more complete and coherent product or pattern.

Trigger Questions:
- How can this idea be joined or connected with _____ to create a more complete or comprehensive answer?
- How could these different _____ be grouped together into a more general class or category?
- How could these separate _____ be reorganized

or rearranged to produce a comprehensive understanding of the big picture?

3.   APPLICATION (APPLIED THINKING)—using knowledge for practical purposes to solve problems and resolve issues.

Trigger Questions:
- How can this idea be used to _____?
- How can this theory be put into practice to _____?
- What could be done to improve or strengthen _____?
- What could be done to prevent or reduce _____?

4.   BALANCED THINKING—carefully considering reasons for and against a particular position or viewpoint.

Trigger Questions:
- Have I considered both sides of _____?
- What are the strengths (advantages) and weaknesses (disadvantages) of _____?
- What evidence supports and contradicts _____?
- What are arguments for and counterarguments against _____?

(continued)

Box 6.4 *(continued)*

5. MULTIDIMENSIONAL THINKING—thinking that involves viewing yourself and the world around you from different angles or vantage points.

   Trigger Questions:
   - Have I taken into consideration all factors that could influence _____ or be influenced by _____?
   - How would _____ affect different dimensions of myself (emotional, physical, etc.)?
   - What broader impact would _____ have on the social and physical world around me?
   - How might people living in different times (e.g., past and future) experience _____?
   - How would people from different cultural backgrounds interpret or react to _____?

6. CRITICAL THINKING (EVALUATION)—making critical judgments or assessments.

   Trigger Questions for Evaluating *Empirical Evidence:*
   - What examples support the argument that _____?
   - What research evidence is there for _____?
   - What statistical data document or back up this _____?

   Trigger Questions for Evaluating *Logical Consistency:*
   - If _____ is true, does it follow that _____ is also true?
   - If I believe in _____, should I practice _____?
   - To draw this conclusion means I'm assuming that _____?

   Trigger Questions for Evaluating *Morality (Ethics):*
   - Is _____ fair?
   - Is _____ just?
   - Is this action consistent with the professed or stated values of _____?

   Trigger Questions for Evaluating Beauty (Aesthetics):
   - Does _____ meet established criteria for judging artistic beauty?
   - What is the aesthetic merit or value of _____?

   - Does _____ contribute to or detract from the beauty of the environment?

   Trigger Questions for Evaluating *Practicality (Usefulness):*
   - Will _____ work?
   - What practical value does this _____ have?
   - What potential benefits and drawbacks would result if this _____ were put into practice?

   Trigger Questions for Evaluating *Priority (Order of Importance or Effectiveness):*
   - Which one of these _____ is the most important?
   - Is this _____ the best option or choice available?
   - How do these _____ rank from first to last (best to worst) in terms of their effectiveness?

7. CREATIVE THINKING—generating ideas that are unique, original, or distinctively different.
   Trigger Questions:
   - What could be invented to _____?
   - Imagine what would happen if _____?
   - What might be a different way to _____?
   - How would this change if _____?
   - What would be an innovative approach to _____?

Note: Save these higher-level thinking questions and use them when completing different academic tasks required in your courses (e.g., preparing for exams, writing papers or reports, and participating in class discussions or study group sessions). Get in the habit of periodically stepping back to reflect on your thinking and ask yourself what form of thinking you're engaging in (analysis, synthesis, application, etc.). You could even keep a "thinking log" or "thinking journal" to increase self-awareness of the thinking strategies you're using and developing. This strategy will not only help you acquire higher-level thinking skills, it will also help you communicate these skills in job interviews and letters of application for career positions.

Think About It—Journal Entry 6.11

Review the higher-level thinking skills listed in questions in **Box 6.4** above. Identify one trigger question listed under each of the seven forms of thinking and fill in the blank with an idea or issue being covered in a course you're taking this term.

Strategies for Increasing Creativity

In addition to self-questioning strategies, the following attitudes and practices can be used to stimulate creative thinking.

> "All thinking begins with wonder."
>
> —*Socrates, classic Greek (Athenian) philosopher and founding father of Western philosophy*

- **Be flexible.** Think about ideas and objects in alternative and unconventional ways. The power of flexible and unconventional thinking was well illustrated in the movie "Apollo 13," based on the true story of an astronaut who saved his life by creatively using duct tape as an air filter. The inventor of the printing press (Johannes Gutenberg) made his groundbreaking discovery while watching a machine being used to crush grapes at a wine harvest. He thought that the same type of machine could be used for a different purpose—to press letters onto paper (Dorfman, Shames, & Kihlstrom, 1996).
- **Be experimental.** Play with ideas; try them out to see whether they'll work or work better than the status quo. Studies show that creative people tend to be mental risk-takers who are willing to experiment with different ideas and techniques (Sternberg, 2001). Consciously resist the temptation to settle for the security of familiarity. When people cling rigidly to what's conventional or traditional, they're clinging to the comfort or security of what's most familiar and predictable; this often blocks originality, ingenuity, and openness to change. Tom Kelley, cofounder of the famous IDEO design firm in Palo Alto, California, has found that innovative thinking emerges from an exploratory mindset that's "open to new insights every day" (Kelley & Littman, 2005).
- **Get mobile.** Stand up and move around while you're thinking. Research shows that taking a walk—either inside or outside—stimulates the production of creative ideas (Oppezzo & Schwartz, 2014). Even by standing up, our brain gets approximately 10% more oxygen than it does when sitting down (Sousa, 2011). Since oxygen provides fuel for the brain, our ability to think creatively is energized when we're up on our feet and moving around.
- **Get it down.** Creative ideas can often pop into our mind at the most unexpected times. Scholars refer to the sudden birth of creative ideas as *incubation*—just like incubated eggs can hatch at any time, so too can original ideas suddenly hatch and pop into our consciousness. However, just as great ideas can suddenly come to mind, they can also slip out of mind as soon as we start thinking about

something else. You can prevent this slippage from happening by having the right equipment on hand to record your creative ideas before they slip away. Carry a pen and a small notepad, a packet of sticky notes, or a portable electronic recording device at all times to immediately record original ideas the instant you have them.

- **Get diverse.** Seek ideas from diverse social and informational sources. Bouncing your ideas off of different people and getting their feedback about your ideas is a good way to generate mental energy, synergy (multiplication of ideas), and serendipity (accidental discoveries). Studies show that creative people venture well beyond the boundaries of their particular area of training or specialization (Baer, 1993; Kaufman & Baer, 2002). They have wide-ranging interests and knowledge, which they draw upon and combine to generate new ideas (Riquelme, 2002). So, be on the lookout to combine the knowledge and skills you acquire from different subjects and different people, and use them to create bridges to new ideas.

- **Take breaks.** If you're having trouble discovering a solution to a problem, stop working on it for a while and come back to it later. Creative solutions often come to mind after you stop thinking about the problem you're trying to solve. What often happens when you work intensely on a problem or challenging task for a sustained period of time, your attention can get rigidly riveted on just one approach to its solution (German & Barrett, 2005; Maier, 1970). By taking your mind off of it and returning to it later, your focus of attention is likely to shift to a different feature or aspect of the problem. This new focus may enable you to view the problem from a different angle or vantage point, which can lead to a breakthrough idea that was blocked by your previous perspective (Anderson, 2010). Furthermore, taking a break allows the problem to incubate in your mind at a lower level of consciousness and stress, which can sometimes give birth to a sudden solution.

- **Reorganize the problem.** When you're stuck on a problem, try rearranging its parts or pieces. Reorganization can transform the problem into a different pattern that may enable you to suddenly see a solution you previously overlooked—similar to how changing the order of letters in a word jumble can help you find the hidden word. You can use the same strategy to change the wording of any problem you're working on, or by recording ideas on index cards (or sticky notes) and laying them out in different sequences and patterns.

  If you're having trouble solving a problem that involves a sequence of steps (e.g., a math problem), try reversing the sequence and start by working from the end or middle. The new sequence makes you to take a different approach to the problem; this forces you to come at it from a different direction, which can lead you to an alternative path to its solution.

" I make progress by having people around who are smarter than I am—and listening to them. And I assume that everyone is smarter about something than I am."

—Henry Kaiser, successful industrialist, known as the father of American shipbuilding

" Eureka! (literally translated: "I have found it!")

—Attributed to Archimedes, ancient Greek mathematician and inventor when he suddenly discovered (while sitting in a bathtub) how to measure the purity of gold

" Creativity consists largely of re-arranging what we know in order to find out what we do not know."

—George Keller, prolific American architect and originator of the Union Station design for elevated train stations

Think About It—Journal Entry 6.12

The popularity of sticky notes is no doubt due to their versatility—you can post them on almost anything, remove them from where they were stuck (without a mess), and re-stick them somewhere else.

Think creatively for a minute. In what ways might you use sticky notes in a course or to handle a challenge you face in college?

_____

_____

_____

_____

_____

"

"Genius is 1% inspiration and 99% perspiration."

—*Thomas Edison, scientist and creator of more than 1,000 inventions, including the light bulb, phonograph, and motion picture camera*

- **Be persistent.** Studies show that creativity takes time, dedication, and hard work (Ericsson, 2006; Ericsson & Charness, 1994). Creative insights typically don't occur effortlessly, but emerge after repeated reflection and sustained commitment.

Chapter Summary and Highlights

Higher-level thinking (also known as higher-order thinking) refers to a more advanced level of thought than that used to acquire factual knowledge. It involves reflecting on knowledge acquired and taking it to a higher level—by performing additional mental action on it—such as evaluating its validity, integrating it with other ideas, or applying it to solve problems.

In this chapter, seven major forms of higher-level thinking skills were identified along with strategies for developing each of them:

1. *Analysis (Analytical Thinking)*—breaking down information to identify its key parts and underlying elements;
2. *Synthesis (Integrative Thinking)*—building up ideas by connecting them to form a larger whole or more comprehensive system;
3. *Application (Applied Thinking)*—putting knowledge into practice to solve problems and resolve issues;
4. *Multidimensional Thinking*—taking multiple perspectives (i.e., viewing issues from different vantage points);
5. *Balanced Thinking*—carefully considering arguments for and against a particular argument or position;
6. *Critical Thinking*—evaluating (judging the quality of) arguments, conclusions, and ideas;
7. *Creative Thinking*—generating ideas that are unique, original, or distinctively different.

Besides achieving academic excellence in college, there are other key benefits of developing higher-level thinking skills.

1. Higher-level thinking is essential for success in today's "information age"—a time when new information is being generated at faster rates than at any other time in human history. The majority of new workers in the

information age no longer work with their hands, they will work with their heads (Miller, 2003). Employers now value college graduates who have inquiring minds and possess higher-level thinking skills (Harvey, et al., 1997; Peter D. Hart Research Associates, 2006).

2. **Higher-level thinking skills are vital for citizens in a democratic nation.** Authoritarian political systems, such as dictatorships and fascist regimes, suppress critical thought and demand submissive obedience to authority. In contrast, citizens of a democracy are able to control their political destiny by making wise choices about the political leaders they elect. Thus, effective use of higher-level thinking skills, such as critical thinking, is an essential civic responsibility for people living in a democratic nation.

3. **Higher-level thinking is an important safeguard against prejudice, discrimination, and hostility.** Racial, ethnic, and national prejudices are often rooted in narrow, self-centered or group-centered thinking (Paul & Elder, 2014). Oversimplified, dualistic thinking can lead individuals to categorizing others into either "in" groups (us) or "out" groups (them). Such dualistic thinking can lead, in turn, to ethnocentrism—the tendency to view one's own racial or ethnic group as the superior "in" group and see other groups as inferior "out" groups. Development of higher-level thinking skills, such as taking multiple perspectives and using balanced thinking, counteracts the type of dualistic, ethnocentric thinking that leads to prejudice, discrimination, and hate crimes.

4. **Higher-level thinking helps preserve mental and physical health.** Simply put: Those who use their mind don't lose their mind. As they age, mentally active people are less likely to suffer memory loss or experience dementia (Wilson, Mendes, & Barnes, 2002). Thinking is not only a mental activity, it's also a physical activity that exercises the brain, much like physical activity exercises muscles in other parts of the body. Thinking requires higher levels of energy, which stimulates biological activity among brain cells, invigorates them, and reduces the likelihood they will deteriorate with age.

©Kendall Hunt Publishing Company.

Contrary to common belief, problem solving and other forms of higher-level thinking will not "fry" your brain but will stimulate and exercise it, reducing the likelihood that you'll experience Alzheimer's disease and other causes of memory loss in later life.

Learning More through the World Wide Web: Internet-Based Resources

For additional information on thinking skills, see the following websites:

Higher-Level Thinking Skills: http://edorigami.wikispaces.com/Bloom%27s+Digital+Taxonomy

Critical Thinking:
www.criticalthinking.org

Creative Thinking:
www.amcreativityassoc.org

Thinking Errors:
www.psychologytoday.com/blog/what-mentally-strong-people-dont-do/201501/10-thinking-errors-will-crush-your-mental-strength

www.factcheck.org (site for evaluating the factual accuracy of statements made by politicians in TV ads, debates, speeches, interviews, and news releases)

References

Anderson, J. R. (2010). *Cognitive psychology and its implications.* New York: Worth Publishers.

Anderson, L. W., & Krathwohl, D. R. (Eds.). (2001). *A taxonomy for learning, teaching, and assessing: A revision of Bloom's taxonomy of educational objectives.* New York: Addison Wesley Longman.

Baer, J. M. (1993). *Creativity and divergent thinking.* Hillsdale, NJ: Erlbaum.

Basadur, M., Runco, M. A., & Vega, L. A. (2000). Understanding how creative thinking skills, attitudes and behaviors work together: A causal process model. *Journal of Creative Behavior*, Vol. 34, (2), pp 77–100.

Conley, D. T. (2005). *College knowledge: What it really takes for students to succeed and what we can do to get them ready.* San Francisco: Jossey-Bass.

De Bono, E. (2007). *How to have creative ideas.* London, UK: Vermillion.

Donald, J. G. (2002). *Learning to think: Disciplinary perspectives.* San Francisco: Jossey-Bass.

Dorfman, J., Shames, J., & Kihlstrom, J. F. (1996). Intuition, incubation, and insight. In G. Underwood (Ed.), *Implicit cognition* (pp. 257–296). New York: Oxford University Press.

Ericsson, K. A. (2006). The influence of experience and deliberate practice on the development of superior expert performance. In K. A. Ericsson, N. Charness, P. Feltovich, & R. R. Hoffman, (Eds.). *Cambridge handbook of expertise and expert performance* (pp. 685–706). Cambridge, UK: Cambridge University Press.

Ericsson, K. A., & Charness, N. (1994). Expert performance: Its structure and acquisition. *American Psychologist*, 49(8), 725–747.

Fairbairn, G. J., & Winch, C. (1996). *Reading, writing and reasoning: A guide for students* (2nd ed.). Buckingham: OU Press.

Flavell, J. H. (1979). Metacognition and cognitive monitoring: A new area of cognitive- developmental inquiry. *American Psychologist*, 34(10), 906–911.

Gardiner, L. F. (2005). Transforming the environment for learning: A crisis of quality. *To Improve the Academy*, 23, 3–23.

German, T. P., & Barrett, H. C. (2005). Functional fixedness in a technologically sparse culture. *Psychological Science*, 16, 1–5.

Halpern, D. F. (2013). *Thought & knowledge: An introduction to critical thinking* (5th ed.). New York: Psychology Press.

Hartman, H. J. (Ed.) (2001). *Metacognition in learning and instruction: Theory, research and practice.* Dordrecht: Kluwer Academic Publishers.

Harvey, L., Moon, S., Geall, V., & Bower, R. (1997). *Graduates work: Organizational change and students' attributes*, Birmingham, Centre for Research into Quality, University of Central England.

Higher Education Research Institute (HERI) (2009). *The American college teacher: National norms for 2007–2008.* Los Angeles: HERI, University of California, Los Angeles.

Intergovernmental Council on Climate Change (2013). *Climate change 2013: The physical science basis.* Working Group I Contribution to the Fifth Assessment Report of the Intergovernmental Council on Climate Change. Switzerland: Intergovernmental Panel on Climate Change. Retrieved from http://www.ipcc.ch/report/ar5/wg1/.

Joint Science Academies Statement (2005). *Global response to climate change.* Retrieved from http://nationalacademies.org/onpi/06072005.pdf.

Kaufman, J. C., & Baer, J. (2002). Could Steven Spielberg manage the Yankees? Creative thinking in different domains. *Korean Journal of Thinking & Problem Solving*, 12(2), 5–14.

Kelley, T., & Littman, J. (2005). *The ten faces of innovation: IDEO's strategies for beating the devil's advocate & driving creativity throughout your organization.* New York: Currency/Doubleday.

King, A. (1990). Enhancing peer interaction and learning in the classroom through reciprocal questioning. *American Educational Research Journal, 27*(4), 664–687.

King, A. (1995). Guided peer questioning: A cooperative learning approach to critical thinking. *Cooperative Learning and College Teaching, 5*(2), 15–19.

King, A. (2002). Structuring peer interaction to promote high-level cognitive processing. *Theory into Practice, 41*(1), 33–39.

Maier, N. R. F. (1970). *Problem solving and creativity in individuals and groups.* Belmont, CA: Brooks/Cole.

Martin, R. L. (2007). *The opposable mind: How successful leaders win through integrative thinking.* Boston: Harvard Business School Press.

Miller, M. A. (2003, September/October). The meaning of the baccalaureate. *About Campus*, pp. 2–8.

Milton, O. (1982). *Will that be on the final?* Springfield, IL: Charles C. Thomas. National Resources Defense Council (2005). *Global warming: A summary of recent findings on the changing global climate.* Retrieved from http://www.nrdc.org/globalwarming/science/2005.asp.

National Resources Defense Council. (2012). *Global warming: An introduction to climate change.* Retrieved from www.nrdc.org/globalwarming.

Oppezzo, M., & Schwartz, D. L. (2014). Give your ideas some legs: The positive effect of walking on creative thinking. *Journal of Experimental Psychology: Learning, Memory, and Cognition, 40*(4), 1142–1152.

Pascarella, E., & Terenzini, P. (1991). *How college affects students: Findings and insights from twenty years of research.* San Francisco: Jossey-Bass.

Pascarella, E., & Terenzini, P. (2005). *How college affects students: A third decade of research* (Vol. 2). San Francisco: Jossey-Bass.

Paul, R., & Elder, L. (2004). *The nature and functions of critical and creative thinking.* Dillon Beach, CA: Foundation for Critical Thinking.

Paul, R., & Elder, L. (2014). *Critical thinking: Tools for taking charge of your professional and personal life.* Upper Saddle River, NJ: Pearson Education.

Perry, W. G. (1970, 1999). *Forms of intellectual and ethical development during the college years: A scheme.* New York: Holt, Rinehart & Winston.

Peter D. Hart Research Associates, 2006. *How should colleges prepare students to succeed in today's global economy?* The Association of American Colleges and Universities by Peter D. Hart Research Associates, Inc.

Resnick, L. B. (1986). *Education and learning to think.* Washington, DC: National Academy Press.

Riquelme, H. (2002). Can people creative in imagery interpret ambiguous figures faster than people less creative in imagery? *Journal of Creative Behavior, 36*(2), 105–116.

Runco, M. A. (2004). Creativity. *Annual Review of Psychology, 55*, 657–687.

Seabrook, J. (2008). *Flash of genius and other true stories of invention*, New York: St. Martin's Press.

Shelton, et al., 2003 Evaluation of parameters affecting quantitative detection of Escherichia coli O157 in enriched water samples using immunomagnetic electrochemiluminescence. *J. Microbiology Methods, Dec; 55*(3): 717–25.

Sousa, D. A. (2011). *How the brain learns.* Thousand Oaks, CA: Sage.

Stark, J. S., Lowther, R. J., Bentley, M. P., Ryan, G. G., Martens, M. L., Genthon, P. A., et al. (1990). *Planning introductory college courses: Influences on faculty.* Ann Arbor: National Center for Research to Improve Postsecondary Teaching and Learning, University of Michigan. (ERIC Document Reproduction Services No. 330 277 370.)

Staudinger, U. M. (2008). A psychology of wisdom: History and recent developments. *Research in Human Development, 5*, 107–120.

Sternberg, R. J. (2001). What is the common thread of creativity? *American Psychologist, 56*(4), 360–362.

Wilson, R., Mendes, C., Barnes, L., and others (2002). Participation in cognitively stimulating activities and risk of incident Alzheimer's disease. *Journal of the American Medical Association, 287*(6), 742–748.

Chapter 6 Exercises

6.1 Quote Reflections

Review the sidebar quotes contained in this chapter and select two that were especially meaningful or inspirational to you.

For each quote, provide a three- to five-sentence explanation why you chose it.

6.2 Reality Bite

Trick or Treat: Confusing Test or Challenging Test?

Students in Professor Plato's philosophy course just got their first exam back and they're going over the test together in class. Some students are angry because they feel the professor deliberately included "trick questions" to confuse them. Professor Plato responds by saying that his test questions were not designed to trick the class but to "challenge them to think."

Reflection and Discussion Questions

1. What do you think may have led some students to conclude that the professor was trying to trick or confuse them?
2. What type of test questions do you suspect the professor created to "challenge students to think"?
3. On future tests, what might the students do to reduce the likelihood that they'll feel tricked again?
4. On future tests, what might Professor Plato do to reduce the likelihood that students will complain about being asked "trick questions"?

6.3 Faculty Interview

Make an appointment to visit a faculty member on campus, either in a course you're taking this term, or in a field of study you're likely to pursue as your major. During your visit, ask the following questions:

1. In your field of study, what key questions do scholars ask?
2. How are answers to these questions investigated and discovered?
3. How do scholars in your field demonstrate critical and creative thinking?
4. What types of thinking skills does it take for students to succeed or excel in your field?

6.4 Self-Assessment of Higher-Level Thinking Characteristics

Thinking at a higher level is not just an intellectual process, it's also a personal attribute. Listed below are attributes of higher-level thinkers, accompanied by specific behaviors associated with each attribute. As you read the behaviors under each of the general attributes, place a checkmark (✓) next to any behavior that's true of you now and an asterisk (*) next to any behavior you think you need to work on.

1. *Tolerant and Accepting*

   ＿＿ Don't tune out ideas that conflict with your own

   ＿＿ Keep your emotions under control when someone criticizes your personal viewpoint

   ＿＿ Feel comfortable discussing controversial issues

   ＿＿ Try to find common ground with others holding opposing viewpoints

2. *Inquisitive and Open Minded*

___ Eager to continue learning new things from different people and different experiences

___ Willing to seek out others who hold viewpoints different than your own

___ Find differences of opinion and opposing viewpoints to be interesting and stimulating

___ Attempt to understand why people have opposing viewpoints

3. *Reflective and Tentative*

___ Take time to consider all perspectives or sides of an issue before drawing conclusions, making choices, or reaching decisions

___ Give fair consideration to ideas that others may instantly disapprove of or find distasteful

___ Acknowledge the complexity, ambiguity and uncertainty of certain issues, and am willing to say: "I need to give this more thought" or "I need more evidence before I can draw a conclusion"

___ Periodically reexamine your own viewpoints to determine whether they should be maintained or changed

4. *Honest and Courageous*

___ Willing to examine your views to see if they're biased or prejudiced

___ Willing to challenge others' ideas that are based on personal bias or prejudice

___ Willing to express viewpoints that may not conform to those of the majority

___ Willing to change previously held opinions and personal beliefs when they're contradicted by sound arguments or new evidence

Look back at the list and count the number of checkmarks and asterisks you placed in each of the four general areas:

	Checkmarks	Asterisks
Tolerant and Accepting:	___	___
Inquisitive and Open Minded:	___	___
Reflective and Tentative:	___	___
Honest and Courageous:	___	___

Reflection questions:

- Under which of the four attributes did you place (a) the most *checkmarks*, (b) the most *asterisks*? What do you think accounts for the difference?

- What could you do in college to strengthen your weakest area (the attribute below which you had the most asterisks)?

6.5 Chapter 5 Reflection

How can you use critical thinking to be a more successful student? Explain. List three action steps you can do to make this happen.

How can you use critical thinking to improve your personal life? Explain.

How can you use creative thinking to be a more successful student? Explain. List three action steps you can do to make this happen.

How can you use creative thinking to improve your personal life? Explain.

Notes

Notes

Diversity and the Community College Experience

LEARNING ABOUT AND FROM HUMAN DIFFERENCES

This chapter clarifies what "diversity" truly means and demonstrates how experiencing diversity can deepen:

- Learning,
- Promote critical and creative thinking, and
- Contribute to your personal and professional development.

Simply stated, we learn more from people who differ from us than we do from people similar to us. There is more diversity among college students today than at any other time in history. This chapter will help you capitalize on this learning opportunity.

Gain greater appreciation of human differences and develop skills for making the most of diversity in college and beyond.

 Think About It—Journal Entry 7.1

Complete the following sentence:

When I hear the word *diversity*, the first thing that comes to my mind is . . .

_____

_____

_____

What Is Diversity?

Literally translated, the word *diversity* derives from the Latin root *diversus*, meaning "various" or "variety." Thus, human diversity refers to the variety that exists in humanity (the human species). The relationship between humanity and diversity may be compared to the relationship between sunlight and the variety of colors that make up the visual spectrum. Similar to how sunlight passing through a prism disperses into the variety of colors that comprise the visual spectrum, the human spe-

FIGURE 7.1: **Humanity and Diversity**

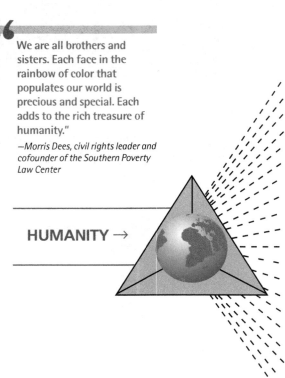

> "We are all brothers and sisters. Each face in the rainbow of color that populates our world is precious and special. Each adds to the rich treasure of humanity."
>
> —*Morris Dees, civil rights leader and cofounder of the Southern Poverty Law Center*

HUMANITY →

SPECTRUM
of
DIVERSITY

Gender (male-female)
Age (stage of life)
Race (e.g., White, Black, Asian)
Ethnicity (e.g., Native American, Hispanic, Irish, German)
Socioeconomic status (job status/income)
National *citizenship* (citizen of U.S. or another country)
Native (first-learned) *language*
National *origin* (nation of birth)
National *region* (e.g., raised in north/south)
Generation (historical period when people are born and live)
Political ideology (e.g., liberal/conservative)
Religious/spiritual beliefs (e.g., Christian/Buddhist/Muslim)
Family status (e.g., single-parent/two-parent family)
Marital status (single/married)
Parental status (with/without children)
Sexual orientation (heterosexual/homosexual/bisexual)
Physical ability/disability (e.g., able to hear/deaf)
Mental ability/disability (e.g., mentally able/challenged)
Learning ability/disability (e.g., absence/presence of dyslexia)
Mental health/illness (e.g., absence/presence of depression)

_ _ _ _ _ _ = dimension of diversity

*This list represents some of the major dimensions of human diversity; it does not constitute a complete list of all possible forms of human diversity. Also, disagreement exists about certain dimensions of diversity (e.g., whether certain groups should be considered races or ethnic groups).

cies on planet earth is dispersed into a variety of different groups that comprise the human spectrum (humanity). **Figure 7.1** illustrates this metaphorical relationship between diversity and humanity.

As depicted in the above figure, human diversity is manifested in a multiplicity of ways, including differences in physical features, national origins, cultural backgrounds, and sexual orientations. Some dimensions of diversity are easily detectable, others are very subtle, and some are invisible.

 Think About It—Journal Entry 7.2

Look at the diversity spectrum in Figure 7.1 and look over the list of groups that make up the spectrum. Do you notice any groups missing from the list that should be added, either because they have distinctive backgrounds or because they've been targets of prejudice and discrimination?

Diversity includes discussion of equal rights and social justice for minority groups, but it's a broader concept that involves much more than political issues. In a national survey of American voters, the vast majority of respondents agreed that diversity is more than just "political correctness" (National Survey of Women Voters, 1998). Diversity is also an *educational* issue—an integral element of a college education that contributes to the learning, personal development, and career preparation of *all* students. It enhances the quality of the college experience by bringing multiple perspectives and alternative approaches to *what* is being learned (the content) and *how* it's being learned (the process).

Note

Diversity is a human *issue that embraces and benefits* all *people; it's not a code word for "some" people. Although one major goal of diversity is to promote appreciation and equitable treatment of particular groups of people who've experienced discrimination, it's also a* learning *experience that strengthens the quality of a college education, career preparation, and leadership potential.*

What Is Racial Diversity?

A *racial group (race)* is a group of people who share distinctive physical traits, such as skin color or facial characteristics. The variation in skin color we now see among humans is largely due to biological adaptations that have evolved over thousands of years among groups of humans who migrated to different climatic regions of the world. Currently, the most widely accepted explanation of the geographic origin of modern humans is the "Out of Africa" theory. Genetic studies and fossil evidence indicate that all Homo sapiens inhabited Africa 150,000–250,000 years ago; over time, some migrated from Africa to other parts of the world (Mendez, et al., 2013; Meredith, 2011; Reid & Hetherington, 2010). Darker skin tones developed among humans who inhabited and reproduced in hotter geographical regions nearer the equator (e.g., Africans). Their darker skin color helped them adapt and survive by providing them with better protection from the potentially damaging effects of intense sunlight (Bridgeman, 2003). In contrast, lighter skin tones developed over time among humans inhabiting colder climates that were farther from the equator (e.g., Scandinavia). Their lighter skin color enabled them to absorb greater amounts of vitamin D supplied by sunlight, which was in shorter supply in those regions of the world (Jablonksi & Chaplin, 2002).

Currently, the U.S. Census Bureau has identified five races (U.S. Census Bureau, 2012):

White: a person whose lineage may be traced to the original people inhabiting Europe, the Middle East, or North Africa.

Black or African American: a person whose lineage may be traced to the original people inhabiting Africa.

American Indian or Alaska Native: a person whose lineage may be traced to the original people inhabiting North and South America (including Central America), and who continue to maintain their tribal affiliation or attachment.

Asian: a person whose lineage may be traced to the original people inhabiting the Far East, Southeast Asia, or the Indian subcontinent, including: Cambodia, China, India, Japan, Korea, Malaysia, Pakistan, the Philippine Islands, Thailand, and Vietnam.

Native Hawaiian or Other Pacific Islander: a person whose lineage may be traced to the original people inhabiting Hawaii, Guam, Samoa, or other Pacific islands.

It's important to keep in mind that racial categories are not based on scientific evidence; they merely represent group classifications constructed by society (Anderson & Fienberg, 2000). No identifiable set of genes distinguishes one race from another; in fact, there continues to be disagreement among scholars about what groups of people constitute a human race or whether distinctive races actually exist (Wheelright, 2005). In other words, you can't do a blood test or some type of internal genetic test to determine a person's race. Humans have simply decided to categorize themselves into races on the basis of certain external differences in their physical appearance, particularly the color of their outer layer of skin. The U.S. Census Bureau could have decided to divide people into "racial" categories based on other physical characteristics, such as eye color (blue, brown, and green), hair color (brown, black, blonde, or red), or body length (tall, short, or mid-sized).

AUTHOR'S EXPERIENCE

My father stood approximately six feet tall and had straight, light brown hair. His skin color was that of a Western European with a very slight suntan. My mother was from Alabama; she was dark in skin color with high cheekbones and had long curly black hair. In fact, if you didn't know that my father was of African American descent, you would not have thought he was black.

All of my life I've thought of myself as African American and all people who know me have thought of me as African American. I've lived half of a century with that as my racial identity. Several years ago, I carefully reviewed records of births and deaths in my family history and discovered that I had less than 50% African lineage. Biologically, I am no longer black; socially and emotionally, I still am. Clearly, my "race" has been socially constructed, not biologically determined.

— Aaron Thompson

While humans may display diversity in the color or tone of their external layer of skin, the reality is that all members of the human species are remarkably similar at an internal biological level. More than 98% of the genes of all humans are exactly the same, regardless of what their particular race may be (Bronfenbrenner, 2005). This large amount of genetic overlap accounts for our distinctively "human" appearance, which clearly distinguishes us from all other living species. All humans have internal organs that are similar in structure and function, and despite variations in the color of our outer layer of skin, when it's cut, all humans bleed in the same color.

AUTHOR'S EXPERIENCE

I was sitting in a coffee shop in the Chicago O'Hare airport while proofreading my first draft of this chapter. I looked up from my work for a second and saw what appeared to be a white girl about 18 years of age. As I lowered my head to return to work, I did a double-take and looked at her again because something about her seemed different or unusual. When I looked more closely at her the second time, I noticed that although she had white skin, the features of her face and hair appeared to be those of an African American. After a couple of seconds of puzzlement, I figured it out: she was an *albino* African American. That satisfied my curiosity for the moment, but then I began to wonder: Would it still be accurate to say she was "black" even though her skin was not black? Would her hair and facial features be sufficient for her to be considered or classified as black? If yes, then what would be the "race" of someone who had black skin tone, but did not have the typical hair and facial features characteristic of black people? Is skin color the defining feature of being African American or are other features equally important?

I was unable to answer these questions, but found it amusing that all of these thoughts were crossing my mind while I was working on a chapter dealing with diversity. On the plane ride home, I thought again about that albino African American girl and realized that she was a perfect example of how classifying people into "races" isn't based on objective, scientific evidence, but on subjective, socially constructed categories.

—*Joe Cuseo*

Categorizing people into distinct racial or ethnic groups is becoming even more difficult because members of different ethnic and racial groups are increasingly forming cross-ethnic and interracial families. By 2050, the number of Americans who identify themselves as being of two or more races is projected to more than triple, growing from 5.2 million to 16.2 million (U.S. Census Bureau, 2008).

Think About It—Journal Entry 7.3

What race(s) do you consider yourself to be?

Would you say you identify strongly with your racial identity, or are you rarely conscious of it?

Why?

What Is Cultural Diversity?

"Culture" may be defined as a distinctive pattern of beliefs and values learned by a group of people who share the same social heritage and traditions. In short, culture is the whole way in which a group of people has learned to live (Peoples & Bailey, 2011); it includes their style of speaking (language), fashion, food, art and music, as well as their beliefs and values. **Box 7.1** contains a summary of key components of culture that a group may share.

Box 7.1

Key Components of Culture

Language: How members of the culture communicate through written or spoken words; their particular dialect; and their distinctive style of nonverbal communication (body language).

Space: How cultural members arrange themselves with respect to social–spatial distance (e.g., how closely they stand next to each other when having a conversation).

Time: How the culture conceives of, divides, and uses time (e.g., the speed or pace at which they conduct business).

Aesthetics: How cultural members appreciate and express artistic beauty and creativity (e.g., their style of visual art, culinary art, music, theater, literature, and dance).

Family: The culture's attitudes and habits with respect to interacting with family members (e.g., customary styles of parenting their children and caring for their elderly).

Economics: How the culture meets its members' material needs, and its customary ways of acquiring and distribut-ing wealth (e.g., general level of wealth and gap between the very rich and very poor).

Gender Roles: The culture's expectations for "appropri-ate" male and female behavior (e.g., whether or not women are able to hold the same leadership positions as men).

Politics: How decision-making power is exercised in the culture (e.g., democratically or autocratically).

Science and Technology: The culture's attitude toward and use of science or technology (e.g., the degree to which the culture is technologically "advanced").

Philosophy: The culture's ideas or views on wisdom, goodness, truth, and social values (e.g., whether they place greater value on individual competition or collec-tive collaboration).

Spirituality and Religion: Cultural beliefs about a supreme being and an afterlife (e.g., its predominant faith-based views and belief systems about the supernatural).

Note

The reality of our own culture is not the reality of other cultures. Our perceptions of the outside world are shaped (and sometimes distorted) by our prior cultural experiences.

 Think About It—Journal Entry 7.4

Look at the components of culture cited in the previous list. Add another aspect of culture to the list that you think is important or influential. Explain why you think this is an important element of culture.

_____

_____

_____

AUTHOR'S EXPERIENCE

I was watching a basketball game between the Los Angeles Lakers and Los Angeles Clippers when a short scuffle broke out between the Lakers' Paul Gasol—who is Spanish—and the Clippers' Chris Paul—who is African American. After the scuffle ended, Gasol tried to show Paul there were no hard feelings by patting him on the head. Instead of interpreting Gasol's head pat as a peace-making gesture, Paul took it as a putdown and returned the favor by slapping (rather than patting) Paul in the head.

This whole misunderstanding stemmed from a basic difference in nonverbal communication between the two cultures. Patting someone on the head in European cultures is a friendly gesture; European soccer players often do it to an opposing player to express no ill will after a foul or collision. However, this same nonverbal message meant something very different to Chris Paul—an African American raised in urban America.

—Joe Cuseo

What Is an Ethnic Group?

A group of people who share the same culture is referred to as an *ethnic group*. Thus, "culture" refers to *what* an ethnic group shares in common (e.g., language and traditions) and "ethnic group" refers to the *people* who share the same culture that's been *learned* through common social experiences. Members of the same racial group—whose shared physical characteristics have been *inherited*—may be members of different ethnic groups. For instance, white Americans belong to the same racial group, but differ in terms of their ethnic group (e.g., French, German, Irish) and Asian Americans belong to the same racial group, but are members of different ethnic groups (e.g., Japanese, Chinese, Korean).

Currently, the major cultural (ethnic) groups in the United States include:

- Native Americans (American Indians)
  - Cherokee, Navaho, Hopi, Alaskan natives, Blackfoot, etc.
- European Americans (Whites)
  - Descendents from Western Europe (e.g., United Kingdom, Ireland, Netherlands), Eastern Europe (e.g., Hungary, Romania, Bulgaria), Southern Europe (e.g., Italy, Greece, Portugal), and Northern Europe or Scandinavia (e.g., Denmark, Sweden, Norway)
- African Americans (Blacks)
  - Americans whose cultural roots lie in the continent of Africa (e.g., Ethiopia, Kenya, Nigeria) and the Caribbean Islands (e.g., Bahamas, Cuba, Jamaica)
- Hispanic Americans (Latinos)
  - Americans with cultural roots in Mexico, Puerto Rico, Central America (e.g., El Salvador, Guatemala, Nicaragua), and South America (e.g., Brazil, Columbia, Venezuela)
- Asian Americans
  - Americans whose cultural roots lie in East Asia (e.g., Japan, China, Korea), Southeast Asia (e.g., Vietnam, Thailand, Cambodia), and South Asia (e.g., India, Pakistan, Bangladesh)
- Middle Eastern Americans
  - Americans with cultural roots in Iraq, Iran, Israel, etc.

Think About It—Journal Entry 7.5

What ethnic group(s) are you a member of, or do you identify with? What would you say are the key cultural values shared by your ethnic group(s)?

> "I'm the only person from my race in class."
>
> —*Hispanic student commenting on why he felt uncomfortable in his class on race, ethnicity, and gender*

European Americans are still the majority ethnic group in the United States; they account for more than 50% of the American population. Native Americans, African Americans, Hispanic Americans, and Asian Americans are considered to be *minority* ethnic groups because each of these groups represents less than 50% of the American population.

As with racial grouping, classifying humans into different ethnic groups can be very arbitrary and subject to debate. Currently, the U.S. Census Bureau classifies Hispanics as an ethnic group rather than a race. However, among Americans who checked "some other race" in the 2000 Census, 97% were Hispanic. This finding suggests that Hispanic Americans consider themselves to be a racial group, probably because that's how they're perceived and treated by non-Hispanics (Cianciatto, 2005). It's noteworthy that the American media used the term "racial profiling" (rather than ethnic profiling) to describe Arizona's controversial 2010 law that allowed police to target Hispanics who "look" like illegal aliens from Mexico, Central America, and South America. Once again, this illustrates how race and ethnicity are subjective, socially constructed concepts that reflect how people perceive and treat different social groups, which, in turn, affects how members of these groups perceive themselves.

The Relationship between Diversity and Humanity

As previously noted, diversity represents variations on the same theme: being human. Thus, humanity and diversity are interdependent, complementary concepts. To understand human diversity is to understand both our differences and *similarities* (Public Service Enterprise Group, 2009). Diversity appreciation includes appreciating both the unique perspectives of different cultural groups as well as universal aspects of the human experience that are common to all groups—whatever their particular cultural background happens to be. Members of all racial and ethnic groups live in communities, develop personal relationships, have emotional needs, and undergo life experiences that affect their self-esteem and personal identity. Humans of all races and ethnicities experience similar emotions and reveal those emotions with similar facial expressions (see **Figure 7.2**).

FIGURE 7.2

Humans all over the world display the same facial expressions when experiencing and expressing different emotions. See if you can detect the emotions being expressed in the following faces.
(To find the answers, turn your book upside down.)

Answers: The emotions shown. Top, left to right: anger, fear, and sadness.
Bottom, left to right: disgust, happiness, and surprise.

All images ©JupiterImages Corporation.

Other characteristics that anthropologists have found to be shared by all humans in every corner of the world include: storytelling, poetry, adornment of the body, dance, music, decoration with artifacts, families, socialization of children by elders, a sense of right and wrong, supernatural beliefs, and mourning of the dead (Pinker, 2000). Although different cultural groups may express these shared experiences in different ways, they are universal experiences common to all human cultures.

Think About It—Journal Entry 7.6

In addition to those already mentioned, can you think of another important human experience that is universal—that is experienced by all humans?

_____

_____

_____

_____

_____

You may have heard the question: "We're all human, aren't we?" The answer to this important question is "yes and no." Yes, we are all the same, but not in the same way. A good metaphor for understanding this apparent contradiction is to visualize humanity as a quilt in which we're all united by the common thread of humanity—the universal bond of being human. (Much like the quilt below.) The different patches comprising the quilt represent diversity—the distinctive or unique cultures that comprise our shared humanity. The quilt metaphor acknowledges the identity and beauty of all cultures. It differs from the old American "melting pot" metaphor, which viewed cultural differences as something to be melted down and eliminated. It also differs from the old "salad bowl" metaphor that depicted America as a hodgepodge or mishmash of cultures thrown together without any common connection. In contrast, the quilt metaphor suggests that the unique cultures of different human groups should be preserved, recognized, and valued; at the same time, these cultural differences join together to form a seamless, unified whole. This blending of diversity and unity is captured in the Latin expression _E pluribus unum_ ("Out of many, one")—the motto of the United States—which you'll find printed on all its currency.

©steven r. hendricks/Shutterstock.com

Note

When we appreciate diversity in the context of humanity, we capitalize on the variety and versatility of human differences while preserving the collective strength and synergy of human unity.

Cultural differences can exist within the same society (multicultural society), within a single nation (domestic diversity), or across different nations (international diversity).

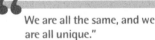

> "We are all the same, and we are all unique."
>
> _—Georgia Dunston, African American biologist and research specialist in human genetics_

> "We have become not a melting pot but a beautiful mosaic."
>
> _—Jimmy Carter, 39th president of the United States and winner of the Nobel Peace Prize_

AUTHOR'S EXPERIENCE

When I was 12 years old and living in New York City, I returned from school one Friday and my mother asked me if anything interesting happened at school that day. I told her that the teacher went around the room asking students what they had for dinner the night before. At that moment, my mother became a bit concerned and nervously asked me: "What did you tell the teacher?" I said: "I told her and the rest of the class that I had pasta last night because my family always eats pasta on Thursdays and Sundays." My mother exploded and fired back the following question at me in a very agitated tone, "Why didn't you tell her we had steak or roast beef?" For a moment, I was stunned and couldn't figure out what I'd done wrong or why I should have lied about eating pasta. Then it dawned on me: My mom was embarrassed about being Italian American. She wanted me to hide our family's ethnic background and make it sound like we were very "American."

As I grew older, I understood why my mother felt the way she did. She grew up in America's "melting pot" generation—a time when different American ethnic groups were expected to melt down and melt away their ethnicity. They were not to celebrate their diversity; they were to eliminate it.

—*Joe Cuseo*

What Is Individuality?

It's important to keep in mind that there are individual differences among members of any racial or ethnic group that are greater than the average difference between groups. Said in another way, there's more variability (individuality) within groups than between groups. For example, among members of the same racial group, individual differences in their physical attributes (e.g., height and weight) and psychological characteristics (e.g., temperament and personality) are greater than any average difference that may exist between their racial group and other racial groups (Caplan & Caplan, 2008).

Note

While it's valuable to learn about differences between different human groups, there are substantial individual differences among people within the same racial or ethnic group that should neither be ignored nor overlooked. Don't assume that individuals with the same racial or ethnic characteristics share the same personal characteristics.

> "I realize that I'm black, but I like to be viewed as a person, and this is everybody's wish."
>
> —*Michael Jordan, Hall of Fame basketball player*

As you proceed through your college experience, keep the following key distinctions in mind:

- Humanity. All humans are members of the *same group*—the human species.
- Diversity. All humans are members of *different groups*—such as, different racial and ethnic groups.
- Individuality. Each human is a *unique individual* who differs from all other members of any group to which he or she may belong.

> "Every human is, at the same time, like all other humans, like some humans, and like no other human."
>
> —*Clyde Kluckhohn, American anthropologist*

Major Forms or Types of Diversity in Today's World

Ethnic and Racial Diversity

America is rapidly becoming a more racially and ethnically diverse nation. Minorities now account for 36.6% of the total population—an all-time high; in 2011, for the first time in U.S. history, racial and ethnic minorities made up more than half (50.4%) of all children born in America (Nhan, 2012). By the middle of the 21st century, minority groups are expected to comprise 54% of the American population and more than 60% of the nation's children will be members of minority groups (U.S. Census Bureau, 2008).

More specifically, by 2050 the American population is projected to be more than 30% Hispanic (up from 15% in 2008), 15% Black (up from 13% in 2008), 9.6% Asian (up from 5.3% in 2008), and 2% Native Americans (up from 1.6% in 2008). The Native Hawaiian and Pacific Islander population is expected to more than double between 2008 and 2050. During this same timeframe, the percentage of white Americans will decline from 66% (2008) to 46% (2050). As a result of these demographic trends, today's ethnic and racial minorities will become the "new majority" of Americans by the middle of the 21st century (see **Figure 7.3**).

FIGURE 7.3: **The "New Majority"**

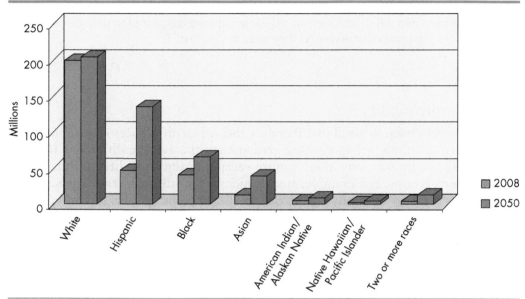

©Kendall Hunt Publishing Company

The growing racial and ethnic diversity of America's population is reflected in the growing diversity of students enrolled in its colleges and universities. In 1960, whites made up almost 95% of the total college population; in 2010, that percentage had decreased to 61.5%. Between 1976 and 2010, the percentage of ethnic minority students in higher education increased from 17% to 40% (National Center for Education Statistics, 2011). This rise in ethnic and racial diversity on American campuses is particularly noteworthy when viewed in light of the historical treatment of minority groups in the United States. In the early 19th century, education was not a right, but a privilege available only to those who could afford to attend private schools. It was experienced largely by Protestants of European descent (Luhman, 2007).

 Think About It—Journal Entry 7.7

1.   What diverse groups do you see represented on your campus?

2. Are there groups on campus you didn't expect to see or to see in such large numbers?

3. Are there groups on campus you expected to see but don't see or, see in smaller numbers than you expected?

> Of all the civil rights for which the world has struggled and fought for 5,000 years, the right to learn is undoubtedly the most fundamental."
>
> —W. E. B. Du Bois, African American sociologist, historian, and civil rights activist

The rise in ethnic and racial diversity on American campuses is particularly noteworthy when viewed in light of the historical treatment of minority groups in the United States. Members of certain minority groups were left out of the educational process altogether, or were forced to be educated in racially segregated settings. For example, Americans of color were once taught in separate, segregated schools that were typically inferior in terms of educational facilities. It was not until the groundbreaking Supreme Court ruling in *Brown v. Board of Education* (1954) that the face of education for people of color changed with the ruling that "separate educational facilities are inherently unequal." The decision made it illegal for Kansas and 20 other states to deliver education in segregated classrooms.

Box 7.2

Diversity in America's Community Colleges

58% of community college students are women

53% are 22 years of age or older

Among full-time students, 50% are employed part-time and 27% are employed full-timeAmong part-time

students, 50% are employed full-time and 33% are employed part-time

39% are the first in their family to attend college

36% are members of a minority ethnic or racial group

17% are single parents

Source: American Association of Community Colleges (2009)

My mother was a direct descendent of slaves and moved with her parents from the Deep South at the age of 17. My father lived in an all-Black coal mining camp, into which my mother and her family moved in 1938. My father remained illiterate because he was not allowed to attend public schools in eastern Kentucky. In the early 1960s my brother, my sister, and I were integrated into the White public schools. Physical violence and constant verbal harassment caused many other Blacks to forgo their education and opt for jobs in the coal mines at an early age. But my father remained constant in his advice to me: "It doesn't matter if they call you n_____; but don't you ever let them beat you by walking out on your education." He would say to me, "Son, you will have opportunities that I never had. Just remember, when you do get that education, you'll never have to go in those coal mines and have them break your back. You can choose what you want to do, and then you can be free man."

My parents, who could never provide me with monetary wealth, truly made me proud of them by giving me the gift of insight and an aspiration for achievement.

—*Aaron Thompson*

Socioeconomic Diversity

"Being born in the elite in the U.S. gives you a constellation of privileges that very few people in the world have ever experienced. Being born poor in the U.S. gives you disadvantages unlike anything in Western Europe, Japan and Canada."

—David I. Levine, economist and social mobility researcher

Human diversity also exists among groups of people in terms of their socioeconomic status (SES), which is determined by their level of education, level of income, and the occupational prestige of the jobs they hold. Groups are stratified (divided) into lower, middle, or upper classes, and groups occupying lower social strata have less economic resources and social privileges (Feagin & Feagin, 2007).

Young adults from high-income families are more than seven times likely to have earned a college degree and hold a prestigious job than those from low-income families (Olson, 2007). Sharp discrepancies also exist in income level among different racial, ethnic, and gender groups. In 2012, the median income for non-Hispanic white households was $57,009, compared to $39,005 for Hispanics and $33,321 for African Americans (DeNavas-Walt, Proctor, & Smith, 2013). From 2005 to 2009, household wealth fell by 66% for Hispanics, 53% for Blacks, and 16% for Whites, largely due to the housing and mortgage collapse—which had a more damaging effect on lower-income families (Kochlar, Fry, & Taylor, 2011).

Despite its overall wealth, the United States is one of the most impoverished of all developed countries in the world (Shah, 2008). The poverty rate in the United States is almost twice the rate of other economically developed countries around the world (Gould & Wething, 2013). In 2012, more than 16% of the American population, and almost 20% of American children, lived below the poverty line ($23,050 yearly income for a family of four) (U.S. Census Bureau, 2013).

 Think About It—Journal Entry 7.8

Are you the first in your family to attend college?

Whether yes or no, how does that make you feel?

International Diversity

If it were possible to reduce the world's population to a village of precisely 100 people, with all existing human ratios remaining about the same, the demographics of this world village would look something like this:

61 would be Asians; 13 would be Africans; 12 would be Europeans; 9 would be Latin Americans; and 5 would be North Americans (citizens of the United States and Canada)

50 would be male, 50 would be female

75 would be non-white; 25 white

67 would be non-Christian; 33 would be Christian

80 would live in substandard housing

16 would be unable to read or write

50 would be malnourished and 1 would be dying of starvation

33 would be without access to a safe water supply

39 would lack access to modern sanitation

24 would have no electricity (and of the 76 who have electricity, most would only use it for light at night)

8 people would have access to the Internet

1 would have a college education

1 would have HIV

2 would be near birth; 1 near death

5 would control 32% of the entire world's wealth; all 5 would be U.S. citizens

48 would live on less than $2 a day

20 would live on less than $1 a day (Family Care Foundation, 1997–2012).

In this world village, English would not be the most common language spoken—it would be third, following Chinese and Spanish (Lewis, Paul, & Fennig, 2014).

The need for American college students to develop an appreciation of international diversity is highlighted by a study conducted by an anthropologist who went "undercover" to pose as a student in a university residence hall. She found that the biggest complaint international students had about American students was their lack of knowledge of other countries and the misconceptions they held about people from different nations (Nathan, 2005). When you take the time to learn about other countries and the cultures of people who inhabit them, you move beyond being just a citizen of your own nation, you become *cosmopolitan*—a citizen of the world.

Generational Diversity

Humans are also diverse with respect to the historical time period in which they grew up. The term "generation" refers to a cohort (group) of individuals born during the same period in history whose attitudes, values, and habits have been shaped by events that took place in the world during their formative years of development. People growing up in different generations are likely to develop different attitudes and beliefs because of the different historical events they experienced during their upbringing.

Box 7.3 contains a brief summary of different generations, the key historical events they experienced, and the personal characteristics commonly associated with each generational group (Lancaster & Stillman, 2002).

Box 7.3

Generational Diversity: A Snapshot Summary

- The Traditional Generation (a.k.a. "Silent Generation") (born 1922–1945). This generation was influenced by events such as the Great Depression and World Wars I and II. Characteristics associated with people growing up at this time include loyalty, patriotism, respect for authority, and conservatism.
- The Baby Boomer Generation (born 1946–1964). This generation was influenced by events such as the Vietnam War, Watergate, and the civil rights movement. Characteristics associated with people growing up at this time include idealism, emphasis on self-fulfillment, and concern for social justice and equal rights.
- Generation X (born 1965–1980). This generation was influenced by Sesame Street, the creation of MTV, AIDS, and soaring divorce rates. They were the first "latchkey children"—youngsters who used their own key to let themselves into their home after school—because their mother (or single mother) was working outside the home. Characteristics associated with people growing up at this time include self-reliance, resourcefulness, and ability to adapt to change.
- Generation Y (a.k.a. "Millennials") (born 1981–2002). This generation was influenced by the September 11, 2001, terrorist attack on the United States, the shooting of students at Columbine High School, and the collapse of the Enron Corporation. Characteristics associated with people growing up at this time include a prefer-

ence for working and playing in groups, familiarity with technology, and willingness to engage in volunteer service in their community (the "civic generation"). This is also the most ethnically diverse generation, which may explain why they're more open to diversity than previous generations and are more likely to view diversity positively.

> "You guys [in the media] have to get used to it. This is a new day and age, and for my generation that's a very common word. It's like saying 'bro.' That's how we address our friends. That's how we talk."
>
> *—Matt Barnes, 33-year-old, biracial professional basketball player, explaining to reporters after being fined for using the word "niggas" in a tweet to some of his African American teammates*

- Generation Z (a.k.a. "The iGeneration") (born 1994–present). This generation includes the latter half of Generation Y. They grew up during the wars in Afghanistan and Iraq, terrorism, the global recession, and climate change. Consequently, they have less trust in political systems and industrial corporations than previous generations. During their formative years, the world wide web was in place, so they're quite comfortable with technology and rely heavily on the Internet, Wikipedia, Google, Twitter, MySpace, Facebook, Instant Messaging, image boards, and YouTube. They expect immediate gratification through technology and accept the lack of privacy associated with social networking. For these reasons, they're also referred to as the "digital generation."

 Think About It—Journal Entry 7.9

Look back at the characteristics associated with your generation. Which of these characteristics accurately reflect your personal characteristics and those of your closest friends? Which do not?

Sexual Diversity: LGBT, LGBTQ, LGBTQA, TBL

These acronyms refer to lesbian, gay, bisexual, transgender, queer or questioning, and asexual or ally but all of the different identities within "LGBT" are often grouped together. These groups are very present on college campuses and there are specific needs and concerns related to each individual identity.

Humans experience and express sexuality in diverse ways. "Sexual diversity" refers to differences in human *sexual orientation*—the gender (male or female) an individual is physically attracted to, and *sexual identity*—the gender an individual identifies with or considers himself or herself or to be. The spectrum of sexual diversity includes:

Heterosexuals—males who are sexually attracted to females, and females who are sexually attracted to males

Gays—males who are sexually attracted to males

Lesbians—females who are sexually attracted to females

Bisexuals—individuals who are sexually attracted to males and females

Transgender—individuals who do not identify with the gender they were assigned at birth, or don't feel they belong to a single gender (e.g., transsexuals, transvestites, and bigender) .

Other terms are often grouped and discussed in these diverse communities. They are:

Asexual: A person who generally does not feel sexual attraction or desire to any group of people. Asexuality is not the same as celibacy.

Ally: Typically any non-LGBT person who supports and stands up for the rights of LGBT people, although LGBT people can be allies, such as a lesbian who is an ally to a transgender person.

Biphobia: Aversion toward bisexuality and bisexual people as a social group or as individuals. People of any sexual orientation can experience such feelings of aversion. Biphobia is a source of discrimination against bisexuals, and may be based on negative bisexual stereotypes or irrational fear.

Cisgender: Types of gender identity where an individual's experience of their own gender matches the sex they were assigned at birth.

Coming Out: The process of acknowledging one's sexual orientation and/or gender identity to other people. For most LGBT people, this is a lifelong process.

Gender expression: A term that refers to the ways in which we each manifest masculinity or femininity. It is usually an extension of our "gender identity," our innate sense of being male, female, etc. Each of us expresses a particular gender every day—by the way we style our hair, select our clothing, or even the way we stand. Our appearance, speech, behavior, movement, and other factors signal that we feel—and wish to be understood as—masculine or feminine, or as a man or a woman.

Gender identity: The sense of "being" male, female, genderqueer, agender, etc. For some people, gender identity is in accord with physical anatomy. For transgender people, gender identity may differ from physical anatomy or expected social roles. It is important to note that gender identity, biological sex, and sexual orientation are separate and that you cannot assume how someone identifies in one category based on how they identify in another category.

Genderqueer: A term that refers to individuals or groups who "queer" or problematize the hegemonic notions of sex, gender, and desire in a given society. Genderqueer people possess identities that fall outside of the widely accepted sexual binary (i.e., "men" and "women"). Genderqueer may also refer to people who identify as both transgendered AND queer—that is, individuals who challenge both gender and sexuality regimes and see gender identity and sexual orientation as overlapping and interconnected.

Heterosexual: A person who is only attracted to members of the opposite sex. Also called "straight."

Homophobia: A range of negative attitudes and feelings toward homosexuality or people who are identified or perceived as being lesbian, gay, bisexual, or transgender (LGBT). It can be expressed as antipathy, contempt, prejudice, aversion, or hatred; may be based on irrational fear; and is sometimes related to religious beliefs.

Homosexual: A clinical term for people who are attracted to members of the same sex. Some people find this term offensive.

Intersex: A person whose sexual anatomy or chromosomes do not fit with the traditional markers of "female" and "male." For example: people born with both "female" and "male" anatomy (penis, testicles, vagina, uterus); people born with XXY chromosomes.

In the closet: Describes a person who keeps their sexual orientation or gender identity a secret from some or all people.

Queer: 1) An umbrella term sometimes used by LGBTQA people to refer to the entire LGBT community. 2) An alternative that some people use to "queer" the idea of the labels and categories such as lesbian, gay, bisexual, etc. Similar to the concept of genderqueer. It is important to note that the word queer is an in-group term, and a word that can be considered offensive to some people, depending on their generation, geographic location, and relationship with the word.

Questioning: For some, the process of exploring and discovering one's own sexual orientation, gender identity, or gender expression.

Pansexual: A person who experiences sexual, romantic, physical, and/or spiritual attraction for members of all gender identities/expressions, not just people who fit into the standard gender binary (i.e., men and women).

Sexual orientation: The type of sexual, romantic, and/or physical attraction someone feels toward others. Often labeled based on the gender identity/expression of the person and who they are attracted to. Common labels: lesbian, gay, bisexual, pansexual, etc.

Transphobia: The fear or hatred of transgender people or gender nonconforming behavior. Like biphobia, transphobia can also exist among lesbian, gay, and bisexual people as well as among heterosexual people.

Transsexual: A person whose gender identity is different from their biological sex, who may undergo medical treatments to change their biological sex, oftentimes to align it with their gender identity, or they may live their lives as another sex.

For more information:
- http://itspronouncedmetrosexual.com/2013/01/a-comprehensive-list-of-lgbtq-term-definitions/
- http://gillfoundation.org/grants/gender-expression-toolkit/gender-expression/

College campuses across the country are increasing their support for GLBT (gay, lesbian, bisexual, transgendered) students, creating centers and services to facilitate their acceptance and adjustment. These centers and services play an important role in combating homophobia and related forms of sexual prejudice on campus, while promoting awareness and tolerance of all forms of sexual diversity. By accepting individuals who span the spectrum of sexual diversity, we acknowledge and appreciate the reality that heterosexuality isn't the one-and-only form of human sexual expression (Dessel, 2012). This growing acknowledgment is reflected in the Supreme Court's historic decision to legalize same-sex marriage nationwide (Dolan & Romney, 2015).

The Benefits of Experiencing Diversity

Thus far, this chapter has focused on *what* diversity is; we now turn to *why* diversity is worth experiencing. National surveys show that by the end of their first year in college, almost two-thirds of students report "stronger" or "much stronger" knowledge of people from different races and cultures than they had when they first began college, and the majority of them became more open to diverse cultures, viewpoints and values (HERI, 2013, 2014). Students who develop more openness to and knowledge of diversity are likely to experience the following benefits.

Diversity Increases Self-Awareness and Self-Knowledge

Interacting with people from diverse backgrounds increases self-knowledge and self-awareness by enabling you to compare your life experiences with others whose experiences may differ sharply from your own. When you step outside yourself to contrast your experiences with others from different backgrounds, you move beyond ethnocentrism and gain a *comparative perspective*—a reference point that positions you to see how your particular cultural background has shaped the person you are today.

> It is difficult to see the picture when you are inside the frame."
> —*An old saying (author unknown)*

A comparative perspective also enables us to learn how our cultural background has advantaged or disadvantaged us. For instance, learning about cross-cultural differences in education makes us aware of the limited opportunities people in other countries have to attend college and how advantaged we are in America—where a college education is available to everyone, regardless of their race, gender, age, or prior academic history.

Note

The more you learn from people who are different than yourself, the more you learn about yourself.

Diversity Deepens Learning

Research consistently shows that we learn more from people who differ from us than we do from people similar to us (Pascarella, 2001; Pascarella & Terenzini, 2005). Learning about different cultures and interacting with people from diverse cultural groups provides our brain with more varied routes or pathways through which to connect (learn) new ideas. Experiencing diversity "stretches" the brain beyond its normal "comfort zone," requiring it to work harder to assimilate something unfamiliar. When we encounter the unfamiliar, the brain has to engage in extra effort to understand it by comparing and contrasting it to something we already know (Acredolo & O'Connor, 1991; Nagda, Gurin, & Johnson, 2005). This added expenditure of mental energy results in the brain forming neurological connections that are deeper and more durable (Willis, 2006). Simply stated, humans learn more from diversity than they do from similarity or familiarity. In contrast, when we restrict the diversity of people with whom we interact (out of habit or prejudice), we limit the breadth and depth of our learning.

Diversity Promotes Critical Thinking

Studies show that students who experience high levels of exposure to various forms of diversity while in college—such as participating in multicultural courses and campus events and interacting with peers of different ethnic backgrounds—report the greatest gains in:

- thinking *complexity*—ability to think about all parts and sides of an issue (Association of American Colleges & Universities, 2004; Gurin, 1999),
- *reflective* thinking—ability to think deeply about personal and global issues (Kitchener, Wood, & Jensen, 2000), and
- *critical* thinking—ability to evaluate the validity of their own reasoning and the reasoning of others (Gorski, 2009; Pascarella, et al., 2001).

These findings are likely explained by the fact that when we're exposed to perspectives that differ from our own, we experience "cognitive dissonance"—a state of cognitive (mental) disequilibrium or imbalance that "forces" our mind to consider multiple perspectives simultaneously; this makes our thinking less simplistic, more complex, and more comprehensive (Brookfield, 1987; Gorski, 2009).

Diversity Stimulates Creative Thinking

Cross-cultural knowledge and experiences enhance personal creativity (Leung, et al., 2008; Maddux & Galinsky, 2009). When we have diverse perspectives at our disposal, we have more opportunities to shift perspectives and discover "multiple partial solutions" to problems (Kelly, 1994). Furthermore, ideas acquired from diverse people and cultures can "cross-fertilize," giving birth to new ideas for tackling old problems (Harris, 2010). Research shows that when ideas are generated freely and exchanged openly in groups comprised of people from diverse backgrounds, powerful "cross-stimulation" effects can occur, whereby ideas from one group member trigger new ideas among other group members (Brown, Dane, & Durham, 1998). Research also indicates that seeking out diverse alternatives, perspectives, and viewpoints enhances our ability to reach personal goals (Stoltz, 2014).

Note

By drawing on ideas generated by people from diverse backgrounds and bouncing your ideas off them, divergent or expansive thinking is stimulated; this leads to synergy (multiplication of ideas) and serendipity (unexpected discoveries).

In contrast, when different cultural perspectives are neither sought nor valued, the variety of lenses available to us for viewing problems is reduced, which, in turn, reduces our capacity to think creatively. Ideas are less likely to diverge (go in different directions); instead, they're more likely to converge and merge into the same cultural channel—the one shared by the homogeneous group of people doing the thinking.

"When the only tool you have is a hammer, you tend to see every problem as a nail."
—*Abraham Maslow, humanistic psychologist, best known for his self-actualization theory of human motivation*

"What I look for in musicians is generosity. There is so much to learn from each other and about each other's culture. Great creativity begins with tolerance."
—*Yo-Yo Ma, French-born, Chinese-American virtuoso cellist, composer, and winner of multiple Grammy Awards*

"When all men think alike, no one thinks very much."
—*Walter Lippmann, distinguished journalist and originator of the term "stereotype"*

Diversity Enhances Career Preparation and Career Success

Whatever line of work you decide to pursue, you're likely to find yourself working with employers, coworkers, customers, and clients from diverse cultural backgrounds. America's workforce is now more diverse than at any other time in history and will grow ever more diverse throughout the 21st century; by 2050, the proportion of American workers from minority ethnic and racial groups will jump to 55% (U.S. Census Bureau, 2008).

National surveys reveal that policymakers, business leaders, and employers seek college graduates who are more than just "aware" of or "tolerant" of diversity. They want graduates who have actual *experience* with diversity (Education Commission of the States, 1995) and are able to collaborate with diverse coworkers, clients, and customers (Association of American Colleges & Universities, 2002; Hart Research Associates, 2013). Over 90% of employers agree that all students should have experiences in college that teach them how to solve problems with people whose views differ from their own (Hart Research Associates, 2013).

The current "global economy" also requires skills relating to international diversity. Today's work world is characterized by economic interdependence among nations, international trading (imports/exports), multinational corporations, international travel, and almost instantaneous worldwide communication—due to rapid advances in the world wide web (Dryden & Vos, 1999; Friedman, 2005). Even smaller companies and corporations have become increasingly international in nature (Brooks, 2009). As a result, employers in all sectors of the economy now seek job candidates who possess the following skills and attributes: sensitivity to human differences, ability to understand and relate to people from different cultural backgrounds, international knowledge, and ability to communicate in a second language (Fixman, 1990; Hart Research Associates, 2013; National Association of Colleges & Employers, 2007; Office of Research, 1994).

As a result of these domestic and international trends, *intercultural competence* has become an essential skill for success in the 21st century (Thompson & Cuseo, 2014). Intercultural competence may be defined as the ability to appreciate and learn from human differences and to interact effectively with people from diverse cultural backgrounds. It includes "knowledge of cultures and cultural practices (one's own and others), complex cognitive skills for decision making in intercultural contexts, social skills to function effectively in diverse groups, and personal attributes that include flexibility and openness to new ideas" (Wabash National Study of Liberal Arts Education, 2007).

> The benefits that accrue to college students who are exposed to racial and ethnic diversity during their education carry over in the work environment. The improved ability to think critically, to understand issues from different points of view, and to collaborate harmoniously with co-workers from a range of cultural backgrounds all enhance a graduate's ability to contribute to his or her company's growth and productivity."
>
> —*Business/Higher Education Forum*

> Technology and advanced communications have transformed the world into a global community, with business colleagues and competitors as likely to live in India as in Indianapolis. In this environment, people need a deeper understanding of the thinking, motivations, and actions of different cultures, countries and regions."
>
> —*The Partnership for 21st Century Skills*

Think About It—Journal Entry 7.10

What intercultural skills do you think you already possess?

What intercultural skills do you think you need to develop?

Overcoming Barriers to Diversity

Before we can capitalize on the benefits of diversity, we need to overcome obstacles that have long impeded our ability to appreciate and seek out diversity. These major impediments are discussed below.

Ethnocentrism

FIGURE 7.4:
Optical Illusion

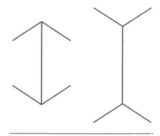

©Kendall Hunt Publishing Company.

A major advantage of culture is that it builds group solidarity, binding its members into a supportive, tight-knit community. Unfortunately, culture not only binds us, it can also blind us from taking different cultural perspectives. Since culture shapes thought and perception, people from the same ethnic (cultural) group run the risk of becoming *ethnocentric*—centered on their own culture to such a degree they view the world solely through their own cultural lens (frame of reference) and fail to consider or appreciate other cultural perspectives (Colombo, Cullen, & Lisle, 2013). Optical illusions are a good example of how our particular cultural perspective can influence (and distort) our perceptions. Compare the lengths of the two lines in **Figure 7.4**.

If you perceive the line on the right to be longer than the one on the left, your perception has been shaped by Western culture. People from Western cultures, such as Americans, perceive the line on the right to be longer. However, both lines are actually equal in length. (If you don't believe it, take out a ruler and measure them.) Interestingly, this perceptual error isn't made by people from non-Western cultures—whose living spaces and architectural structures are predominantly circular (e.g., huts or igloos)—in contrast to rectangular-shaped buildings with angled corners that typify Western cultures (Segall, Campbell, & Herskovits, 1966).

The optical illusion depicted in Figure 7.4 is just one of a number of illusions experienced by people in certain cultures, but not others (Shiraev & Levy, 2013). Cross-cultural differences in susceptibility to optical illusions illustrate how strongly our cultural experiences can influence and sometimes misinform our perception of reality. People think they are seeing things objectively (as they actually are) but they're really seeing things subjectively—as viewed from their particular cultural perspective.

If our cultural experience can influence our perception of the physical world, it can certainly shape our perception of social events and political issues. Research in psychology indicates that the more exposure humans have to somebody or something, the more familiar it becomes and the more likely it will be perceived positively and judged favorably. The effect of familiarity is so prevalent and powerful that social psychologists have come to call it the "familiarity principle"—that is, what is familiar is perceived as better or more acceptable (Zajonc, 1968, 1970, 2001). Thus, we need to be mindful that the familiarity of our cultural experiences can bias us toward seeing our culture as normal or better. By remaining open to the viewpoints of people who perceive the world from different cultural vantage points, we minimize our cultural blind spots, expand our range of perception, and position ourselves to perceive the world with greater clarity and cultural sensitivity.

©James Michael Doresey/Shutterstock.com

People whose cultural experiences involve living and working in circular structures would not be fooled by the optical illusion in Figure 7.4.

Stereotyping

"Stereotype" derives from two different roots: *stereo*—to look at in a fixed way—and *type*—to categorize or group together, as in the word "typical." Thus, to stereotype is to view individuals of the same type (group) in the same (fixed) way.

Stereotyping overlooks or disregards individuality; all people sharing the same group characteristic (e.g., race or gender) are viewed as having the same personal characteristics—as in the expression: "You know how they are; they're all alike." Stereotypes can also involve *bias*—literally meaning "slant"—a slant that can tilt toward the positive or the negative. Positive bias results in favorable stereotypes (e.g., "Asians are great in science and math"); negative bias leads to unfavorable stereotypes (e.g., "Asians are nerds who do nothing but study"). Here are some other examples of negative stereotypes:

- Muslims are religious terrorists.
- Whites can't jump (or dance).
- Blacks are lazy.
- Irish are alcoholics.
- Gay men are feminine; lesbian women are masculine.
- Jews are cheap.
- Women are weak.

While few people would agree with these crass stereotypes, overgeneralizations are often made about members of certain groups. Such negative overgeneralizations malign the group's reputation, rob group members of their individuality, and can weaken their self-esteem and self-confidence (as illustrated by the following experience).

AUTHOR'S EXPERIENCE

When I was six years old, I was told by a six-year-old girl from a different racial group that all people of my race could not swim. Since I couldn't swim at that time and she could, I assumed she was correct. I asked a boy, who was a member of the same racial group as the girl, whether her statement was true. He responded emphatically: "Yes, it's true!" Since I was from an area where few other African Americans were around to counteract this belief about my racial group, I continued to buy into this stereotype until I finally took swimming lessons as an adult. After many lessons, I am now a lousy swimmer because I didn't even attempt to swim until I was an adult. Moral of this story: Group stereotypes can limit the confidence and potential of individual members of the stereotyped group.

—*Aaron Thompson*

Whether you are male or female, don't let gender stereotypes limit your career options.

Think About It—Journal Entry 7.11

1. Have you ever been stereotyped based on your appearance or group membership? If so, what was the stereotype and how did it make you feel?

2. Have you ever unintentionally perceived or treated a person in terms of a group stereotype rather than as an individual? What assumptions did you make about that person? Was that person aware of, or affected by, your stereotyping?

_____

_____

_____

_____

Prejudice

If all members of a stereotyped group are judged and evaluated in a negative way, the result is *prejudice*. The word "prejudice" literally means to "pre-judge." Typically, the prejudgment is negative and involves *stigmatizing*—ascribing inferior or unfavorable traits to people who belong to the same group. Thus, prejudice may be defined as a negative stereotype held about a group of people that's formed before the facts are known.

People who hold a group prejudice typically avoid contact with members of that group. This enables the prejudice to continue unchallenged because there's little opportunity for the prejudiced person to have a positive experience with members of the stigmatized group that could contradict or disprove the prejudice. Thus, a vicious cycle is established in which the prejudiced person continues to avoid contact with individuals from the stigmatized group; this, in turn, continues to maintain and reinforce the prejudice

> When you see me, do not look at me with disgrace. Know that I am an African-American Birthed by a woman of style and grace. Be proud To stand by my side. Hold your head high Like me. Be proud. To say you know me. Just as I stand by you, proud to be me.
>
> —Poem by Brittany Beard, first-year student

Think About It—Journal Entry 7.12

Prejudice and discrimination can be subtle and only begin to surface when the social or emotional distance among members of different groups grows closer. Rate your level of comfort (high, moderate, or low) with the following situations.

Someone from another racial group:

1. Going to your school	high	moderate	low
2. Working in your place of employment	high	moderate	low
3. Living on your street as a neighbor	high	moderate	low
4. Living with you as a roommate	high	moderate	low
5. Socializing with you as a personal friend	high	moderate	low
6. Being your most intimate friend or romantic partner	high	moderate	low
7. Being your partner in marriage	high	moderate	low

> See that man over there? Yes.
> Well, I hate him.
> But you don't know him. That's why I hate him."
>
> —Gordon Allport, influential social psychologist and author of The Nature of Prejudice

For any item you rated "low," what do you think was responsible for the low rating?

> "We see what is behind our eyes."
>
> *—Chinese proverb*

Once prejudice has been formed, it often remains intact and resistant to change through the psychological process of *selective perception*—the tendency for biased (prejudiced) people to see what they *expect* to see and fail to see what contradicts their bias (Hugenberg & Bodenhausen, 2003). Have you ever noticed how fans rooting for their favorite sports team tend to focus on and "see" the calls of referees that go against their own team, but don't seem to react (or even notice) the calls that go against the opposing team? This is a classic example of selective perception. In effect, selective perception transforms the old adage, "seeing is believing," into "believing is seeing." This can lead prejudiced people to focus their attention on information that's consistent with their prejudgment, causing them to "see" what supports or reinforces it and fail to see information that contradicts it.

Making matters worse, selective perception is often accompanied by *selective memory*—the tendency to remember information that's consistent with one's prejudicial belief and to forget information that's inconsistent with it or contradicts it (Judd, Ryan, & Parke, 1991). The mental processes of selective perception and selective memory often work together and often work *unconsciously*. As a result, prejudiced people may not even be aware they're using these biased mental processes or realize how these processes are keeping their prejudice permanently intact (Baron, Byrne, & Brauscombe, 2008).

 Think About It—Journal Entry 7.13

Have you witnessed selective perception or selective memory—people seeing or recalling what they believe is true (due to bias), rather than what's actually true? What happened and why do you think it happened?

Discrimination

Literally translated, the term *discrimination* means "division" or "separation." Whereas prejudice involves a belief, attitude or opinion, discrimination involves an *act* or *behavior.* Technically, discrimination can be either positive or negative. A discriminating eater may only eat healthy foods, which is a positive quality. However, discrimination is most often associated with a harmful act that results in a prejudiced person treating another individual, or group of individuals, in an unfair manner. Thus, it could be said that discrimination is prejudice put into action. For instance, to fire or not hire people on the basis of their race, gender, or sexual orientation is an act of discrimination.

Box 7.4 below contains a summary of the major forms of discrimination, prejudice, and stereotypes that have plagued humanity. As you read through the following list, place a check mark next to any item that you, a friend, or family member has experienced.

Box 7.4

Stereotypes, Prejudices, and Forms of Discrimination: A Snapshot Summary

- **Ethnocentrism:** viewing one's own culture or ethnic group as "central" or "normal," while viewing different cultures as "deficient" or "inferior."

  Example: Viewing another culture as "abnormal" or "uncivilized" because its members eat animals our culture views as unacceptable to eat, although we eat animals their culture views as unacceptable to eat.

- **Stereotyping:** viewing all (or virtually all) members of the same group in the same way—as having the same personal qualities or characteristics.

  Example: "If you're Italian, you must be in the Mafia, or have a family member who is."

- **Prejudice:** negative prejudgment about another group of people.

  Example: Women can't be effective leaders because they're too emotional.

- **Discrimination:** unequal and unfair treatment of a person or group of people—prejudice put into action.

  Example: Paying women less than men for performing the same job, even though they have the same level of education and job qualifications.

- **Segregation:** intentional decision made by a group to separate itself (socially or physically) from another group.

  Example: "White flight"—white people moving out of neighborhoods when people of color move in.

- **Racism:** belief that one's racial group is superior to another group and expressing that belief in attitude (prejudice) or action (discrimination).

Example: Confiscating land from American Indians based on the unfounded belief that they are "uncivilized" or "savages."

- **Institutional Racism:** racial discrimination rooted in organizational policies and practices that disadvantage certain racial groups.

> "Let us all hope that the dark clouds of racial prejudice will soon pass away and . . . in some not too distant tomorrow the radiant stars of love and brotherhood will shine over our great nation."
>
> —*Martin Luther King, Jr., Civil rights leader, humanitarian, and youngest recipient of the Nobel Peace Prize*

Example: Race-based discrimination in mortgage lending, housing, and bank loans.

- **Racial Profiling:** investigating or arresting someone solely on the basis of the person's race, ethnicity, or national origin—without witnessing actual criminal behavior or possessing incriminating evidence.

  Example: Police making a traffic stop or conducting a personal search based solely on an individual's racial features.

- **Slavery:** forced labor in which people are considered to be property, held against their will, and deprived of the right to receive wages.

  Example: Enslavement of Blacks, which was legal in the United States until 1865.

- **"Jim Crow" Laws:** formal and informal laws created by Whites to segregate Blacks after the abolition of slavery.

(continued)

Box 7.4 *(continued)*

Example: laws in certain parts of the United States that once required Blacks to use separate bathrooms and be educated in separate schools.

- Apartheid: an institutionalized system of "legal racism" supported by a nation's government. (Apartheid derives from a word in the Afrikaan language, meaning "apartness.")

Example: South Africa's national system of racial segregation and discrimination that was in place from 1948 to 1994.

Never, never, and never again shall it be that this beautiful land will again experience the oppression of one by another."

—*Nelson Mandela, anti-apartheid revolutionary, first Black president of South Africa after apartheid, and winner of the Nobel Peace Prize*

- Hate Crimes: criminal action motivated solely by prejudice toward the crime victim.

Example: Acts of vandalism or assault aimed at members of a particular ethnic group or persons of a particular sexual orientation.

- Hate Groups: organizations whose primary purpose is to stimulate prejudice, discrimination, or aggression toward certain groups of people based on their ethnicity, race, religion, etc.

Example: The Ku Klux Klan—an American terrorist group that perpetrates hatred toward all non-white races.

- Genocide: mass murdering of a particular ethnic or racial group.

Example: The Holocaust, in which millions of Jews were systematically murdered during World War II. Other examples include the murdering of Cambodians under the Khmer Rouge regime, the murdering of Bosnian Muslims in the former country of Yugoslavia, and the slaughter of the Tutsi minority by the Hutu majority in Rwanda.

- Classism: prejudice or discrimination based on social class, particularly toward people of lower socioeconomic status.

Example: Acknowledging the contributions made by politicians and wealthy industrialists to America, while ignoring the contributions of poor immigrants, farmers, slaves, and pioneer women.

- Religious Intolerance: denying the fundamental human right of people to hold religious beliefs, or to hold religious beliefs that differ from one's own.

Example: An atheist who forces nonreligious (secular) beliefs on others, or a member of a religious group who believes that people who hold different religious beliefs are infidels or "sinners" whose souls will not be saved.

Rivers, ponds, lakes and streams— they all have different names, but they all contain water. Just as religions do— they all contain truths."

—*Muhammad Ali, three-time world heavyweight boxing champion, member of the International Boxing Hall of Fame, and recipient of the Spirit of America Award as the most recognized American in the world*

- Anti-Semitism: prejudice or discrimination toward Jews or people who practice the religion of Judaism.

Example: Disliking Jews because they're the ones who "killed Christ."

- Xenophobia: fear or hatred of foreigners, outsiders, or strangers.

Example: Believing that immigrants should be banned from entering the country because they'll undermine our economy and increase our crime rate.

- Regional Bias: prejudice or discrimination based on the geographical region in which an individual is born and raised.

Example: A northerner thinking that all southerners are racists.

- Jingoism: excessive interest and belief in the superiority of one's own nation—without acknowledging its mistakes or weaknesses—often accompanied by an aggressive foreign policy that neglects the needs of other nations or the common needs of all nations.

Example: "Blind patriotism"—failure to see the shortcomings of one's own nation and viewing any questioning or criticism of one's own nation as being disloyal or "unpatriotic." (As in the slogan, "America: right or wrong" or "America: love it or leave it!")

Above all nations is humanity."

—*Motto of the University of Hawaii*

- Terrorism: intentional acts of violence committed against civilians that are motivated by political or religious prejudice.

Example: The September 11, 2001, attacks on the United States.

(continued)

Box 7.4 *(continued)*

- Sexism: prejudice or discrimination based on sex or gender.

    Example: Believing that women should not pursue careers in fields traditionally filled only by men (e.g., engineering or politics) because they lack the innate qualities or natural skills to do so.

- Heterosexism: belief that heterosexuality is the only acceptable sexual orientation.

    Example: Believing that gays should not have the same legal rights and opportunities as heterosexuals.

- Homophobia: extreme fear or hatred of homosexuals.

    Example: Creating or contributing to anti-gay websites, or "gay bashing" (acts of violence toward gays).

- Ageism: prejudice or discrimination toward certain age groups, particularly toward the elderly.

    Example: Believing that all "old" people have dementia and shouldn't be allowed to drive or make important decisions.

- Ableism: prejudice or discrimination toward people who are disabled or handicapped (physically, mentally, or emotionally).

    Example: Intentionally avoiding social contact with people in wheelchairs.

 Think About It—Journal Entry 7.14

As you read through the above list, did you, a friend, or family member experience any of the form(s) of prejudice listed? If yes, what happened and why do you think it happened?

_____

_____

_____

_____

> I grew up in a very racist family. Even just a year ago, I could honestly say 'I hate Asians' with a straight face and mean it. My senior AP language teacher tried hard to teach me not to be judgmental. He got me to be open to others, so much so that my current boyfriend is half Chinese."
>
> —First-year college student

Strategies for Overcoming Stereotypes and Prejudices

We may hold prejudices, stereotypes, or subtle biases that bubble beneath the surface of our conscious awareness. The following practices and strategies can help us become more aware of our unconscious biases and relate more effectively to individuals from diverse groups.

Consciously avoid preoccupation with physical appearances. Remember the old proverb: "It's what inside that counts." Judge others by the quality of their inner qualities, not by the familiarity of their outer features. Get beneath the superficial surface of appearances and relate to people not in terms of how they look but who they are and how they act.

> Stop judging by mere appearances, and make a right judgment."
>
> —Bible, John 7:24

Form impressions of others on a person-to-person basis, not on the basis of their group membership. This may seem like an obvious and easy thing to do, but research shows that humans have a natural tendency to perceive individuals from unfamiliar groups as being more alike (or all alike) than members of their own group (Taylor, Peplau, & Sears, 2006). Thus, we need to remain mindful of this tendency and make a conscious effort to perceive and treat individuals of diverse

> You can't judge a book by the cover."
>
> —1962 hit song by Elias Bates, a.k.a. Bo Diddley (Note: a "bo diddley" is a one-stringed African guitar)

groups as unique human beings, not according to some general (stereotypical) rule of thumb.

Note

It's valuable to learn about different cultures and the common characteristics shared by members of the same culture; however, this shouldn't be done while ignoring individual differences. Don't assume that all individuals who share the same cultural background share the same personal characteristics.

 Think About It—Journal Entry 7.15

Your comfort level while interacting with people from diverse groups is likely to depend on how much prior experience you've had with members of those groups. Rate the amount or variety of diversity you have experienced in the following settings:

1. The high school you attended	high	moderate	low
2. The college or university you now attend	high	moderate	low
3. The neighborhood in which you grew up	high	moderate	low
4. Places where you have been employed	high	moderate	low

Which setting had the *most* and the *least* diversity?

_____

_____

_____

_____

What do you think accounted for this difference?

_____

_____

_____

_____

_____

> "I am very happy with the diversity here, but it also frightens me. I have never been in a situation where I have met people who are Jewish, Muslim, atheist, born-again, and many more."
>
> —First-year student (quoted in Erickson, Peters, & Strommer, 2006)

Place yourself in situations and locations on campus where you will come in regular contact with individuals from diverse groups. Distancing ourselves from diversity ensures we'll never experience diversity and benefit from it. Research in social psychology shows that relationships are more likely to form among people who come in regular contact with one another (Latané, et al., 1995), and research on diversity reveals that when there's regular contact between members of different racial or ethnic groups, stereotyping is sharply reduced and intercultural friendships are more likely to develop (Pettigrew, 1997, 1998). You can create these conditions by making an intentional attempt to sit near diverse students in the classroom, library, or student café, and by joining them for class discussion groups or group projects.

Take advantage of social media to "chat" virtually with students from diverse groups on your own campus, or students on other campuses. Electronic communication can be a convenient and comfortable way to initially interact with members of diverse groups with whom you have had little prior experience. After interacting *online*, you're more likely to feel more comfortable about interacting *in person*.

Engage in co-curricular experiences involving diversity. Review your student handbook to find co-curricular programs, student activities, student clubs, or campus organizations that emphasize diversity awareness and appreciation. Studies indicate that participation in co-curricular experiences relating to diversity promotes critical thinking (Pascarella & Terenzini, 2005) and reduces unconscious prejudice (Blair, 2002).

Consider spending time at the multicultural center on your campus, or joining a campus club or organization that's devoted to diversity awareness (e.g., multicultural or international student club). Putting yourself in these situations will enable you to make regular contact with members of cultural groups other than your own; it also sends a clear message to members of these groups that you value their culture because you've taken the initiative to connect with them on "their turf."

If your campus sponsors multicultural or cross-cultural retreats, strongly consider participating in them. A retreat setting can provide a comfortable environment in which you can interact personally with diverse students without being distracted by your customary social circle and daily routine.

If possible, participate in a study abroad or travel study program that gives you the opportunity to live in another country and interact directly with its native citizens. In addition to coursework, you can gain international knowledge and a global perspective by participating in programs that enable you to actually *experience* a different country. You can do this for a full term or for a shorter time period (e.g., January, May, or summer term). To prepare for international experiences, take a course in the language, culture, or history of the nation to which you will be traveling.

Research on students who participate in study abroad programs indicates that these experiences promote greater appreciation of cross-cultural differences, greater interest in world affairs, and greater commitment to peace and international cooperation (Bok, 2006; Kaufmann, et al., 1992). Additional research shows that study abroad benefits students' personal development, including improved self-confidence, sense of independence, and ability to function in complex environments (Carlson, et al., 1990; IES Abroad News, 2002).

Incorporate diversity courses into your planned schedule of classes. Review your college catalog (bulletin) and identify courses that are designed to promote understanding or appreciation of diversity. These courses may focus on diverse cultures found within the United States (sometimes referred to as multicultural courses) or diverse cultures associated with different countries (sometimes referred to as international or cross-cultural courses).

> "
> Empirical evidence shows that the actual effects on student development of emphasizing diversity and of student participation in diversity activities are overwhelmingly positive."
>
> —*Alexander Astin*, What Matters in College

In a national study of college students who experienced multicultural courses, it was discovered that students of all racial and ethnic groups made significant gains in learning and intellectual development (Smith, 1997; Smith, et al., 1997).

Taking courses focusing on international diversity can help you develop the global perspective needed for success in today's international economy and enhance the quality of your college transcript (Brooks, 2009; Cuseo, et al., 2013; National Association of Colleges & Employers, 2003).

Be on the lookout for diversity implications associated with topics you're reading about or discussing in class. Consider the multicultural and cross-cultural ramifications of material you're studying and use examples of diversity to support or illustrate your points. If you're allowed to choose a topic for a research project, select one that relates to diversity or has implications for diversity.

Seek out the views and opinions of classmates from diverse backgrounds. Discussions among students of different races and cultures can reduce prejudice and promote intercultural appreciation, but only if each member's cultural identity and perspective is sought out and valued by members of the discussion group (Baron, Byrne, & Brauscombe, 2008). During class discussions, you can demonstrate leadership by seeking out views and opinions of classmates from diverse backgrounds and ensuring that the ideas of people from minority groups are included and respected. Also, after class discussions, you can ask students from different backgrounds if there was any point made or position taken in class that they would have strongly questioned or challenged.

If there is little or no diversity among students in class, encourage your classmates to look at the topic from diverse perspectives. For instance, you might ask: "If there were international students here, what might they be adding to our discussion?" or, "If members of certain minority groups were here, would they be offering a different viewpoint?"

If you are given the opportunity to form your own discussion groups and group project teams, join or create groups composed of students from diverse backgrounds. You can gain greater exposure to diverse perspectives by intentionally joining or forming learning groups with students who differ in terms of gender, age, race, or ethnicity. Including diversity in your discussion groups not only creates social variety, it also enhances the quality of your group's work by allowing members to gain access to and learn from multiple perspectives. For instance, in learning groups that are diverse with respect to age, older students will bring a broad range of life experiences that younger students can draw upon and learn from, while younger students can provide a more contemporary and idealistic perspective to the group's discussions. Gender diversity is also likely to infuse group discussions with different learning styles and approaches to understanding issues. Studies show that males are more likely to be "separate knowers"—they tend to "detach" themselves from the concept or issue being discussed so they can analyze it. In contrast, females are more likely to be "connected knowers"—they tend to relate personally to concepts and connect them with their own experiences and the experiences of others. For example, when interpreting a poem, males are more likely to ask: "What techniques can I use to analyze it?" In contrast, females would be more likely to ask: "What is the poet trying to say to me?" (Belenky, et al., 1986). It's also been found that females are more likely to work collaboratively during group discussions and collect the ideas of other members; in contrast, males are more likely to adopt a competitive approach and debate the ideas of others (Magolda, 1992). Both of these styles of learning are valuable and you can capitalize on these different styles by forming gender-diverse discussion groups.

> "The classroom can provide a 'public place' where community can be practiced."
>
> —*Susanne Morse*, Renewing Civic Capacity: Preparing College Students for Service and Citizenship.

Form collaborative learning teams with students from diverse backgrounds. A learning *team* is more than a discussion group that tosses around ideas; it moves beyond discussion to *collaboration*—its members "co-labor" (work together) to reach the same goal. Research from kindergarten through college indicates that when students collaborate in teams, their academic performance and interpersonal skills are strengthened (Cuseo, 1996). Also, when individuals from different racial groups work collaboratively toward the same goal, racial prejudice is reduced and interracial friendships are more likely to be formed (Allport, 1954; Amir, 1976; Brown, et al., 2003; Dovidio, Eller, & Hewstone, 2011). These positive developments may be explained, in part, by the fact that when members of diverse groups come together on the same team, nobody is a member of an "out" group ("them"); instead, everybody belongs to the same "in" group ("us") (Pratto, et al., 2000; Sidanius, et al., 2000).

In an analysis of multiple studies involving more than 90,000 people from 25 different countries, it was found that when interaction between members of diverse groups took place under the conditions described in **Box 7.5**, prejudice was significantly reduced (Pettigrew & Tropp, 2000) and the greatest gains in learning took place (Johnson, Johnson, & Smith, 1998; Slavin, 1995).

Box 7.5

Tips for Teamwork: Creating Diverse and Effective Learning Teams

1. Intentionally form learning teams with students who have different cultural backgrounds and life experiences. Teaming up only with friends or classmates whose backgrounds and experiences are similar to yours can actually impair your team's performance because teammates can get off track and onto topics that have nothing to do with the learning task (e.g., what they did last weekend or what they're planning to do next weekend).

2. Before jumping into group work, take some time to interact informally with your teammates. When team members have some social "warm up" time (e.g., time to learn each other's names and learn something about each other), they feel more comfortable expressing their ideas and are more likely to develop a stronger sense of team identity. This feeling of group solidarity can create a foundation of trust among group members, enabling them to work together as a team, particularly if they come from diverse (and unfamiliar) cultural backgrounds.

   The context in which a group interacts can influence the openness and harmony of their interaction. Group members are more likely to interact openly and collaboratively when they work in a friendly, informal environment that's conducive to relationship building. A living room or a lounge area provides a warmer and friendlier team-learning atmosphere than a sterile classroom.

3. Have teammates work together to complete a single work product. One jointly created product serves to highlight the team's collaborative effort and collective achievement (e.g., a completed sheet of answers to questions, or a comprehensive list of ideas). Creating a common final product helps keep individuals thinking in terms of "we" (not "me") and keeps the team moving in the same direction toward the same goal.

4. Group members should work interdependently—they should depend on each other to reach their common goal and each member should have equal opportunity to contribute to the team's final product. Each teammate should take responsibility for making an indispensable contribution to the team's end product, such as contributing: (a) a different piece of *information* (e.g., a specific chapter from the textbook or a particular section of class notes), (b) a particular form of *thinking* to the learning task (e.g., analysis, synthesis, or application), or (c) a different *perspective* (e.g., national, international, or global). Said in another way, each group member should assume personal responsibility for a piece that's needed to complete the whole puzzle.

   Similar to a sports team, each member of a learning team should have a specific role to play. For instance,

(continued)

Box 7.5 *(continued)*

each teammate could perform one of the following roles:

- manager—whose role is to assure that the team stays on track and keeps moving toward its goal;
- moderator—whose role is to ensure that all teammates have equal opportunity to contribute;
- summarizer—whose role is to monitor the team's progress, identifying what has been accomplished and what still needs to be done;
- recorder—whose role is to keep a written record of the team's ideas.

5. After concluding work in diverse learning teams, take time to reflect on the experience. The final step in any learning process, whether it be learning from a lecture or learning from a group discussion, is to step back from the process and thoughtfully review it. Deep learning requires not only effortful action but also thoughtful reflection (Bligh, 2000; Roediger, Dudai, & Fitzpatrick, 2007). You can reflect on your experiences with diverse learning groups by asking yourself questions that prompt you to process the ideas shared by members of your group and the impact those ideas had on you. For instance, ask yourself (and your teammates) the following questions:

What major similarities in viewpoints did all group members share? (What were the common themes?)

- What major differences of opinion were expressed by diverse members of our group? (What were the variations on the themes?)
- Were there particular topics or issues raised during the discussion that provoked intense reactions or emotional responses from certain members of our group?
- Did the group discussion lead any individuals to change their mind about an idea or position they originally held?

When contact among people from diverse groups takes place under the five conditions described in this box, group work is transformed into *teamwork* and promotes higher levels of thinking and deeper appreciation of diversity. A win-win scenario is created: Learning and thinking are strengthened while bias and prejudice are weakened (Allport, 1979; Amir, 1969; Aronson, Wilson, & Akert, 2013; Cook, 1984; Sherif, et al., 1961).

Think About It—Journal Entry 7.16

Have you had an experience with a member of an unfamiliar racial or cultural group that caused you to change your attitude or viewpoint toward that group? Explain.

_____

_____

_____

_____

_____

Take a stand against prejudice or discrimination by constructively disagreeing with students who make stereotypical statements and prejudicial remarks. By saying nothing, you may avoid conflict, but your silence may be perceived by others to mean that you agree with the person who made the prejudicial remark. Studies show that when members of the same group observe another member of their own group making prejudicial comments, prejudice tends to increase among all group members—probably due to peer pressure of group conformity (Stangor, Sechrist, & Jost, 2001). In contrast, if a person's prejudicial remark is challenged by a member of one's own group, particularly a fellow member who is liked and respected, that person's prejudice decreases along with similar prejudices held by other members of the group (Baron, Byrne, & Brauscombe, 2008). Thus, by taking a leadership role and challenging peers who make prejudicial remarks, you're likely to reduce that person's prejudice as well as the prejudice of others who hear the remark. In addition, you help create a campus climate in which students experience greater satisfaction with with their college experience and are more likely to complete their college degree. Studies show that a campus climate which is hostile toward students from minority groups lowers students' level of college satisfaction and college completion rates of both minority and majority students (Cabrera, et al., 1999; Eimers & Pike, 1997; Nora & Cabrera, 1996).

Note

By actively opposing prejudice on campus, you demonstrate diversity leadership and moral character. You become a role model whose actions send a clear message that valuing diversity is not only the smart thing to do, it's the right *thing to do.*

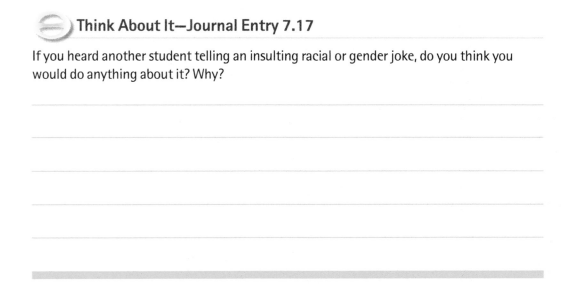

Think About It—Journal Entry 7.17

If you heard another student telling an insulting racial or gender joke, do you think you would do anything about it? Why?

Chapter Summary and Highlights

Diversity refers to the variety of groups that comprise humanity (the human species). Humans differ from one another in multiple ways, including physical features, religious beliefs, mental and physical abilities, national origins, social backgrounds, gender, and sexual orientation. Diversity involves the important political issue of securing equal rights and social justice for all people; however, it's also an important *educational* issue—an integral element of the college experience that enriches learning, personal development, and career preparation.

When a group of people share the same traditions and customs, it creates a culture that serves to bind people into a supportive, tight-knit community. However, culture can also lead its members to view the world solely through their own cultural lens (known as ethnocentrism), which can blind them to other cultural perspectives. Ethnocentrism can contribute to stereotyping—viewing individual members of another cultural group in the same (fixed) way, in which they're seen as having similar personal characteristics.

Stereotyping can result in prejudice—a biased prejudgment about another person or group of people that's formed before the facts are known. Stereotyping and prejudice often go hand in hand because if the stereotype is negative, members of the stereotyped group are then judged negatively. Discrimination takes prejudice one step further by converting the negative prejudgment into behavior that results in unfair treatment of others. Thus, discrimination is prejudice put into action.

Once stereotyping and prejudice are overcome, we are positioned to experience diversity and reap its multiple benefits—which include sharper self-awareness, deeper learning, higher-level thinking, and better career preparation.

The increasing diversity of students on campus, combined with the wealth of diversity-related educational experiences found in the college curriculum and co-curriculum, presents you with an unprecedented opportunity to infuse diversity into your college experience. Seize this opportunity and capitalize on the power of diversity to increase the quality of your college education and your prospects for success in the 21st century.

Learning More through the World Wide Web: Internet-Based Resources

For additional information on diversity, see the following websites:

Stereotyping: ReducingStereotypeThreat.org at www.reducingstereotypethreat.org

Prejudice & Discrimination: Southern Poverty Law Center at www.splcenter.org/

Human Rights:
Amnesty International at www.amnesty.org/en/discrimination
Center for Economic & Social Justice at www.cesj.org

Sexism in the Media:
"Killing Us Softly" at www.youtube.com/watch?v=PTlmho_RovY

LGBT Acceptance & Support: "It Gets Better Project," at www.itgetsbetter.org

References

Acredolo, C., & O'Connor, J. (1991). On the difficulty of detecting cognitive uncertainty. *Human Development, 34,* 204–223.

Allport, G. W. (1954). *The nature of prejudice.* Cambridge, MA: Addison-Wesley.

Allport, G. W. (1979). *The Nature of prejudice* (3rd ed.). Reading, MA: Addison-Wesley.

American Association of Community Colleges (2009). 2009 Fact Sheet. Retrieved from http://www.aacc.nche.edu/About/Documents/factsheet2009.pdf.

Amir, Y. (1969). Contact hypothesis in ethnic relations. *Psychological Bulletin, 71,* 319–342.

Amir, Y. (1976). The role of intergroup contact in change of prejudice and ethnic relations. In P. A. Katz (Ed.), *Towards the elimination of racism* (pp. 245–308). New York: Pergamon Press.

Anderson, M. & Fienberg, S. 2000. *Race and ethnicity and the controversy over the US Census.* Current Sociology; 48(3): 87–110.

Aronson, E., Wilson, T. D., & Akert, R. M. (2013). *Social psychology* (8th ed.). Upper Saddle River, NJ: Pearson/Prentice Hall.

Association of American Colleges & Universities (AAC&U) (2002). *Greater expectations: A new vision for learning as a nation goes to college.* Washington, DC: Author.

Association of American Colleges & Universities (AAC&U) (2004). *Our students' best work.* Washington, DC: Author.

Baron, et. al., 2008. Social Psychology, 12th Edition. Allyn & Bacon, Boston, MA.

Belenky, M. F., Clinchy, B., Goldberger, N. R., & Tarule, J. M. (1986). *Women's ways of knowing: The development of self, voice, and mind.* New York: Basic Books.

Blair, I. V. (2002). The malleability of automatic stereotypes and prejudice. *Personality and Social Psychology Review, 6*(3), 242–261.

Bligh, D.A. (2000). *What's the use of lectures?* San Francisco: Jossey Bass.

Bok, D. 2006. *Our Underachieving Colleges: A Candid Look at How Much Students Learn and Why they Should be Learning More.* Princeton, New Jersey: Princeton University Press, 2006.

Bridgeman, B. 2003. Psychology and Evolution: The Origins of Mind. Thousand Oaks, Ca.: Sage Publications.

Bronfenbrenner, U. (Ed.) (2005). *Making human beings human: Bioecological perspectives on human development.* Thousand Oaks, CA: Sage.

Brookfield, S. D. (1987). *Developing critical thinkers.* San Francisco: Jossey-Bass.

Brooks, I. 2009. Organisational Behaviour, 4th Edition. Englewood Cliffs, NJ: Prentice Hall.

Brown, T. D., Dane, F. C., & Durham, M. D. (1998). Perception of race and ethnicity. *Journal of Social Behavior and Personality, 13*(2), 295–306.

Brown, K. T, Brown, T. N., Jackson, J. S., Sellers, R. M., & Manuel, W. J. (2003).

Teammates on and off the field? Contact with Black teammates and the racial attitudes of White student athletes. *Journal of Applied Social Psychology, 33,* 1379–1403.

Cabrera, A., Nora, A., Terenzini, P., Pascarella, E., & Hagedorn, L. S. (1999). Campus racial climate and the adjustment of students to college: A comparison between White students and African American students. *The Journal of Higher Education, 70*(2), 134–160.

Caplan, P. J., & Caplan, J. B. (2008). *Thinking critically about research on sex and gender* (3rd ed.). New York: HarperCollins College Publishers.

Carlson, et al., 1990. Individual differences in the behavioral effects of stressors attributable to lateralized differences in mesocortical dopamine systems. *Society for Neuroscience absracts 16.*233.

Ciancotto, J. (2005). *Hispanic and Latino same-sex couple households in the United States: A report from the 2000 Census.* New York: The National Gay and Lesbian Task Force Policy Institute and the National Latino/a Coalition for Justice.

Colombo, G., Cullen, R., & Lisle, B. (2013). *Rereading America: Cultural contexts for critical thinking and writing* (9th ed.). Boston: Bedford Books of St. Martin's Press.

Cook, S. W. (1984). Cooperative interaction in multiethnic contexts. In N. Miller & M. B. Brewer (Eds.), *Groups in contact: The psychology of desegregation (pp. 291–302).* New York: Academic Press.

Cuseo, J. B. (1996). *Cooperative learning: A pedagogy for addressing contemporary challenges and critical issues in higher education.* Stillwater, OK: New Forums Press.

Cuseo, J. B. et al., 2013. *Thriving in Community College & Beyond: Strategies for Academic Success and Personal Development.* Kendall Hunt Publishing Company, Dubuque, Ia.

DeNavas-Walt, C., Proctor, B. D., & Smith, J. C. (2013). *Income, poverty, and health insurance coverage in the United States, 2012.* U.S. Census Bureau, Current Population Reports, P60–245, Washington, DC: U.S. Government Printing Office.

Dessel, A. (2012). Effects of intergroup dialogue: Public school teachers and sexual orientation prejudice. *Small Group Research, 41*(5), 556–592.

Dolan, M., & Romney, L. (2015). "Law in California is now a right for all." *Los Angeles Times.* June 27, pp. A1 & A8.

Dovidio, J. F., Eller, A., & Hewstone, M. (2011). Improving intergroup relations through direct, extended and other forms of indirect contact. *Group Processes & Intergroup Relations, 14,* 147–160.

Dryden, G., & Vos, J. (1999). *The learning revolution: To change the way the world learns.* Torrance, CA and Auckland, New Zealand: The Learning Web.

Education Commission of the States (1995). *Making quality count in undergraduate education.* Denver, CO: ECS Distribution Center.

Eimers, M. T., & Pike, G. R. (1997). Minority and nonminority adjustment to college: Differences or similarities. *Research in Higher Education, 38* (1), 77–97.

Erickson, B. L., Peters, C. B., & Strommer, D. W. (2006). *Teaching first-year college students.* San Francisco: Jossey-Bass.

Family Care Foundation. (1997–2012). *If the world were a village of 100 people.* Retrieved from http://www.familycare. org/special-interest/if-the-world-were-a-village-of-100-people/.

Feagin, J. R., & Feagin, C. B., 2007. Racial and Ethnic Relations, 8th Edition. Englewood Cliffs, NJ. Prentice Hall.

Fixman, C. S. (1990). The foreign language needs of U.S. based corporations. *Annals of the American Academy of Political and Social Science, 511,* 25–46.

Friedman, T. L. 2005. *The world is flat: A brief history of the twenty-first century: Revitalizing the civic mission of schools.* Alexandria, VA.

Gorski, P. C. (2009). *Key characteristics of a multicultural curriculum.* Critical Multicultural Pavilion: Multicultural Curriculum Reform (An EdChange Project). Retrieved from www.edchange.org/multicultural/curriculum/characteristics.html.

Gould, E. & Wething, H. 2013 *Health Care, the Market and Consumer Choice. Inquiry 50* (1):85–86.

Gurin, P. (1999). New research on the benefits of diversity in college and beyond: An empirical analysis. *Diversity Digest* (spring). Retrieved from http://www.diversityweb.org/Digest/Sp99/benefits.html.

Harris, 2010. Leading system transformation. *School Leadership and Management 30* (Jul).

Hart Research Associates (2013). *It takes more than a major: Employer priorities for college learning and student success.* Washington, DC: Author.

HERI (Higher Education Research Institute) (2013). *Your first college year survey 2012.* Los Angeles, CA: Cooperative Institutional Research Program, University of California-Los Angeles.

HERI (Higher Education Research Institute) (2014). *Your first college year survey 2014.* Los Angeles, CA: Cooperative Institutional Research Program, University of California-Los Angeles.

Hugenberg, K., & Bodenhausen, G. V. (2003). Facing prejudice: Implicit prejudice and the perception of facial threat. *Psychological Science, 14,* 640–643.

IES Abroad News (2002). Study abroad: A lifetime of benefits. Retrieved from www.iesabroad.org/study-abroad/news/study-abroad-lifetime-benefits.

Jablonski, N. G., & Chaplin, G. (2002). Skin deep. *Scientific American* (October), 75–81.

Johnson, D., Johnson, R., & Smith, K. (1998). Cooperative learning returns to college: What evidence is there that it works? *Change, 30,* 26–35.

Judd, C. M., Ryan, C. S., & Parke, B. (1991). Accuracy in the judgment of in-group and out-group variability. *Journal of Personality and Social Psychology, 61,* 366–379.

Kaufmann, N. L., Martin, J. M., & Weaver, H. D. (1992). *Students abroad: Strangers at home: Education for a global society.* Yarmouth, ME: Intercultural Press.

Kelly, K. (1994). *Out of control: The new biology of machines, social systems, and the economic world.* Reading, MA: Addison-Wesley.

Kitchener, K., Wood, P., & Jensen, L. (2000, August). *Curricular, co-curricular, and institutional influence on real-world problem-solving.* Paper presented at the annual meeting of the American Psychological *Associa*tion, Boston.

Kochlar, R., Fry, R., & Taylor, P. (2011). "Wealth gaps rise to record highs between Whites, Blacks, Hispanics, twenty-to-one." *Pew Research Social and Demographics Trends* (July). Retrieved from http://www.pewsocialtrends.org/2011/07/26/wealth-gaps-rise-to-record-highs-between-whites-blacks-hispanics/.

Lancaster, L., & Stilman, D. (2002). *When generations collide: Who they are. Why they clash.* New York: HarperCollins.

Latané, B., Liu, J. H., Nowak, A., Bonevento, N., & Zheng, L. (1995). Distance matters: Physical space and social impact. *Personality and Social Psychology Bulletin, 21,* 795–805.

Leung, A. K., Maddux, W. W., Galinsky, A. D., & Chie-yue, C. (2008). Multicultural experience enhances creativity: The when and how. *American Psychologist, 63*(3), 169–181.

Lewis, M., Paul, G. W., & Fenning, C. D. (Eds.) (2014). Ethnologue: languages of the world, seventeeth edition. Dallas, Texas: SIL International. Online version: http://www.ethnologue.com.

Luhman, R. (2007). *The sociological outlook.* Lanham, MD: Rowman & Littlefield.

Maddux, W.W. & Galinsky, A.D. 2009. *Cultural borders and mental barriers: the relationship between living abroad and creativity.* Journal of Personality and Social Psychology, 96(5):1047-61.

Magolda, M. B. B. (1992). *Knowing and reasoning in college.* San Francisco: Jossey-Bass.

Mendez, F., Krahn, T., Schrack, B., Krahn, A. M., Veeramah, K., Woerner, A., Fomine, F. L. M., Bradman, N., Thomas, M., Karafet, T., & Hammer, M. (2013). An African American paternal lineage adds an extremely ancient root to the human Y chromosome phylogenetic tree. *The American Journal of Human Genetics, 92,* 454–459.

Meredith, M. (2011). *Born in Africa: The quest for the origins of human Life.* New York: Public Affairs.

Nagda, B. R., Gurin, P., & Johnson, S. M. (2005). Living, doing and thinking diversity: How does pre-college diversity experience affect first-year students' engagement with college diversity? In R. S. Feldman (Ed.), *Improving the first year of college: Research and practice* (pp. 73–110). Mahwah, NJ: Lawrence Erlbaum.

Nathan, R. (2005). *My freshman year: What a professor learned by becoming a student.* London: Penguin.

National Association of Colleges & Employers, 2003, 2007

National Association of Colleges and Employers (NACE). (2003). Job outlook 2003 survey. Bethlehem, PA: Author.

National Center for Education Statistics. (2011). *Digest of education statistics, table 237. Total fall enrollment in degree-granting institutions, by level of student, sex, attendance status, and race/ ethnicity: Selected years, 1976 through 2010.* Alexandria, VA: U.S. Department of Education. Retrieved from http://neces. ed/gov/programs/digest/d11/tables/dt11_237.asp

National Association of Colleges and Employers (NACE). (2003). Job outlook 2003 survey. Bethlehem, PA: Author.

National Association of Colleges and Employers (NACE). (2007). Job outlook 2007 survey. Bethlehem, PA: Author

National Survey of Women Voters (1998). *Autumn overview report conducted by DYG Inc.* Retrieved from http://www.diversityweb.org/research_and_trends/research_evaluation_impact_/campus_community_connections/national_poll.cfm

Nhan, D. (2012). "Census: Minorities constitute 37 percent of U.S. population." *National Journal: The Next America-Demographics 2012.* Retrieved from http://www.nationaljournal.com/thenextamerica/demographics/census-minorities- constitute-37-percent-of-u-s-population-20120517

Nora, A., & Cabrera, A. (1996). The role of perceptions of prejudice and discrimination on the adjustment of minority college students. *The Journal of Higher Education, 67* (2), 119–148.

Office of Research (1994). *What employers expect of college graduates: International knowledge and second language skills.* Washington, DC: Office of Educational Research and Improvement, U.S. Department of Education.

Olson, L. (2007). What does "ready" mean? *Education Week, 40,* 7–12.

Pascarella, E. T. (2001, November/December). Cognitive growth in college: Surprising and reassuring findings from the National Study of Student Learning. *Change,* pp. 21–27.

Pascarella, E. T. & Terenzini, P. T. 2005. *How College Affects Students, Volume 2, A Third Decade of Research.* San Francisco, CA: Jossey-Bass.

Pascarella, E., Palmer, B., Moye, M., & Pierson, C. (2001). Do diversity experiences influence the development of critical thinking? Journal of College Student Development, 42(3), 257–291.

Peoples, J., & Bailey, G. (2011). *Humanity: An introduction to cultural anthropology.* Belmont, CA: Wadsworth, Cengage Learning.

Pettigrew, T. F. (1997). Generalized intergroup contact effects on prejudice. *Personality and Social Psychology Bulletin, 23,* 173–185.

Pettigrew, T. F. (1998). Intergroup contact theory. *Annual Review of Psychology, 49,* 65–85.

Pettigrew, T. F. & Tropp, L. R. (2000). Does intergroup contact reduce prejudice? Recent meta-analytic findings. S. Oskamp (Ed.), *Reducing prejudice and discrimination* (pp. 93–114). Mahwah, NJ: Lawrence Erlbaum Associates.

Pinker, S. (2000). *The language instinct: The new science of language and mind.* New York: Perennial.

Pratto, F., Liu, J. H., Levin, S., Sidanius, J., Shih, M., Bachrach, H., & Hegarty, P. (2000). Social dominance orientation and the legitimization of inequality across cultures. *Journal of Cross-Cultural Psychology, 31,* 369–409.

Public Service Enterprise Group (PSEG) (2009). *Diversity.* Retrieved from www.pseg.com/info/environment/sustainability/2009/.../diversity.jsp

Reid, G. B. R., & Hetherington, R. (2010). *The climate connection: Climate change and modern evolution.* Cambridge, UK: Cambridge University Press.

Roediger, H. L., Dudai, Y., & Fitzpatrick, S. M. (2007). *Science of memory: concepts.* New York, NY: Oxford University Press.

Segall, M. H., Campbell, D. T., & Herskovits, M. J. (1966). *The influence of culture on visual perception.* Indianapolis: Bobbs-Merrill.

Shah, A. (2009). *Global issues: Poverty facts and stats.* Retrieved from http://www.globalissues.org/artoc;e/26/poverty-facts-and-stats.

Sherif, M., Harvey, D. J., White, B. J., Hood, W. R., & Sherif, C. W. (1961). *The Robbers' cave experiment.* Norman, OK: Institute of Group Relations.

Shiraev, E. D., & Levy, D. (2013). *Cross-cultural psychology: Critical thinking and contemporary applications* (5th ed.). Upper Saddle River, NJ: Pearson Education.

Sidanius, J., Levin, S., Liu, H., & Pratto, F. (2000). Social dominance orientation, anti-egalitarianism, and the political psychology of gender: An extension and cross-cultural replication. *European Journal of Social Psychology, 30,* 41–67.

Slavin, R. E. (1995). *Cooperative learning* (2nd ed.). Boston: Allyn & Bacon.

Smith, D. G., Guy L., Gerbrick, G. L., Figueroa, M. A., Watkins, G. H., Levitan, T., Moore L. C., Merchant, P. A., Beliak, H. D., & Figueroa, B. (1997). *Diversity works: The emerging picture of how students benefit.* Washington, DC: Association of American Colleges and Universities.

Stangor, C., Sechrist, G. B., & Jost, J. T. (2001). Changing racial beliefs by providing consensus information. *Personality and Social Psychology Bulletin, 27,* 484–494.

Stoltz, P. G. (2014). *Grit: The new science of what it takes to persevere, flourish, succeed.* San Luis Obispo: Climb Strong Press.

Taylor, S. E., Peplau, L. A., & Sears, D. O. (2006). *Social psychology* (12th ed.). Upper Saddle River, NJ: Pearson/Prentice-Hall.

Thompson, A., & Cuseo, J. (2014). *Diversity and the college experience.* Dubuque, IA: Kendall Hunt.

U.S. Census Bureau (2008). *Bureau of Labor Statistics.* Washington, DC: Author.

U.S Census Bureau (2013). *Poverty.* Retrieved from https://www.census.gov/hhes/www/poverty/data/threshld/.

Wabash National Study of Liberal Arts Education (2007). *Liberal Arts outcomes.* Retrieved from http:www.liberalarts.wabash.edu/ study-overview/.

Wheelright, J. (2005, March). Human, study thyself. *Discover,* pp. 39–45.

Willis, J. (2006). *Research-based strategies to ignite student learning: Insights from a neurologist and classroom teacher.* Alexandria, VA: ASCD.

Zajonc, R. B. (1968). Attitudinal effects of mere exposure. *Journal of Personality and Social Psychology, 9,* Monograph Supplement, No. 2, part 2.

Zajonc, R. B. (1970). Brainwash: Familiarity breeds comfort. *Psychology Today,* (February), pp. 32–35, 60–62.

Zajonc, R. B. (2001). Mere exposure: A gateway to the subliminal. *Current Directions in Psychological Science, 10,* 224–228.

Chapter 7 Exercises

7.1 Quote Reflections

Review the sidebar quotes contained in this chapter and select two that were especially meaningful or inspirational to you.

For each quote, provide a three- to five-sentence explanation why you chose it.

7.2 Reality Bite

Hate Crime: A Racially Motivated Murder

Jasper County, Texas, has a population of approximately 31,000 people. In this county, 80% of the people are White, 18% are Black, and 2% are of other races. The county's poverty rate is considerably higher than the national average, and its average household income is significantly lower. In 1998, the mayor, the president of the Chamber of Commerce, and two councilmen were Black. From the outside, Jasper appeared to be a town with racial harmony, and its Black and White leaders were quick to state that there was no racial tension in Jasper.

However, one day, James Byrd Jr.—a 49-year-old African American man—was walking home along a road one evening and was offered a ride by three White males. Rather than taking Byrd home, Lawrence Brewer (age 31), John King (age 23), and Shawn Berry (age 23), three men linked to White-supremacist groups, took Byrd to an isolated area and began beating him. They then dropped his pants to his ankles, painted his face black, chained Byrd to their truck, and dragged him for approximately three miles. The truck was driven in a zigzag fashion to inflict maximum pain on the victim. Byrd was decapitated after his body collided with a culvert in a ditch alongside the road. His skin, arms, genitalia, and other body parts were strewn along the road, while his torso was found dumped in front of a Black cemetery. Medical examiners testified that Byrd was alive for much of the dragging incident.

When they were brought to trial, the bodies of Brewer and King were covered with racist tattoos; they were eventually sentenced to death. As a result of the murder, Byrd's family created the James Byrd Foundation for Racial Healing. A wrought iron fence that separated Black and White graves for more than 150 years in Jasper Cemetery was removed in a special unity service. Members of the racist Ku Klux Klan have since visited the gravesite of Byrd several times, leaving racist stickers and other marks that angered the Jasper community and Byrd's family.

Source: Louisiana Weekly (February 3, 2003).

Reflection Questions

1. What factors do you think were responsible for this incident?
2. Could this incident have been prevented? If yes, how? If no, why not?
3. How likely do you think an incident like this could take place in your hometown or near your college campus?
4. If this event happened to take place place in your hometown, how do you think members of your community would react?

7.3 Gaining Awareness of Your Group Identities

We are members of multiple groups at the same time and our membership in these overlapping groups can influence our personal development and identity. In the following figure, consider the shaded center circle to be yourself and the six unshaded circles to be six different groups you belong to and that you think have influenced your development.

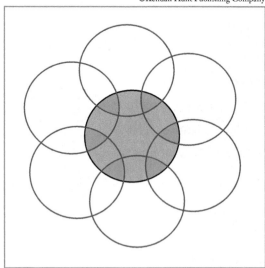

Fill in the unshaded circles with the names of groups to which you think you belong that have had the most influence on your personal development and identity. You can use the diversity spectrum (**p. 166**) to help you identify different groups to which you may be a member. Don't feel you have to fill in all six circles. What's more important is to identify those groups that you think have had a significant influence on your personal development or identity.

Reflection Questions:

1. Which one of your groups has had the greatest influence on your personal development or identity? Why?

2. Have you ever felt limited or disadvantaged by being a member of any your group(s) to which you belonged? Why?

3. Have you ever felt advantaged or privileged by your membership in any group(s)? Why?

7.4 Intercultural Interview

1. Identify a person on your campus who is a member of an ethnic or racial group that you've had little previous contact. Ask that person for an interview, and during the interview, include the following questions:

   - What does "diversity" mean to you?
   - What prior experiences have affected your current viewpoints or attitudes about diversity?
   - What would you say have been the major influences and turning points in your life?
   - Who would you cite as your positive role models, heroes, or sources of inspiration?
   - What societal contributions made by your ethnic or racial group would you like others to be aware of and acknowledge?
   - What do you hope will never again be said about your ethnic or racial group?

2. If you were the interviewee instead of the interviewer, how would you have answered the above questions?

3. What do you think accounts for the differences (and similarities) between your answers to the above questions and those provided by the person you interviewed?

7.5 Hidden Bias Test

Go to www.tolerance.org/activity/test-yourself-hidden-bias and take one or more of the hidden bias tests on this website. These tests assess subtle bias with respect to gender, age, ethnic minority groups, religious denominations, sexual orientations, disabilities, and body weight.

1. After completing the test, answer the following questions:

2. Did the results reveal any biases you weren't unaware of?

3. Did you think the assessment results were accurate or valid?

4. What do you think best accounts for or explains your results?

If your closest family member and best friend took the test, how do you think their results would compare with yours?

Chapter 7 Reflection

After reading this chapter, has your definition of diversity changed? Explain.

List and describe five ways appreciating diversity will assist you in being successful in college and/or life.

1.

2.

3.

4.

5.

Are there any areas of diversity you feel you need to be more comfortable with? What are the areas and HOW will you become more comfortable with them?

Notes

Notes

Deep Learning

STRATEGIC NOTE-TAKING, READING, AND STUDYING

This chapter will help you apply research on human learning and the human brain to become a more effective and efficient learner. It takes you through three key stages of the learning process—from the first stage of acquiring information through lectures and readings, through the second stage of studying and retaining the information you acquire, through the final stage of retrieving (recalling) the information you studied. The ultimate goal of this chapter is to supply you with a set of powerful strategies that can be used to promote learning that's *deep* (not surface-level memorization), *durable* (long-lasting), and retrievable (accessible to you when you need it).

Chapter Preview

Develop a collection of effective strategies for studying smarter, learning deeply, and retaining longer what you have learned.

Learning Goal

 Think About It—Journal Entry 8.1

Thought Starter

What would you say is the key difference between learning and memorizing?

Learning is the fundamental mission of all colleges and universities. One of the major goals of a college education is to help students become independent, self-directed learners. Learning doesn't stop after college graduation; it's a lifelong process that is essential for success in the 21st century. The ongoing information technology revolution, coupled with global interdependence, is creating a greater need for effective learning skills that can be used throughout life and in different cultural and occupational contexts. Today's employers value job applicants who have "learned how to learn" and will continue to be "lifelong learners" (SECFHE, 2006).

FIGURE 8.1: Network of Brain Cells

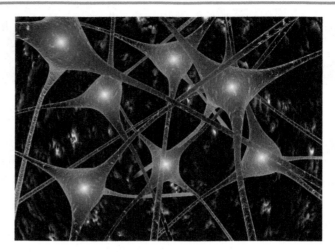

Deep learning involves making connections between what you're trying to learn and what you already know. When you learn something deeply, it's stored in the brain as a link in an interconnected network of brain cells.

©Jurgen Ziewe/Shutterstock.com

What Is Deep Learning?

When students learn deeply, they dive below the surface of shallow memorization; they go further by building mental bridges between what they're trying to learn and what they already know (Piaget, 1978; Vygotsky, 1978). Knowledge isn't acquired by simply pouring information into the brain as if it were an empty jar. It's a matter of attaching or connecting new ideas to ideas that are already stored in the brain. When this happens, facts are transformed into *concepts*—networks of connected or interrelated ideas. In fact, when something is learned deeply, the human brain actually makes a physical (neurological) connection between separate nerve cells (LeDoux, 2002). (See **Figure 8.1**.)

Studies suggest that most college students don't engage in deep learning (Arum & Roksa, 2011; Kuh, 2005; Nathan, 2005). They may show up for class most of the time, cram for their exams, and get their assignments done right before they're due. These learning strategies may enable students to survive college, but not thrive in college and achieve academic excellence.

Stages in the Learning and Memory Process

Learning deeply and retaining what you've learned is a process that involves three key stages:

1. **Sensory input (perception).** Taking information into the brain;
2. **Memory formation (storage).** Transforming that information into knowledge and storing it in the brain;
3. **Memory recall (retrieval).** Bringing that knowledge back to mind when you need it.

These three stages are summarized visually in **Figure 8.2**. These stages of the learning and memory process are similar to the way information is processed by a computer: (1) information is entered onto the screen (input), (2) that information is saved in a memory file (storage), and (3) the saved information is recalled and used

FIGURE 8.2: **Key Stages in the Learning and Memory Process**

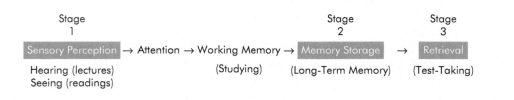

©Kendall Hunt Publishing Company.

when it's needed (retrieval). This three-stage process can serve as a framework for using the two major routes through which knowledge is acquired in college: from lectures and readings.

Effective Lecture-Listening and Note-Taking Strategies

The importance of developing effective listening skills in the college classroom was highlighted in a classic study of more than 400 students who were given a listening test at the start of their college experience. At the end of their first year in college, 49% of those students who scored low on the listening test were on academic probation—compared to only 4.4% of students who scored high on the listening test. On the other hand, 68.5% of students who scored high on the listening test were eligible for the honors program at the end of their first year—compared to only 4.17% of those students who had low listening test scores (Conaway, 1982).

 Think About It—Journal Entry 8.2

Do you think writing notes in class helps or hinders your ability to pay attention to and learn from your instructors' lectures?

Why?

Studies show that information delivered during lectures is the number one source of test questions (and answers) on college exams (Brown, 1988; Kuhn, 1988). When lecture information isn't recorded in students' notes and appears on a test, it has only a 5% chance of being recalled (Kiewra, et al., 2000). Students who write notes during lectures achieve higher course grades than students who just listen to lectures (Kiewra, 1985, 2005), and students with a more complete set of lecture notes are more likely to demonstrate higher levels of overall academic achievement (Johnstone & Su, 1994; Kiewra & DuBois, 1998).

Contrary to a popular belief that writing while listening interferes with the ability to listen, students report that taking notes actually increases their attention and concentration in class (Hartley, 1998; Hartley & Marshall, 1974). Studies also show that when students write down information that's presented to them, they're more likely to remember the most important aspects of that information when tested later (Bligh, 2000). One study discovered that students with grade point averages (GPAs) of 2.53 or higher record more information in their notes and retain a larger percentage of the most important information than do students with GPAs of less than 2.53 (Einstein, Morris, & Smith, 1985). These findings aren't surprising when you consider that hearing information, writing it and then seeing it after it's been written produces three different memory traces (tracks) in the brain, thus tripling your chances of remembering it.

Furthermore, when notes are taken, you're left with a written record of lecture information that can be studied later to improve your test performance. In contrast, if you take few or no notes, you're left with little or no information to study for upcoming exams. As previously noted, the majority of questions on professors' exams come from information contained in their lectures. So, come to class with the attitude that your instructors are dispensing answers to test questions as they speak and your job is to pick out and record these answers so you can pick up points on the next exam.

Note

Points your professors make in class that make it into your notes turn into points earned on your exams (and higher grades in your courses).

You can get the most out of lectures by employing effective strategies at three key times: before, during, and after class.

Pre-Lecture Strategies: What to Do *Before* Class

1. Check your syllabus to see where you are in the course and determine how the upcoming class fits into the total course picture. By checking the course syllabus before individual class sessions you'll see how each part (class) relates to the whole (course). This strategy capitalizes on the brain's natural tendency to seek larger patterns and see the "big picture." The human brain is naturally inclined to connect parts into a whole (Caine & Caine, 2011). It looks for meaningful patterns and connections rather than isolated bits and pieces of information (Jensen, 2008). In **Figure 8.3**, notice how your brain naturally ties together and fills in the missing information to perceive a whole pattern that is meaningful.

2. Get to class early so that you can review your notes from the previous class session and from any reading assignments relating to the day's lecture topic. Research indicates that when students review information related to an upcoming lecture topic, they take more accurate and complete lecture notes (Jairam & Kiewra, 2009; Kiewra, 2005). Thus, a good way to improve your ability to learn from lectures is to review your notes from the previous class session and read textbook information related to the lecture topic—*before* hearing the lecture. Reviewing previously learned information activates your prior knowledge, enabling you to connect lecture material to what you already know—a powerful way to promote deep learning (Bruner, 1990; Piaget, 1978; Vygotky, 1978).

FIGURE 8.3: **Triangle Illusion**

You perceive a white triangle in the middle of this figure. However, if you use three fingers to cover up the three corners of the white triangle that fall outside the other (background) triangle, the white triangle suddenly disappears. What your brain does is take these corners as starting points and fills in the rest of the information on its own to create a complete or whole pattern that has meaning to you. (Also, notice how you perceive the background triangle as a complete triangle, even though parts of its three sides sides are missing.)

©Kendall Hunt Publishing Company

Listening and Note-Taking Strategies: What to Do *During* Class

1. Give lectures your undivided attention. As previously noted, research shows that in all subject areas, the majority of test questions appearing on college exams come from the professor's lectures and students who take better class notes get better course grades (Brown, 1988; Cuseo, et al., 2013; Kiewra, 2000). Studies also show that the more time students spend surfing the web or using Facebook during lectures, the lower their test scores. These results hold true for all students, regardless of how they scored on college admissions tests (Ravizza, Hambrick, & Fenn, 2014).

   Remember that like all humans, not all professors are created equal. You'll have some that are more dynamic and easier to pay attention to than others. It's the less dynamic ones that will tempt you to lose attention and stop taking notes. Don't let the less engaging or less entertaining professors lower your course grades. Instead view them as a challenge; step up your focus of attention, continue taking notes to keep yourself engaged, and leave the course with the satisfaction of earning a good grade.

2. Take your own notes in class. Don't rely on someone else to take notes for you. Taking notes in your own words focuses your attention and ensures the notes you take make sense to you. Research indicates that students who record and review their own notes on information presented to them earn higher scores on memory tests for that information than do students who review notes taken by others (Jairam & Kiewra, 2009; Kiewra, 2005). Taking your own notes in your own words makes them *meaningful to you*. While it's a good idea to collaborate with classmates to compare notes for completeness and accuracy, or to pick up points you may have missed, you shouldn't rely on someone else to do your note-taking for you.

3. Take notes in longhand rather than typing them on a laptop. Studies show that when students use a keyboard to type notes, they're more likely to mindlessly punch in the exact words used by the instructor, rather than transforming the instructor's words into words that are meaningful to them. When tested on understanding and memory for key concepts presented in class, students who took notes in longhand outperformed those who typed notes on a keyboard (Mueller & Oppenheimer, 2014). This may be due to the fact that the movements made during handwriting leave a motor (muscle) memory trace in the brain, which deepens learning and strengthens memory (Herbert, 2014).

4. **Be alert to cues for the most important information contained in lectures.** Since the human attention span is limited, it's impossible to attend to and make note of everything. Thus, we need to use our attention *selectively* to detect and select information that matters most. Here are some strategies for identifying and recording the most important information delivered by professors during lectures:

    *   Pay particular attention to information your instructors put *in print*—on the board, on a slide, or in a handout. If your instructor has taken the time and energy to write it out or type it out, this is usually a good clue that the information is important and you'll likely see it again—on an exam.
    *   Pay special attention to information presented during the *first and last few minutes of class*. Instructors are most likely to provide valuable reminders, reviews, and previews at the start and end of a class session.
    *   Look for *verbal and nonverbal cues* that signal the instructor is delivering important information. Don't just tune in when your professors are writing something down and tune out at other times. It's been found that students record almost 90% of material written on the board, but less than 50% of important ideas that professors state but don't write on the board (Johnstone & Su, 1994; Locke, 1977; Titsworth & Kiewra, 2004). So, don't fall into the reflex-like routine of just taking notes when you see your instructor writing notes. Instead, listen actively to ideas you *hear* your instructor saying and take notes on these ideas as well. **Box 8.1** contains strategies for detecting clues to important information that professors are delivering orally in class.

Box 8.1

Detecting When Instructors Are Delivering Important Information during Lectures

Look for *verbal* cues, such as:

*   Phrases signaling important information (e.g., "The point here is . . ." or "What's most significant about this is . . .").
*   Information that's repeated or rephrased in a different way (e.g., "In other words, . . ", or "To put it another way . . . ").
*   Stated information that's followed by a question to check understanding (e.g., "Is that clear?" "Do you follow that?" "Does that make sense?" or "Are you with me?").

Watch for *vocal* (*tone of voice*) cues, such as:

*   Information delivered in a louder tone or at a higher pitch than usual—which may indicate excitement or emphasis.

*   Information delivered at a slower rate or with more pauses than usual—which may be your instructor's way of giving you more time to write down these important ideas.

Keep an eye out for *nonverbal* cues, such as:

*   Information delivered by your instructor with more than the usual:
    a. Facial expressiveness (e.g., raised or furrowed eyebrows);
    b. Body movement (e.g., gesticulation and animation);
    c. Eye contact (e.g., looking directly and intently at the faces of students to see if they're following or understanding what's being said).
*   Your instructor moving closer to the students (e.g., moving away from the podium or blackboard).
*   Your instructor orienting his or her body directly toward the class (i.e., both shoulders directly or squarely facing the class).

5. **Keep taking notes even if you don't immediately understand what your instructor is saying.** If you are uncertain or confused about the material being presented, don't stop taking notes. Having notes on that material will at least leave you with a record to review later—when you have more time to think about it and make sense of it. If you still don't understand it after taking time to review it, seek clarification from your instructor, a classmate, or your textbook.

6. **Take organized notes.** If your instructor continues to make points relating to the same idea, take notes on that idea within the same paragraph. When the instructor shifts to a new idea, skip a few lines and shift to a new paragraph. Be alert to phrases that your instructor may use to signal a shift to a new or different idea (e.g., "Let's turn to . . ." or "In addition to . . ."). Use these phrases as cues for taking notes in paragraph form.

   By recording different ideas in different paragraphs, the organizational quality of your notes improves as will your comprehension and retention of them. Be sure to leave extra space between paragraphs (ideas) to give yourself room to add information that you may have initially missed, or to later translate the professor's words into your own words.

   Another popular strategy for taking organized notes is the *Cornell Note-Taking System*.

   There are several methods to take notes. It is important you find the note-taking method that works best for you. Examples include formal outlining, informal outlining, mapping, charting, and many others. Please refer to: http://www.redlands.edu/docs/Academics/1Five_Methods_of_Notetaking_2015.pdf for more information.

Post-Lecture Strategies: What to Do *After* Class

1. **As soon as class ends, quickly check your notes for missing information or incomplete thoughts.** Information delivered during a lecture is likely to be fresh in your mind immediately after class. A quick check of your notes at this time will allow you to take advantage of your short-term memory. By reviewing and reflecting on your notes, you can help move that information into long-term memory before forgetting takes place. This quick review can be done alone or, better yet, with a motivated classmate. If you both have gaps in your notes, check them out with your instructor before he or she leaves the classroom. Even though it may be weeks before you'll be tested on the material, the quicker you pick up missed points and clear up sources of confusion, the better; it will help you understand upcoming material—especially upcoming material that builds on previously covered material. Catching confusion early in the game also enables you to avoid the mad last-minute rush of students seeking help from the instructor just before test time. You want to reserve the critical time just before exams to study notes you know are complete and accurate, rather than rushing around trying to find missing information and seeking last-minute help on concepts presented weeks earlier.

Think About It—Journal Entry 8.3

Do you tend to stick around a few minutes after class sessions end to review your notes and clear up missing information or confusing points? Why?

_____

_____

_____

_____

What could you do immediately after class to be a more successful student?

_____

_____

_____

_____

_____

2. **Before the next class session meets, reflect on and review your notes to make sense of them.** Your professors will often lecture on information that you may have little prior knowledge about, so it's unrealistic to expect that you will understand everything that's being said the first time you hear it. Instead, set aside time to reflect on and review your notes as soon as possible after class has ended. During this review process, take notes on your notes by:
   - Translating technical information into your own words to make it more meaningful to you; and
   - Reorganizing your notes to get ideas related to the same point in the same place.

Studies show that students who organize their lecture notes into meaningful categories demonstrate superior recall of that information on memory tests—compared to students who simply review the notes they took in class (Howe, 1970; Kiewra, 2005).

Note

Effective note taking is a two-stage process: Stage 1 involves actively taking notes in class and stage 2 takes places after class—when you take time to reflect on your notes and process them more deeply.

AUTHOR'S EXPERIENCE

I spent my first year in college spending a lot of time trying to manipulate my schedule to create large blocks of free time. I took all of my classes in a row without a break to preserve some time at the end of the day for relaxation and hanging out with friends. Seldom did I even look at my notes until it was time to be tested on them. Thus, on the day before the test I was in a panic trying to cram the lecture notes into my head for the upcoming exam. Needless to say, I didn't perform well on many of my first tests. Eventually, a professor told me that if I spent some time each day re-writing my notes I would retain the material longer, increase my grades, and decrease my stress at test time. I employed this system and it worked wonderfully.

—Aaron Thompson

 ## Think About It—Journal Entry 8.4

Rate yourself in terms of how frequently you use these note-taking strategies according to the following scale:

4 = always, 3 = sometimes, 2 = rarely, 1 = never

1.	I take notes aggressively in class.	4	3	2	1
2.	I sit near the front of the class.	4	3	2	1
3.	I sit upright and lean forward while in class.	4	3	2	1
4.	I take notes on what my instructors say, not just what they write on the board.	4	3	2	1
5.	I pay special attention to information presented at the start and end of class.	4	3	2	1
6.	I take notes in paragraph form.	4	3	2	1
7.	I review my notes immediately after class to check that they are complete and accurate.	4	3	2	1

What works for you? What might you try to improve your note-taking skills?

_____

_____

_____

_____

_____

Strategic Reading

Expect to do more reading in college than you did in high school and be ready to be held accountable for the reading you're assigned. Information from assigned readings ranks right behind information from lectures as a source of test questions on college exams (Brown, 1988; Cuseo, et al., 2013). You're likely to find exam questions relating to reading assignments that your professors didn't talk about specifically in class (or even mention in class). College professors often expect you to relate or connect their lectures with material they've assigned you to read. Furthermore, professors often deliver class lectures with the assumption that students have done the assigned reading, so if you haven't done it, you're more likely to have difficulty following what your instructor is saying in class. Thus, you should do the assigned reading but also do it according to the schedule the instructor has established. By completing assigned reading in a timely manner, you will (a) be better positioned to understand class lectures, (b) acquire information that's likely to appear on exams but not covered in class, and (c) improve the quality of your participation in class.

The following research-based strategies can be used to improve your comprehension and retention of material you read.

Pre-Reading Strategies: What to Do *Before* Reading

1. **Before jumping into your assigned reading, first see how it fits into the overall organizational structure of the book and course.** You can do this efficiently by taking a quick look at the book's table of contents to see where the chapter you're about to read is placed in the overall sequence of chapters. Look especially at its relationship to the chapters that immediately precede and follow it. This strategy will give you a sense of how the particular part you're focusing on connects with the bigger picture. Research shows that if students have advanced knowledge about how material they're about to learn is organized—if they see how its parts relate to the whole before they start learning the specific parts—they're better able to comprehend and retain the material (Ausubel, Novak, & Hanesian 1978; Chen & Hirumi, 2009). Thus, the first step toward improving reading comprehension and retention of a book chapter is to see how it relates to the book as a whole.

Think About It—Journal Entry 8.5

When you open a textbook to read a chapter, how do you start the reading process? What's the first thing you do? Why?

2. **Preview the chapter by first reading its boldface headings and any chapter outline, objectives, summary, or end-of-chapter questions that may be included.** Before tackling the chapter's specific content, get in the habit of previewing what's in the chapter to get a general sense of its overall organization. If you dive into the specific details first, you may lose sight of how the smaller details relate to the larger picture. Since the brain's natural tendency is to perceive

and comprehend whole patterns rather than isolated bits of information, start by seeing how the parts of the chapter relate to the whole. Just as looking at the whole picture of a completed jigsaw puzzle beforehand helps you connect its parts, so too does getting a picture of the whole chapter before reading its parts.

3. **Take a moment to think about what you may already know that relates to the main topic of the chapter.** This strategy will activate the areas of your brain where your prior knowledge about that topic is stored, thereby preparing it to make meaningful connections with the material you're about to read.

Strategies to Use *During* the Reading Process

1. **Read selectively to locate the most important information.** Effective reading begins with a plan for identifying what should be noted and remembered. Here are three key strategies you can use while reading to help you determine what information you should focus on and retain.

   • **Use boldface or dark-print headings and subheadings as cues for identifying important information.** These headings organize the chapter's major points; you can use them as "traffic" signs to direct you to the most important information in the chapter. Better yet, turn the headings into questions and read to find answers to them. This question-and-answer routine ensures that you read actively and with a purpose. (You can set up this strategy while previewing the chapter by placing a question mark after each heading contained in the chapter.) Creating and answering questions while reading also keeps you motivated because the questions stimulate curiosity and a desire to find answers to them (Walter, Knudsvig, & Smith, 2003). Another advantage of posing and answering questions about what you're reading is that it's an effective way to prepare for exams—you're practicing exactly what you'll be expected to do on exams—answering questions.

   • **Pay close attention to information that's *italicized*, <u>underlined</u>, CAPITALIZED, or bulleted.** These features call attention to key terms that must be understood and built on before you can proceed to understand higher-level concepts covered later in the reading. Don't simply highlight these words because their special appearance suggests they're important. Read these terms carefully and be sure you understand them before you continue reading.

   • **Pay special attention to the first and last sentences in each paragraph.** These sentences provide an important introduction and conclusion to the key point contained in the paragraph. It's a good idea to reread the first and last sentences of each paragraph before you move on to the next paragraph, particularly when reading material that's cumulative (builds on previously covered material), such as science and math.

Note

Your goal when reading is not just to cover the assigned pages, but to uncover the most important ideas contained on those pages.

2. **Take written notes on important information you find in your reading.** A good way to stop and think deeply about key ideas in your reading is to take notes on those ideas in your own words. Research shows that the common student practice of just highlighting the text (the author's words) is not a particularly effective strategy (Dunlosky, et al., 2013). Highlighting is a passive learning process, whereas note-taking actively engages you in the reading process

> I would advise you to read with a pen in your hand, and enter in a little book of short hints of what you find that is curious, or that might be useful; for this will be the best method of imprinting such particulars in your memory, where they will be ready."
>
> —*Benjamin Franklin, 18th-century inventor, newspaper writer, and cosigner of the Declaration of Independence*

and enables you to transform the text into your own words. Don't slip into the habit of using your textbook simply as a coloring book in which the artistic process of highlighting information in spectacular, kaleidoscopic colors distracts you from the more important process of learning actively and thinking deeply about what you're reading. Highlighting is okay as long it's not the only thing you do while reading; take time to make notes on the material you've highlighted—in your own words—to ensure that you reflect on it and make it personally meaningful. Taking notes on information delivered during lectures will improve your performance on exams; taking notes on your reading assignments will do the same.

> "I had the worst study habits and the lowest grades. Then I found out what I was doing wrong. I had been highlighting with a black magic marker."
>
> —Jeff Altman, American comedian

Used Textbooks

Categorized by Color of Used Highlighters

| Mellow Yellow | Outrageous Orange | Moody Blue | Deep Purple | **Dark Black (Illegible)** |

Highlighting textbooks in psychedelic colors is a very popular reading strategy among college students, but it's a less effective strategy for producing deep learning than taking written notes on what you read.

When you transform what someone else has written into your own words, you're implementing a powerful principle of deep learning: relating what you're trying to learn to what you already know (Demmert & Towner, 2003). A good time for pausing and writing a brief summary of what you've read in your own words is when you encounter a boldface heading because it indicates you're about to encounter a new topic; this is the ideal time to deepen your knowledge of what you just finished reading and use that knowledge to help you understand what's coming next.

Think About It—Journal Entry 8.6

When reading a textbook, do you usually have the following tools on hand?

Highlighter:	yes	no
Pen or pencil:	yes	no
Notebook:	yes	no
Class notes:	yes	no
Dictionary:	yes	no
Glossary:	yes	no

If you don't usually have one or more of the above tools on hand while reading, which one(s) do you plan to have on hand in the future?

_____

_____

_____

_____

3. **Make use of visual aids that accompany the written text.** Don't fall into the trap of thinking that visual aids can or should be skipped because they're merely supplemental or ornamental. Visual aids, such as charts, graphs, diagrams, and concept maps are powerful learning and memory tools for a couple of reasons: (a) they enable you to "see" the information in addition to reading (hearing) it, and (b) they pull together separate ideas into a unified snapshot.

    Visual aids also improve learning and memory of written material by delivering information to the brain through a different sensory modality. In addition, periodically pausing to view visual aids adds variety and a change of pace to the reading process. Breaking up sustained periods of reading with a change of pace and different sensory input helps maintain your interest and attention (Malmberg & Murname, 2002; Murname & Shiffrin, 1991).

4. **Regulate or adjust your reading speed to the type of subject matter you're reading.** As you know, academic subjects vary in terms of their level of technicality and complexity. Reading material in a math or science textbook requires reading at a slower rate with more frequent pauses to check for understanding than reading a novel or a short story.

Post-Reading Strategies: What to Do *After* Reading

1. **End your reading sessions with a short review of the key information you've highlighted and taken notes on.** Rather than ending your reading session by trying to cover a few more pages, reserve the last five minutes to review the key ideas you already covered. Most forgetting of information takes place immediately after we stop focusing on the information and turn our attention to another task (Averell & Heathcote, 2011; Baddeley, 1999). By taking a few minutes at the end of a reading session to review the most important information you've just read, you help your brain "lock" that information into long-term memory before getting involved with another task.

    The graph in **Figure 8.4** represents the results of a classic experiment that tested how well information is recalled at various times after it was originally learned. As you can see on the far left of the graph, most forgetting occurs soon after information has been taken in (e.g., after 20 minutes, more than 60% of it was forgotten). The results of this classic study have been confirmed multiple times (Schacter, 2001) and they underscore the importance of reviewing key information acquired through reading *immediately* after you've read it. By doing so, your memory for that information improves dramatically because you're intercepting the human "forgetting curve" at its steepest point of memory loss—just after information has been taken in.

FIGURE 8.4: The Forgetting Curve

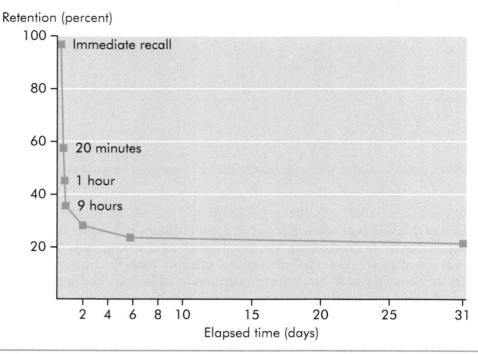

Source: Hermann Ebbinghaus, *Memory: A Contribution to Experimental Psychology*, 1885/1913

2. **After completing a reading assignment, if you're still confused about an important idea or concept contained in the reading, go to another source.** The problem may not be you—it may be the way the author has presented or explained it. You may be able to clear up your confusion by simply consulting another source or resource, such as those listed below.
    - **Look at how another book explains it.** Not all textbooks are created equal; some do a better job of explaining certain concepts than others. Check to see whether your library or campus bookstore has other texts dealing with the same subject as your course. A different book may be able to explain a hard-to-understand concept much better than your assigned textbook.
    - **Seek help from your instructor.** If you completed the reading assignment and made every effort to understand a particular concept but still can't grasp it, most instructors should be willing to assist you.
    - **Seek help from learning assistance professionals or peer tutors in your Learning Center (Academic Support Center).** This is your key campus resource for help with reading assignments, particularly if your instructor is unavailable or unwilling to provide assistance.

Box 8.2

SQ3R: A Method for Improving Reading Comprehension and Retention

A popular system for organizing and remembering key reading strategies, such as those discussed in this chapter, is the *SQ3R* system. SQ3R is an acronym for five steps that can be taken to increase textbook reading comprehension and retention, particularly when reading highly technical or complex material. The following sequences of steps comprise this method:

1. Survey
2. Question
3. Read
4. Recite
5. Review

S = Survey: Get a preview and overview of what you're about to read.

1. Use the chapter's title to activate your thoughts about the subject and get your mind ready to receive information related to it.
2. Read the introduction, chapter objectives, and chapter summary to become familiar with the author's purpose, goals, and key points.
3. Note the boldface headings and subheadings to get a sense of the chapter's organization before you begin reading. This supplies you with a mental structure or framework for making sense of the information you're about to read.
4. Take note of any graphics—such as charts, maps, and diagrams; they provide valuable visual support and reinforcement for the material you're reading.

5. Pay special attention to reading aids (e.g., italics and boldface font); use them to identify, understand, and remember key concepts.

Q = Question: Stay active and curious.

As you read, use boldface headings to formulate questions and read to find answers to those questions. When your mind is actively searching for answers, it becomes more engaged in the learning process. As you read, add any questions of your own that come to mind.

R = Read: Find answers to questions you've created.

Read one section at a time—with your questions in mind—and search for answers to these questions.

R = Recite: Rehearse your answers.

After you complete reading each section, recall the questions you asked and see if you can answer them from memory. If not, look at the questions again and practice your answers until you can recall them without looking. Don't move onto the next section until you're able to answer all questions in the section you've just completed.

R = Review: Look back and get a second view of the whole picture.

Once you've finished the chapter, review all the questions you've created for different parts or sections. See whether you can still answer them without looking. If not, go back and refresh your memory. Also, read the Chapter Summary. If any of the information in the summary seems unfamiliar, go back and find it and make sure you can relate it to what is in the summary.

 Think About It—Journal Entry 8.7

Rate yourself in terms of how frequently you use the following reading strategies, using the following scale:

4 = always, 3 = sometimes, 2 = rarely, 1 = never

1. I read chapter outlines and summaries before I start reading the chapter content.   4   3   2   1

2. I preview a chapter's boldface headings and subheadings before I begin to read the chapter.   4   3   2   1

3. I adjust my reading speed to the type of subject I am reading.   4   3   2   1

4. I look up the meaning of unfamiliar words and unknown terms that I come across before I continue reading.   4   3   2   1

5. I take written notes on information I read.   4   3   2   1

6. I use the visual aids included in my textbooks.   4   3   2   1

7. I finish my reading sessions with a review of important information that I noted or highlighted.   4   3   2   1

What works for you? What might you do to improve reading strategies?

_____

_____

_____

_____

Strategic Studying: Learning Deeply and Remembering Longer

Studying isn't a short sprint that takes place just before test time. Instead, it's more like a long-distance run that takes place over time. Studying the night before an exam should be the last step in a sequence of test-preparation steps that take place well before test time, which include: (a) taking accurate and complete notes in class, (b) doing the assigned reading, and (c) seeking help from professors or peers along the way for any concepts that are unclear or confusing. After these steps have been taken, you are then well-positioned to study the material you've acquired and learn it deeply.

Described below is a series of study strategies you can use to promote deep and durable (long-lasting) learning.

Give Studying Your Undivided Attention

> "You can do several things at once, but only if they are easy and undemanding. You are probably safe carrying on a conversation with a passenger while driving on an empty highway [but] you could not compute the product of 17 x 24 while making a left turn into dense traffic, and you certainly should not try."
>
> —Daniel Kahneman, professor emeritus of Psychology, and author of Thinking Fast and Slow

The human attention span has limited capacity—we have only so much of it available to us at any point in time and we can give all or part of it to whatever task(s) we're working on. As the phrase "paying attention" suggests, it's like paying money, we only have so much of it to spend. Thus, if attention while studying is spent on other activities at the same time (e.g., listening to music, watching TV, or text messaging friends), there's a deduction in the amount of attention paid to studying. In other words, studying doesn't receive our undivided attention.

Studies show that when people multitask they don't pay equal attention to all tasks at the same time; instead, they divide their attention by shifting it back and forth between tasks (Howard, 2014). Their performance on the task that demands the most concentration or deepest thinking is the one that suffers the most (Crawford & Strapp, 1994). When performing complex mental tasks that cannot be done

Multitasking while studying interferes with learning by dividing up attention and driving down comprehension and retention.

automatically or mindlessly, the brain needs quiet, internal reflection time for permanent connections to form between brain cells—which is what must happen if deep, long-lasting learning is to take place (Jensen, 2008). If the brain must simultaneously engage in other tasks or process other sources of external stimulation, this connection-making process is interfered with and learning is impaired.

So, give study time your undivided attention by unplugging all your electronic accessories. You can even use apps to help you do so (e.g., to silence your phone). Another strategy would be to set aside a short block of time to check electronic messages after you've completed a longer block of study time (e.g., as a study break); this allows you to use social media as a reward *after* putting in a stretch of focused study time. Just don't do both at the *same* time.

AUTHOR'S EXPERIENCE

When I was in college there were so many distractions for me. I had a job that I could work as many hours as I wanted to work. I had organizations where I was offered leadership positions. In addition, there were so many attractive girls. Then there were all these demanding classes that required me to study. To be honest, I enjoyed some of these distractions more than others. Well, that's another story for another day and another book. What I did know was that my education was the most important thing to me so I had to prioritize it. Thus, I had to study, learn, and do well in order to graduate. To do this I had to **REDUCE MY DISTRACTIONS!!** So, I developed Thompson's plan of action. They were: 1. Find a friend or two who also wanted to learn who could be study partners. What I realized was that my primary learning style is auditory (this worked well when I needed to study for a test). 2. If I was studying alone, find a place that was quiet where I could not listen to music or turn on the TV (the library was my favorite place to do this). BTW, in today's terms, that means no internet, text, phone, etc. 3. Never study when I am hungry and tired. 4. Give myself enough time to complete the assigned study task where I did not feel I had to rush through the material.

—Aaron Thompson

Make Meaningful Associations

Deep learning doesn't take place by simply absorbing information like a sponge—in exactly the same, prepackaged form as you received it from a textbook or lecture. Instead, deep learning involves actively translating the information you receive into a form that makes sense to you (Biggs & Tang, 2007; Mayer, 2002).

Note

Deep learning is not about teachers transmitting information to students; it's about students transforming that information into knowledge that's meaningful to them.

The brain's natural learning tendency is to translate unfamiliar information into a familiar form that makes sense and has personal meaning. This is illustrated in the experience.

AUTHOR'S EXPERIENCE

When my son was about three years old, we were riding in the car together and listening to a song by the Beatles titled, *Sergeant Pepper's Lonely Hearts Club Band.* You may be familiar with this tune, but in case you're not, there's a part in it where the following lyrics are sung repeatedly: "Sergeant Pepper's Lonely, Sergeant Pepper's Lonely, Sergeant Pepper's Lonely...."

When this part of the song was being played, I noticed that my three-year-old son was singing along. I thought it was pretty amazing for a boy his age to be able to understand and repeat those lyrics. However, when that part of the song came on again, I listened to him more closely and noticed he wasn't singing "Sergeant Pepper's Lonely, Sergeant Pepper's Lonely ..." Instead, he was singing: "Sausage Pepperoni, Sausage Pepperoni ..." (which were his two favorite pizza toppings).

My son's brain was doing what all human brains tend to naturally do. It took unfamiliar information—song lyrics that didn't make any sense to him—and transformed it into a form that was meaningful to him.

—*Joe Cuseo*

You can experience the brain's natural inclination for meaning-making by reading the following passage, which once appeared anonymously on the Internet.

Aoccdrnig to rscheearch at Cmabridge Uinverstisy, it deos't mattaer in what order the ltteers in a word are, the only iprmoetnt thing is that the frist and lsat ltteer be at the rghit pclae. The rset can be a total mses and you can still raed it wouthit a porbelm. This is bcusae the human mind deos not raed ervey lteter by istlef, but the word as a wlohe. Amzanig huh?

Notice how easily you made meaning out of unfamiliar, misspelled words by naturally transforming them into familiar, meaningful words—which were already stored in your brain. Whenever you're learning something new, capitalize on the brain's natural tendency to find meaning by trying to connect what you're trying to understand to what you already know.

Learning the specialized terminology associated with different academic disciplines may seem like learning a foreign language for a student with little or no experience with these terms. However, before you start brutally beating these terms into your brain through sheer repetition, try to find meaning in them. One way to do so is by looking up the term's word root in the dictionary or by identifying its prefix or suffix, which may give away the term's meaning. For instance, suppose you're taking a biology course and studying the autonomic nervous system—the part of the nervous system that operates without conscious awareness or voluntary control (e.g., your heart and lungs). The meaning of this biological term is found in its prefix "auto," meaning self-controlling or "automatic" (e.g., automatic transmission). Once you find meaning in a term, you can learn it faster and retain it longer than by memorizing it through sheer repetition.

If looking up an academic term's root, prefix, or suffix doesn't reveal its meaning, see if you can make it meaningful to you in some other way. Suppose you looked up the root of the term "artery" and nothing about the origins of this term helped you understand its meaning or purpose. You could create your own meaning for this term by taking its first letter (a), and have it stand for "away"—to help you remember that arteries carry blood away from the heart. By so doing, you take a meaningless term and make it personally meaningful and memorable.

 ## Think About It—Journal Entry 8.8

Think of a technical academic term or concept you're learning in a course this term, and create a meaningful association you could use to remember it.

Another way you can make learning meaningful is by *comparing and contrasting* what you're learning with what you already know. When you're studying, get in the habit of asking yourself the following questions:

1. How is this idea similar or comparable to something that I've already learned? (Compare)
2. How is this idea different from what I've already learned? (Contrast)

Research indicates that this simple strategy is one of the most powerful ways to promote learning of academic information (Marzano, Pickering, & Pollock, 2001). When you ask yourself the question, "How is this similar to and different from concepts I already know?" you make the learning process more meaningful and relevant because you're relating what you're trying to learn to what you already know or have already experienced.

Note

When learning, go for meaning first, memorization last. If you can connect what you're trying to learn to what you already know, the deeper you'll learn it and the longer you'll remember it.

Integrate Information from Lectures and Readings

Connect ideas from your lecture notes and reading assignments that relate to the same concept. Get them in the same place by recording them on the same index card under the same category heading. Index cards can be used like a portable file

> "The extent to which we remember a new experience has more to do with how it relates to existing memories than with how many times or how recently we have experienced it."
>
> —*Morton Hunt*, The Universe Within: A New Science Explores the Human Mind

cabinet, whereby each card functions like the hub of a wheel, around which individual pieces of related information can be attached like spokes. In contrast, when ideas pertaining to the same point or concept are spread all over the place, they're more likely to take that form in your mind—leaving them mentally disconnected and leaving you more confused or overwhelmed (and stressed out).

Note

Deep learners ask questions like: How can this specific piece of information be categorized or classified into a larger concept? How does this particular idea relate to or "fit into" something bigger?

Distribute Study Time across Separate Study Sessions

Learning deeply depends not only on how you learn (your method), but when you learn (your timing). Equally important as how much time you spend studying is how you distribute or spread out your study time. Research consistently shows that for students of all abilities and ages, distributing study time across several shorter sessions results in deeper learning and longer retention than channeling all study time into one long session (Brown, Roediger, & McDaniel, 2014; Carey, 2014; Dunlosky, et al., 2013). Distributed practice improves your learning and memory in two major ways:

- It minimizes loss of attention due to fatigue or boredom.
- It reduces mental interference by giving the brain some downtime to cool down and lock in information it has received before being interrupted by the need to deal with additional information (Malmberg & Murnane, 2002; Murname & Shiffrin, 1991). Memory works like a muscle: after it's been exercised, if given some "cool down" time before it's exerted again, it builds greater strength—that is, stronger memory for what it previously learned (Carey, 2014). On the other hand, if the brain's downtime is interfered with by the arrival of additional information, it gets overloaded and its capacity for handling information becomes impaired. That's what cramming does—it overloads the brain with lots of information in a limited period of time. In contrast, distributed study does just the opposite—it uses shorter sessions with downtime between sessions—giving the brain time to slow down and retain the information it's previously processed (studied) and more time to move that information from short-term to long-term memory (Willis, 2006).

"Hurriedly jam-packing a brain is akin to speed-packing a cheap suitcase—it holds its new load for a while, then most everything falls out."

—Benedict Carey, author, How We Learn: Throw Out the Rule Book and Unlock Your Brain's Potential

Distributed study is also less stressful and more motivating than cramming. You're more likely to start studying when you know you won't be doing it for a long stretch of time (or lose any sleep doing it). It's also easier to sustain attention for tasks that are done for a shorter period of time.

Although cramming just before exams is better than not studying at all, it's far less effective than studying that's spread out across time. Instead of frantically cramming total study time into one long session ("massed practice"), use *distributed practice*—"distribute" or space out your study time over several shorter sessions.

Think About It—Journal Entry 8.9

Are you more likely to study in advance of exams or cram just before exams? Explain.

How do you think most students would answer this question?

Use the "Part-to-Whole" Study Method

A natural extension of distributed practice is the part-to-whole method. This method involves breaking up the material you need to learn into smaller parts and studying those parts in separate sessions in advance of the exam; then you use your last study session just before the exam to review (restudy) the parts you previously studied in separate sessions. Thus, your last session isn't a cram session or even a study session, it's a review session.

Research shows that students of all ability levels learn material in college courses more effectively when it's studied in small units and when progression to the next unit takes place only after the previous unit has been mastered or understood (Pascarella & Terenzini, 1991, 2005).

Don't buy into the myth that studying in advance is a waste of time because you'll forget it all by test time. (Procrastinators often use this argument to rationalize their habit of putting off studying until the very last moment, which forces them to cram frantically the night before exams.) Even if you aren't able to recall what you previously studied when you look at it again closer to test time, research shows that once you start reviewing it, you can relearn it in a fraction of the time it took the first time. Since it takes much less time to relearn the material because the brain still has a memory trace for information studied in the earlier sessions (Kintsch, 1994), it proves you didn't completely forget it and that studying it in advance wasn't a waste of time. Another key advantage of breaking material you're learning into smaller parts and studying those parts in advance of major exams is that it allows you to check your understanding of the part you studied before moving on to learning the next part. This is a particularly important advantage in courses where learning the next unit of material builds on your understanding the previous unit (e.g., math and science).

Capitalize on the Power of Visual Learning

The human brain consists of two hemispheres (half spheres)—left and right (see **Figure 8.5**). Each of these hemispheres specializes in a different type of learning. The left hemisphere specializes in verbal learning; it deals primarily with words. In contrast, the right hemisphere specializes in visual–spatial learning; it deals primarily with perceiving images, patterns, and objects that occupy physical place or space. If you involve both hemispheres of the brain while studying, two different memory traces are recorded—one in each major hemisphere (half) of the brain. This process of laying down dual memory traces (verbal and visual) is referred to as *dual coding* (Paivio, 1990). Since two memory traces are better than one, dual coding results in deeper learning and longer retention.

FIGURE 8.5

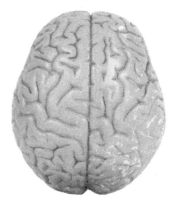

The human brain is comprised of two half spheres (hemispheres): the left hemisphere specializes in verbal learning, and the right hemisphere specializes in visual learning.

©JupiterImages Corporation.

To capitalize on the advantage of dual coding, be sure to use all the visual aids available to you, including those found in your textbook and those provided by your instructor in class. You can also create your own visual aids by representing what you're learning in the form of pictures, symbols, or concept maps—such as flow-charts, timelines, spider webs, wheels with hubs and spokes, or branching tree diagrams. (See **Figure 8.6** for an example of a concept map.) Visit https://coggle.it/ for help in creating your own concept/mind maps. When you transform material you're learning into a visual pattern, you're putting it into a form that's compatible with the brain's tendency to store information in neurological networks (Willis, 2006). Drawing also keeps you actively engaged in the process of learning, and by representing verbal information in visual form, you double the number of memory traces recorded in your brain. As the old saying goes, "A picture is worth a thousand words."

Note

Don't forget that drawings and visual illustrations can be more than just forms of artistic expression; they can also be powerful learning tools—you can draw to learn!

FIGURE 8.6: Concept Map for the Human Nervous System

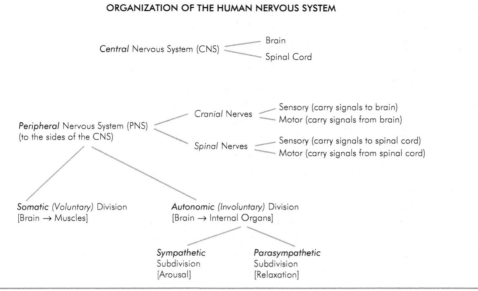

ORGANIZATION OF THE HUMAN NERVOUS SYSTEM

©Kendall Hunt Publishing Company

 Think About It—Journal Entry 8.10

Think of a course you're taking this term in which related pieces of information could be joined together to form a concept map. Make a rough sketch of this map that includes the information you need to remember.

Build Variety into the Study Process

Infusing variety and change of pace into your study routine can increase your motivation to study and your concentration while studying. Here are some practical strategies for doing so.

Mix it up: periodically shift the type of academic tasks you perform during a study session. Changing the nature of the academic work you do while studying increases your alertness and concentration by reducing *habituation*—attention loss that occurs after repeatedly engaging in the same type of mental task (Thompson, 2009). You can combat attention loss due to habituation by varying the type of tasks you perform during a study session. For instance, you can shift periodically among tasks that involve reading, writing by hand, typing on a keyboard, reviewing, reciting, and solving problems. Similar to how athletes benefit from mixing different types of drills into their workouts (e.g., separate drills for building strength, speed, and endurance), studies of human learning show that "interleaving" (mixing) different academic subjects or academic skills while studying results in deeper learning and stronger memory (Brown, Roediger, & McDaniel, 2014; Carey, 2014).

Study in different places. In addition to spreading out your studying at different times, it's also a good idea to spread it out in different places. Studying in different locations provides different environmental contexts for learning; this reduces the amount of mental interference that normally builds up when all information is studied in the same place. The great public speakers in ancient Greece and Rome used this method of changing places to remember long speeches by walking through different rooms while rehearsing their speech, learning each major part of their speech in a different room (Higbee, 2001).

Although it's useful to have set times for studying so that you get into a regular work routine, this doesn't mean you learn best by always studying in the same place. Periodically changing the academic tasks you perform while studying, as well as the environment in which you perform them, has been found to improve attention to (and retention of) what you're studying (Carey, 2014; Druckman & Bjork, 1994).

Break up long study sessions with short study breaks that involve physical activity (e.g., a short jog or brisk walk). Study breaks that include physical activity refresh the mind by giving it a rest from studying. Physical activity also stimulates the mind by increasing blood flow to your brain—helping you retain what you've studied and regain concentration for what you'll study next.

Learning Styles: Identifying Your Learning Preferences

Your learning style is another important personal characteristic you should be aware of when choosing your major. Learning styles refer to individual differences in learning preferences—that is, ways in which individuals prefer to perceive information (receive or take it in) and process information (deal with it after taking it in). Individuals may differ in terms of whether they prefer to take it in information by reading about it, listening to it, seeing an image or diagram of it, or physically touching and manipulating it. Individuals may also vary in terms of whether they like to receive information in a structured and orderly format or in an unstructured form that allows them the freedom to explore, play with, and restructure it in their own way. Once information has been received, individuals may also differ in terms of how they prefer to process or deal with it mentally. Some might like to think about it on their own; others may prefer to discuss it with someone else, make an outline of it, or draw a picture of it.

Probably the most frequently used learning styles test is the Myers-Briggs Type Indicator (MBTI; Myers, 1976; Myers & McCaulley, 1985), which is based on the personality theory of psychologist Carl Jung. The test consists of four pairs of opposing traits and assesses how people vary on a scale (low to high) for each of these four sets of traits.

Learning styles are no more or no less common ways that people learn. We all have a mix of multiple learning styles, thus we have different and multiple ways of learning. Many students may find that they have a dominant learning style but using other styles that are less dominant. In many cases, you might use different styles for different learning circumstances. No style is set in concrete. They can change and there is no perfect mix for greater learning. You have the ability to increase your lesser used methods to make them more dominant while strengthening your dominant one. Since students have different learning styles and academic fields emphasize different styles of learning, it's important to consider how your learning style meshes with the style of learning emphasized by the field you're considering as a major. If the match seems to be close or compatible, then the marriage between you and that major could be one that leads to a satisfying and successful learning experience.

Although there are many (multiple) learning styles, the three that are considered most common are:

- Visual-Spatial Learning (learning by seeing),
- Auditory-Sequential Learning (learning by hearing),
- Kinesthetic Learning (learning by doing).

In addition to taking formal tests to assess which or how many of these are your learning style(s), you can gain awareness of your learning styles through some simple introspection or self-examination. Take a moment to complete the following sentences that are designed to stimulate personal reflection on your learning style:

I learn best if . . .
I learn most from . . .
I enjoy learning when . . .

Knowing your preferred learning style can make studying easier for you. Once you discover your dominant learning style, research some ways you can incorporate your learning style into your study routine (i.e., if your learning style is visual, read over notes or use flashcards; if you are an auditory learner, read your notes out loud to yourself; if you are a kinesthetic learner, rewrite your notes).

To sum up, the most important factor to consider when reaching decisions about a major is whether it is compatible with four characteristics of yourself: (1) your learning style, (2) your abilities, (3) your personal interests, and (4) your values. These four pillars provide the foundation for effective decisions about a college major.

The PEPS Learning Styles Inventory that is packaged with your book will help you identify the ways you learn best. Pay close attention to your detailed report and preference chart and reference it as you read through this chapter (and book). Knowing how you learn best can help you maximize your study strategies.

Learn with and through a variety of senses. When memory is formed in the brain, different sensory aspects of it are stored in different areas. For example, if your brain receives auditory input (e.g., hearing your own words or the words of others), visual input (viewing images, maps or charts), and motor input (movement made when writing, drawing, or manipulating), that information reaches your brain through multiple sensory modalities and is better retained because it: (a) creates more interconnections in areas of the brain where that information is stored, and (b) provides multiple cues for retrieving (recalling) the information (Shams & Seitz, 2011; Willis, 2006; Zull, 2002). Different forms of sensory input are stored as multiple neurological tracks in different parts of the brain, which deepens learning and strengthens memory.

Don't forget that movement is also a sensory channel. When you move, your brain receives kinesthetic stimulation—the sensations generated by your muscles. Memory traces for movement are commonly stored in an area of your brain (the cerebellum) that plays a major role for all types of learning (Middleton & Strick, 1994; Jensen, 2005). Thus, incorporating movement into the process of learning improves your ability to retain what you're studying by adding a motor (muscle)

> "
> I have to *hear* it, *see* it, *write* it, and *talk* about it."
> —First-year college student responding to the question: "How do you learn best?"

> "
> When I have to remember something, it's better for me to do something with my hands so I could physically see it happening."
> —First-year college student

memory trace of it to your brain. You can use movement to help you learn and retain academic information by using your body to act out what you're studying or symbolize it with your hands (Kagan & Kagan, 1998). Suppose you're trying to remember five points about something (e.g., five consequences of the Civil War). When you're studying these points, count them on your fingers as you try to recall each of them.

AUTHOR'S EXPERIENCE

I was talking about memory in class one day and mentioned that when I can't recall how to spell a word, its correct spelling comes back to me after I start writing it. One of my students raised her hand and said the same thing happens to her when she forgets a phone number—it comes back to her when she starts punching it in. Both of these experiences point to the power of movement for promoting learning and memory.

—*Joe Cuseo*

AUTHOR'S EXPERIENCE

Often I forget my grocery list when I head to the grocery store. Instead of turning around and heading home to get the list, if I close my eyes, I can usually "see" most of the list in my head. This is because my strongest learning method is visual. Because of this, I often color code my notes, planner, etc. Knowing my dominant learning style has helped me use it to my advantage.

—*Julie McLaughlin*

Also, remember that talking involves muscle movement of your lips and tongue. Thus, speaking aloud when you're studying, either to a friend or to yourself, can improve memory by supplying kinesthetic stimulation to your brain (in addition to the auditory stimulation your brain receives from hearing what you're saying).

Figure 8.7 shows a map of the outer surface of the human brain; you can see how different parts of the brain are specialized to receive input from different sensory modalities. When multiple sensory modalities are used while learning, multiple memory traces of what you're studying are recorded in separate areas of the brain, resulting in deeper learning and stronger memory for what's been studied.

FIGURE 8.7: **A Map of the Functions Performed by the Outer Surface of the Human Brain**

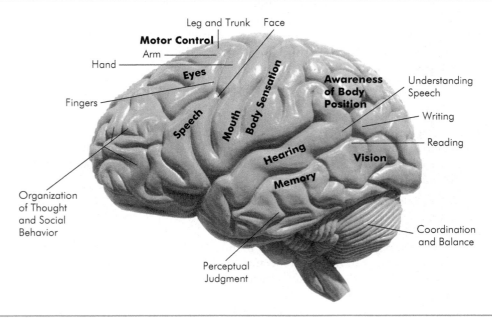

Brain image modified from ©David Huntley/Shutterstock.com

Learn with Emotion

Neural connections run between the emotional and memory centers of the brain (Zull, 1998). Thus, the emotions we're experiencing while learning can affect how deeply we learn. Research indicates that emotional intensity, excitement, and enthusiasm strengthen memory of academic information just as they do for memory of life events and personal experiences. When we're emotionally excited about what we're learning, adrenaline is released and is carried through the bloodstream to the brain. Once adrenaline reaches the brain, it increases blood flow and glucose production, which stimulates learning and strengthens memory (LeDoux, 1998; Rosenfield, 1988). Thus, if you become passionate and enthused about what you're learning, you're more likely to learn it deeply and remember it longer (Howard, 2014; Minninger, 1984).

One way to do this is by keeping in mind the importance or significance of what you're learning. For instance, if you're learning about photosynthesis, remind yourself that you're not just learning a chemical reaction, you're learning about the driving force that underlies all plant life on the planet. If you don't know why the concept you're studying is significant, find out—do a computer search, talk it over with your instructor, or ask an advanced student majoring in the field.

Note

Make learning a "total body experience." Put your whole self into it—your mind, your body, and your heart.

Learn Collaboratively

Simply defined, collaborative learning is the process of two or more people working *interdependently* to advance each other's success—as opposed to working independently or competitively. Learning is strengthened when it takes place in a social context that involves interpersonal interaction. As scholars put it, human knowledge is "socially constructed" or built up through dialogue and an exchange of ideas; conversations with others become internalized as ideas in your mind and influence your way of thinking (Bruffee, 1993). Thus, by having frequent, intelligent conversations with others, you broaden your knowledge base, deepen your learning and elevate the quality of your thinking. (For specific team-learning strategies, see Chapter 3, **pp. 66–68.**)

AUTHOR'S EXPERIENCE

When I was in my senior year of college, I had to take a theory course by independent study because the course would not be offered again until after I planned to graduate. Another senior found himself in the same situation. The instructor allowed both of us to take this course together and agreed to meet with us every two weeks. My fellow classmate and I studied independently for the first two weeks.

I prepared for the biweekly meetings by reading thoroughly, yet I had little understanding of what I had read. After our first meeting, I left with a strong desire to drop the course but decided to stick with it. Over the next two weeks, I spent many sleepless nights trying to prepare for our next meeting and was feeling pretty low about not being the brightest student in my class of two. During the next meeting with the instructor, I found out that the other student was also having difficulty. Not only did I notice, so did the instructor. After that meeting, the instructor gave us study questions and asked us to read separately then get together to discuss the questions. During the next two weeks, my classmate and I met several times to discuss what we were learning (or attempting to learn). By being able to communicate with each other about the issues we were studying, we both ended up gaining greater understanding. Our instructor was delighted to see that he was able to suggest a collaborative learning strategy that worked for both of us.

—*Aaron Thompson*

Self-Monitor: Reflect on What you're Learning and Assess Whether you're Learning it Deeply

Deep learners are *reflective* learners—they are self-aware and mindful of how well they're learning what they're studying. They reflect, check, and self-assess whether they're really getting it. They monitor their comprehension by asking questions such as: "Am I actually understanding this?" and "Do I really know it?"

How do you know if you really know it? Probably the best answer to this question is: "I find meaning in it—I can relate to it personally or put it in terms that make sense to me" (Ramsden, 2003). Listed below are some strategies for checking whether you're truly (deeply) understanding what you're learning. These strategies can be used as indicators or checkpoints for determining whether you're just memorizing or learning at a deep level. They will help you answer the question: "How do I know if I really know it?"

Can you think of an *analogy* between the concept you're learning and something you already know or understand? (e.g., This concept is like _____ or is similar to _____.)

- Can you paraphrase (restate or translate) what you're learning in your own words? If you can take what you're learning and complete the following sentence: "In other words, . . .", it's very likely you've moved beyond surface memorization (and mental regurgitation) to a deeper level of comprehension, because you've transformed what you're learning into a form that makes sense to you. You know you know it if you're not stating it the same way your instructor or textbook stated it, but restating it in words that are your own.
- Can you explain what you're learning to someone who is unfamiliar with it? One of the best ways to gain awareness of how well we know or don't know

something is to explain it to someone who's never heard it before (just ask any teacher). Studies show that students gain a deeper level of understanding for what they're learning when they're asked to explain it to someone else (Chi, et al., 1994). If you can explain it to someone who's unfamiliar with it, that's a good sign you've moved to deeper comprehension because you're able to translate it into language that's understandable to anyone.

- **Can you think of an *example* of what you've learned?** If you can come up with an instance or illustration of what you're learning—that's your own—not one given by your instructor or textbook, this is a good sign that you truly understand it. It shows you've taken an abstract academic concept and connected it to a concrete experience (Bligh, 2000).

- **Can you apply what you're learning to solve a new problem that you haven't seen before?** The ability to apply what you've learned in a different situation is a good indicator of deep learning (Erickson & Strommer, 2005). Learning specialists refer to this mental process as *decontextualization*—taking what you learned in one context (situation) and transferring it to another context (Bransford, Brown, & Cocking, 2000). For instance, you know you've learned a mathematical concept deeply when you can use that concept to solve math problems different from those solved by your instructor or textbook. This is why math instructors rarely include on exams the exact problems they solved in class or were solved in your textbook. They're not trying to "trick" you at test time; they're trying to see whether you've learned the concept deeply.

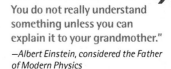

> You do not really understand something unless you can explain it to your grandmother."
>
> —*Albert Einstein, considered the Father of Modern Physics*

> I learn best through teaching. When I learn something and teach it to someone else, I find that it really sticks with me a lot better."
>
> —*College sophomore*

 Think About It—Journal Entry 8.11

Rate yourself in terms of how frequently you use the following learning strategies:

4 = always, 3 = sometimes, 2 = rarely, 1 = never

1. I block out all distracting sources of outside stimulation when I study.   4   3   2   1

2. I try to find meaning in technical terms by looking at their prefix or suffix, or by looking up their etymology (word origin).   4   3   2   1

3. I compare and contrast what I'm currently studying with what I've already learned.   4   3   2   1

4. I organize the information I'm studying into categories or classes.   4   3   2   1

5. I pull together information from my class notes and readings that relate to the same concept or general category.   4   3   2   1

6. I distribute (spread out) my study time over several short sessions in advance of exams and use my last study session before the test to review the information I previously studied.   4   3   2   1

7. I participate in study groups with my classmates.   4   3   2   1

Which works best for you? Why?

_____

_____

_____

_____

_____

Chapter Summary and Highlights

This chapter identified key principles of human learning and supplied specific strategies for learning effectively in college and throughout life. Deep learning goes beyond surface-level memorization. It's connecting new ideas to ideas that have already been learned. Deep learners build mental bridges between what they're trying to learn and what they already know.

Information delivered during lectures is the information that's most likely to appear as items on college exams. Students who don't take good lecture notes have a slim chance of recalling the information at test time. Thus, effective note taking is critical to successful academic performance in college.

Information from reading assignments is the second most common source of test questions on college exams. Professors often don't discuss information in class that's contained in assigned reading. Thus, doing the assigned reading, and doing it in a way that maximizes comprehension and retention, is essential for academic success in college.

Learning from lectures requires active involvement (e.g., actively taking notes while listening to lectures) as does learning from reading (e.g., actively taking notes while reading). Active involvement during the learning process engages your attention and enables information to enter the brain. Reflection on what you have learned keeps it in the brain by locking it into memory. Self-awareness also promotes deep learning. By reflecting on whether you truly understand what you're studying, you become a more self-aware learner and a more successful student.

Cramming total study time into one long session ("massed practice") immediately before exams doesn't promote deep learning or long-term retention. Research consistently shows that *distributed practice*, whereby study time is "distributed" or spread out over several shorter sessions, is more effective—particularly if the last study session just before an exam is used to review (restudy) the parts that were previously studied in separate sessions. Learning is also deepened by engaging as many senses as possible during the learning process.

Lastly, deep learning is enhanced when done *collaboratively*. Research from kindergarten through college shows that students who learn in teams experience significant gains in both academic performance and interpersonal skills.

Learning More through the World Wide Web: Internet-Based Resources

For additional information on learning deeply and strategically, see the following websites:

Strategic Learning & Study Strategies:
https://www.khanacademy.org/coach-res/reference-for-coaches/case-studies-hied/a/help-students-build-study-plans

http://www.dartmouth.edu/~acskills/success/

http://www.isu.edu/success/strategies/handouts.shtml

Brain-Based Learning: http://www.brainrules.net/the-rules

Learning Math and Overcoming Math Anxiety:
www.mathacademy.com/pr/minitext/anxiety

www.onlinemathlearning.com/math-mnemonics.html

References

Anderson, C. J. (2003). The psychology of doing nothing: Forms of decision avoidance result from reason and emotion. *Psychological Bulletin, 129*, 139–167.

Arum, R., & Roska, J. (2011). *Academically adrift: Limited learning on college campuses.* Chicago: The University of Chicago Press.

Ausubel, D., Novak, J., & Hanesian, H. (1978). *Educational psychology: A cognitive view* (2nd ed.). New York: Holt, Rinehart & Winston.

Averell, L., & Heathcote, A. (2011). The form of the forgetting curve and the fate of memories. *Journal of Mathematical Psychology, 55*(1), 25–35

Baddeley, A. D. (1999). *Essentials of human memory.* Hove: Psychology.

Biggs, J., & Tang, C. (2007) *Teaching for quality learning at university* (3rd ed.) Buckingham: SRHE and Open University Press.

Bligh, D.A. (2000). *What's the use of lectures?* San Francisco: Jossey Bass.

Bransford, J. D., Brown, A. L., & Cocking, R. R. (2000). *How people learn: Brain, mind, experience and school.* Washington, DC: National Academies Press.

Brown, R. D. (1988). Self-quiz on testing and grading issues. *Teaching at UNL (University of Nebraska–Lincoln), 10*(2), 1–3.

Brown, P. C., Roediger III, H. L., & McDaniel, M. A. (2014). *Make it stick: The science of successful learning.* Cambridge, MA: The Belknap Press of Harvard University Press.

Bruffee, K. A. (1993). *Collaborative learning: Higher education, interdependence, and the authority of knowledge.* Baltimore: Johns Hopkins University Press.

Bruner, J. (1990) *Acts of Meaning* Cambridge, MA: Harvard University Press.

Caine, R., & Caine, G. (2011). *Natural learning for a connected world: Education, technology and the human brain.* New York, NY. Teachers College Press

Carey, B. (2014). *How we learn.* London: Random House.

Chen, B., & Hirumi, A. (2009). Effects of advance organizers on learning for differentiated learners in a fully Web-based course. *International Journal of Instructional Technology & Distance Learning.* Retrieved from http://itdl.org/Journal/Jun_09/article01.htm

Chi, M., de Leeuw, N., Chiu, M. H., & LaVancher, C. (1994). Eliciting self-explanations improves understanding. *Cognitive Science, 18*, 439–477.

Conaway, M. S. (1982). Listening: Learning tool and retention agent. In A. S. Algier & K. W. Algier, (Eds.), *Improving reading and study skills*, (pp. 51–63). San Francisco: Jossey-Bass.

Crawford, H. J., & Strapp, C. H. (1994). Effects of vocal and instrumental music on visuospatial and verbal performance as moderated by studying preference and personality. *Personality and Individual Differences, 16*(2), 237–245.

Cuseo, J. B., Thompson, A., Campagna, M., & Fecas, V. S. (2013). *Thriving in college & beyond: Research-based strategies for academic success and personal development* (3rd ed.). Dubuque, IA: Kendall Hunt.

Demmert, W. G., Jr., & Towner, J. C. (2003). *A review of the research literature on the influences of culturally based education on the academic performance of Native American students.* Retrieved from the Northwest Regional Educational Laboratory, Portland, Oregon, website: http://educationnorthwest.org/sites/default/files/cbe.pdf.

Druckman, D., & Bjork, R. A. (Eds.). (1994). *Learning, remembering, believing: Enhancing human performance.* Washington, DC: National Academies Press.

Dunlosky, J., Rawson, K. A., Marsh, E. J., Nathan, M. J., & Willingham, D. T. (2013). Improving students' learning with effective learning techniques: Promising directions from cognitive and educational psychology. *Psychological Science in the Public Interest, 14*(1), 4–58.

Einstein, G. O., Morris, J., & Smith, S. (1985). Note-taking, individual differences, and memory for lecture information. *Journal of Educational Psychology, 77*(5), 522–532.

Erickson, B. L., & Strommer, D. W. (2005). Inside the fist-year classroom: Challenges and constraints. In J. L. Upcraft, J. N. Gardner, & B. O. Barefoot, *Challenging and supporting the first-year student* (pp. 241–256). San Francisco: Jossey-Bass.

Hartley, J. (1998). *Learning and studying: a research perspective.* London: Routledge.

Hartley, J., & Marshall, S. (1974). On notes and note taking. *Universities Quarterly, 28,* 225–235.

Hartman, H. J. (2001). *Metacognition in learning and instruction: Theory, research and practice.* Dordrecht: Kluwer Academic Publishers.

Herbert, W. (2014). Ink on paper: Some notes on note taking. Association for Psychological Science (APS). Retrieved from http://www.psychologicalscience.org/index.php/news/were-only-human/ink-on-paper-some-notes-on-note-taking.html

Higbee, K. L. (2001). *Your memory: How it works and how to improve it.* New York: Marlowe.

Howard, P. J. (2014). *The owner's manual for the brain: Everyday applications of mind-brain research* (4th ed.). New York: HarperCollins.

Howe, M. J. (1970). Note-taking strategy, review, and long-term retention of verbal information. *Journal of Educational Psychology, 63,* 285.

Jairam, D., & Kiewra, K. A. (2009). An investigation of the SOAR study method. *Journal of Advanced Academics* (August), 602–629.

Jensen, E. (2005). *Teaching with the brain in mind* (2nd ed.). Alexandria, VA: ASCD.

Jensen, E. (2008). *Brain-based learning.* Thousand Oaks, CA: Corwin Press.

Johnstone, A. H., & Su, W. Y. (1994). Lectures: a learning experience? *Education in Chemistry, 31*(1), 65–76, 79.

Kagan, S., & Kagan, M. (1998). *Multiple intelligences: The complete MI book.* San Clemente, CA: Kagan Cooperative Learning.

Kiewra, K. A. (1985). Students' note-taking behaviors and the efficacy of providing the instructor's notes for review. *Contemporary Educational Psychology, 10,* 378–386.

Kiewra, K. A. (2000). Fish giver or fishing teacher? The lure of strategy instruction. *Teaching at UNL (University of Nebraska–Lincoln), 22*(3), 1–3.

Kiewra, K. A. (2005). *Learn how to study and SOAR to success.* Upper Saddle River, NJ: Pearson Prentice Hall.

Kiewra, K. A., & DuBois, N. F. (1998). *Learning to learn: Making the transition from student to lifelong learner.* Needham Heights, MA: Allyn and Bacon.

Kiewra, K. A., Hart, K., Scoular, J., Stephen, M., Sterup, G., & Tyler, B. (2000). Fish giver or fishing teacher? The lure of strategy instruction. *Teaching at UNL (University of Nebraska–Lincoln), 22*(3).

Kintsch, W. (1994). Text comprehension, memory, and learning. *American Psychologist, 49,* 294–303.

Kuh, G. D, (2005). Student engagement in the first year of college. In M. L. Upcraft, J. N. Gardner, B. O. Barefoot, & Associates, *Challenging and supporting the first-year student: A handbook for improving the first year of college* (pp. 86–107). San Francisco: Jossey-Bass.

Kuhn, L. (1988). What should we tell students about answer changing? *Research Serving Teaching, 1*(8).

LeDoux, J. (1998). *The emotional brain: The mysterious underpinnings of emotional life.* New York: Simon & Schuster.

LeDoux, J. (2002). *Synaptic self: How our brains become who we are.* New York: Penguin Books.

Locke, E. (1977). An empirical study of lecture note-taking among college students. *Journal of Educational Research, 77,* 93–99.

Malmberg, K. J., & Murnane, K. (2002). List composition and the word-frequency effect for recognition memory. *Journal of Experimental Psychology: Learning, Memory, and Cognition, 28,* 616–630.

Marzano, R. J., Pickering, D. J., & Pollock, J. (2001). *Classroom instruction that works: Research-based strategies for increasing student achievement.* Alexandria, VA: Association for Supervision and Curriculum Development.

Mayer, R. E. (2002). Rote versus meaningful learning. *Theory into Practice, 41*(4), 226–232.

Middleton, F., & Strick, P. (1994). Anatomical evidence for cerebellar and basal ganglia involvement in higher brain function. *Science, 226*(51584), 458–461.

Minninger, J. (1984). *Total recall: How to boost your memory power.* Emmaus, PA: Rodale.

Mueller, P. A. & Oppenheimer, D. M (2014). The pen is mightier than the keyboard: Advantages of longhand over laptop note taking. *Psychological Science, 25*(6), 1159–1168.

Murname, K., & Shiffrin, R. M. (1991). Interference and the representation of events in memory. *Journal of Experimental Psychology: Learning, Memory, & Cognition, 17,* 855–874.

Nathan, R. (2005). *My freshman year: What a professor learned by becoming a student.* Ithaca, New York: Cornell University Press.

Paivio, A. (1990). *Mental representations: A dual coding approach.* New York: Oxford University Press.

Pascarella, E., & Terenzini, P. (1991). *How college affects students: Findings and insights from twenty years of research.* San Francisco: Jossey-Bass.

Pascarella, E., & Terenzini, P. (2005). *How college affects students: A third decade of research* (Vol. 2). San Francisco: Jossey-Bass.

Piaget, J. (1978). *Success and understanding.* Cambridge, MA: Harvard University Press.

Ramsden, P. (2003). *Learning to teach in higher education* (2nd ed.). London: RoutledgeFalmer.

Ravizza, S. M., Hambrick, D. Z.. & Fenn, K. M. (2014). Non-academic internet use in the classroom is negatively related to classroom learning regardless of intellectual ability. *Computers & Education, 78,* 109–114.

Rosenfield, I. (1988). *The invention of memory: A new view of the brain.* New York: Basic Books.

Schacter, D. L. (2001). *The seven sins of memory: how the mind forgets and remembers.* Boston: Houghton Mifflin.

SECFHE (2006). *A national dialogue: The Secretary of Education's Commission on the future of higher education.* (U.S. Department of Education Boards and Commissions: A Draft Panel Report). Retrieved from http://www.ed.gov/about/bdscomm/list/hiedfuture/reports/0809-draft.pdf

Shams, W., & Seitz, K. (2011). Influences of multisensory experience on subsequent unisensory processing. *Frontiers in Perception Science, 2*(264), 1–9.

Thompson, R. F. (2009). Habituation: A history. *Neurobiology of Learning and Memory, 92*(2), 127–134.

Titsworth, S., & Kiewra, K. A. (2004). Organizational lecture cues and student notetaking. *Contemporary Educational Psychology, 29,* 447–461.

Vygotsky, L. S. (1978). Internalization of higher cognitive functions. In M. Cole, V. John-Steiner, S. Scribner, & E. Souberman (Eds. & Trans.), *Mind in society: The development of higher psychological processes* (pp. 52–57). Cambridge, MA: Harvard University Press.

Walter, T. W., Knudsvig, G. M., & Smith, D. E. P. (2003). *Critical thinking: Building the basics* (2nd ed.). Belmont, CA: Wadsworth.

Willis, J. (2006). *Research-based strategies to ignite student learning: Insights from a neurologist and classroom teacher.* Alexandria, VA: ASCD.

Zull, J. E. (1998). The brain, the body, learning, and teaching. *The National Teaching & Learning Forum, 7*(3), 1–5.

Zull, J. E. (2002). *The art of changing the brain: Enriching the practice of teaching by exploring the biology of learning.* Sterling, VA: Stylus.

Chapter 8 Exercises

8.1 Quote Reflections

Review the sidebar quotes contained in this chapter and select two that were especially meaningful or inspirational to you.

For each quote, provide a three- to five-sentence explanation why you chose it.

8.2 Reality Bite

Too Fast, Too Frustrating: A Note-Taking Nightmare

Susan Scribe is a first-year student majoring in journalism. She's currently enrolled in an introductory course that is required for her major (Introduction to Mass Media). The instructor in this course lectures at a rapid rate and uses vocabulary that goes right over her head. Since she cannot get all her instructor's words down on paper and cannot understand half the words she does manage to write down, she becomes frustrated and stops taking notes. She wants to do well in this course because it's the first course in her major, but she's afraid she'll fail it because her class notes are so pitiful.

Reflection and Discussion Questions

1. Can you relate to this case personally, or do know any students who are in the same boat as Susan?

2. What would you recommend that Susan do at this point? Why?

8.3 Self-Assessment of Learning Habits

Look back at the ratings you gave yourself for effective note-taking (**Journal Entry 8.4, p. 219**), reading (**Journal Entry 8.7, pp. 225–226**), and studying (**Journal Entry 8.11, pp. 239–240**). Add up your total score for these three sets of learning strategies (the maximum score for each set is 28):

Note Taking = _____

Reading = _____

Studying = _____

Total Learning Strategy Score = _____

Self-Assessment Questions

1. In which learning strategy area did you score lowest?

2. Do you think the area in which you scored lowest has anything to do with your lowest course grade at this point in the term?

3. Of the seven strategies listed under the area you scored lowest, which could you immediately put into practice to improve your performance in the course you're having most difficulty with this term?

4. What's the likelihood that you will put the preceding strategies into practice this term?

8.4 Consulting with a Learning Specialist

Make an appointment to visit your Learning Center or Academic Support Center on campus to discuss the results of your note-taking, reading, and studying self-assessment in Exercise 8.1 (or any other learning self-assessment you may have taken). Ask for recommendations about how you can improve your learning habits in your lowest score area. Following your visit, answer the following questions.

Learning Resource Center Reflection

1. Who did you meet with in the Learning Center?

2. What steps were recommended to you for improving your academic performance?

3. How likely is it that you will take the steps mentioned in the previous question?

   (a) definitely,
   (b) probably,
   (c) possibly, or
   (d) unlikely. Why?

4. Do you plan to see a learning specialist again? (If yes, why? If no, why not?)

8.5 PEPS Learning Style Inventory Reflection

1. Looking at your PEPS preference chart, what surprises you the most? Why?

2. Is your dominant learning style visual, auditory, or kinesthetic? How can you use this to help you be successful in your classes?

3. According to the preference chart, do you prefer more or less structure when it comes to assignment details? How can you use this to your advantage in your college courses?

4. What area on the preference chart would you most like to improve upon? Why? Write a three- to five-step detailed action plan stating how you will improve in this area.

8.6 List and describe at least five principles discussed in this chapter that can help you take better notes in class and improve your reading comprehension.

1.

2.

3.

4.

5.

Now explain how you can put these principles into practice.

Notes

Notes

Test-Taking Skills and Strategies

WHAT TO DO BEFORE, DURING, AND AFTER TESTS

This chapter supplies you with a systematic set of strategies for improving your performance on different types of tests that can be used before, during, and after exams, helping you to become more "test wise" and less "test anxious."

Chapter Preview

Acquire effective strategies to improve your performance on multiple-choice, true–false, and essay tests.

Learning Goal

 Think About It—Journal Entry 9.1

Thought Starter

On which of the following types of tests do you tend to perform better?

a) Multiple-choice tests

b) Essay tests

Why?

_____

_____

_____

_____

Learning in college courses typically takes place in a three-stage process: (1) acquiring information from lectures and readings; (2) studying that information and storing it in your brain as knowledge; and (3) demonstrating that knowledge on exams. The following sections of this chapter contain strategies relating primarily to the third stage of this learning process and they are divided into three categories:

* Strategies to use *in advance* of a test,
* Strategies to use *during* a test, and
* Strategies to use *after* test results are returned.

Pre-Test Strategies: What to Do *in Advance* of Tests

Your ability to remember material on a test that you studied prior to the test depends not only on how long and how well you studied, but also on the type of test questions used to test your memory. You may be able to remember what you've studied if you're tested in one format (e.g., multiple-choice) but not if tested in a different format (e.g., essay). Thus, the type of questions that will appear on an upcoming test should influence the type of study strategies you use to prepare for the test. Test questions can be classified into the following two major categories, depending on the type of memory required to answer them.

1. *Recognition test questions* ask you to select or choose the correct answer from choices that are provided for you. Falling into this category are multiple-choice, true–false, and matching questions. These test questions don't require you to supply or produce the correct answer on your own; instead, you're asked to recognize or pick out the correct answer—similar to picking out the "correct" criminal from a lineup of potential suspects.

2. *Recall test questions* require you to retrieve information you've studied and reproduce it on your own. As the word "recall" implies, you have to re-call ("call back") information and supply it yourself—as opposed to picking it out from information supplied for you. Recall test questions include essay and short-answer questions that require you to provide your own answer—in writing.

Since recognition test questions (e.g., multiple-choice or true–false) ask you to recognize or pick out the correct answer from answers provided for you, reading your class notes and textbook highlights and identifying key information may be an effective study strategy—because it matches the type of mental activity you'll be performing on the exam—reading test questions and identifying correct answers provided to you.

On the other hand, recall test questions, such as essay questions, require you to retrieve information and generate your own answers. They don't involve answer recognition; they require answer *production*—you produce the answer in writing. If you study for essay tests by just looking over your class notes and reviewing your reading highlights, you're using a study strategy that doesn't align with or match what you'll be expected to do on the test itself, which is to supply the correct information yourself. To prepare for essay test questions, you need to practice *retrieval*—recalling the information on your own—without looking at it.

Two essay-test preparation strategies that ensure you engage in memory retrieval are: (a) recitation and (b) creation of retrieval cues. Each of these strategies is described below.

Recitation

Stating aloud the information we want to remember—without looking at that information—is a memory-improvement strategy known as *recitation*. Memory is strengthened substantially when we reproduce on our own what we're trying to remember, instead of simply looking it over or rereading it (Roediger & Karpicke, 2006). Research consistently indicates that this type of self-testing may be the most powerful of all test-preparation strategies (Carey, 2014). Recitation strengthens memory and better prepares you for essay tests because it:

- Requires *more mental effort* to dig out (retrieve) the answer on its own, which strengthens memory for the answer and allows the brain to practice exactly what it's expected to do on essay tests.

- Gives you clear *feedback* about whether or not you know the material. If you can't retrieve and recite it without looking at it, you know for sure that you won't be able to recall it at test time and need to study it further. You can provide yourself with this feedback by putting the question on one side of an index card and the answer on the flip side. If you find yourself flipping over the index card to look at the answer in order to remember it, this shows you can't retrieve the information on your own and you need to study it further. (To create electronic flash cards, see: www.studystack.com or studyblue.com)
- Encourages you to *use your own words*. If you can paraphrase it—rephrase what you're studying in your own words—it's a good indication you really understand it; and if you really understand it, you're more likely to recall it at test time.

Recitation can be done silently, by speaking aloud, or by writing out what you're trying to recall. Speaking aloud or writing out what you're reciting are particularly effective essay-test preparation strategies because they involve physical activity, which ensures that you're actively involved and engaged in the learning process.

Creating Retrieval Cues

Suppose you're trying to remember the name of a person you know; you know you know it, but just can't recall it. If a friend gives you a clue (e.g., the first letter of the person's name or a name that rhymes with it), it's likely to suddenly trigger your memory of that person's name. What your friend did was provide a retrieval cue. A *retrieval cue* is a type of memory reminder (like a string tied around your finger) that brings back to mind what you've temporarily forgotten.

Research shows that students who can't remember previously studied information are better able to recall that information if they're given a retrieval cue. In a classic study, students studied a long list of items, some of which were animals (e.g., giraffe, coyote, and turkey). After they finished studying, students were given a blank sheet of paper and asked to write down the names of those animals. None of the students were able to recall all of the animals that appeared on the list they previously studied. However, when the word "animals" was written on top of the answer sheet to provide students with a retrieval cue, they were able to recall many of the animals they had forgotten (Tulving, 1983). Research findings such as these suggest that category names can serve as powerful retrieval cues. By taking pieces of information you need to recall on an essay test and organizing it into categories, you can then use the category names as retrieval cues at test time. Retrieval cues work because memories are stored in the brain as part of an interconnected network. So, if you're able to recall one piece or segment of the network (the retrieval cue), it can trigger recall of other pieces of information linked to it in the same network (Willingham, 2009).

 ## Think About It—Journal Entry 9.2

Think about items of information you need to remember in a course you're taking this term. Group these items into a category that can be used as a retrieval cue to help you remember them.

1. What's the course?

_____

_____

_____

2. What's the category you've created as a retrieval cue?

_____

_____

_____

3. What items of information would this retrieval cue help you recall?

_____

_____

_____

_____

Another strategy for creating retrieval cues is to come up with your own catchword or catchphrase to "catch" or batch together all related ideas you're trying to remember. Acronyms can serve as catchwords, with each letter acting as a retrieval cue for a batch of related ideas. For instance, suppose you're studying for an essay test in abnormal psychology that will include questions testing your knowledge of different forms of mental illness. You could create the acronym SCOT as a retrieval cue to help you remember to include the following key elements of mental illness in your essay answers: Symptoms (S), Causes (C), Outcomes (O), and Therapies (T).

Strategies to Use *Immediately Before* a Test

1. **Before the exam, take a brisk walk or light jog.** Physical activity increases mental alertness by increasing oxygen flow to the brain; it also decreases tension by increasing the brain's production of emotionally "mellowing" brain chemicals (e.g., serotonin and endorphins).
2. **Come fully armed with all the test-taking tools you need.** In addition to the basic supplies (e.g., no. 2 pencil, pen, blue book, Scantron, calculator, etc.), bring backup equipment in case you experience equipment failure (e.g., an extra pen in case your first one runs out of ink or extra pencils in case your original one breaks).

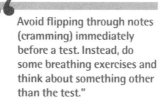

"Avoid flipping through notes (cramming) immediately before a test. Instead, do some breathing exercises and think about something other than the test."

—*Advice to first-year students from a college sophomore*

3. **Get to the classroom as early as possible.** Arriving early allows you to take a few minutes to get into a relaxed pretest state of mind by thinking positive thoughts, taking slow, deep breaths and stretching your muscles.
4. **Sit in the same seat you normally occupy in class.** Research indicates that memory is improved when information is recalled in the same place where it was originally received or reviewed (Sprenger, 1999). Thus, taking a test in the same place where you heard the information delivered will likely improve your test performance.

Studies also show that when students take a test on material in the same environment where they studied the material, they tend to remember more of it at test time than do students who study the material in one place and take a test on that material in a different place (Smith & Vela, 2001). While it's unlikely you will be able to do all your studying in the same room where your test will be taken, it may be possible to do a short, final review session in your classroom or in an empty classroom with similar features. This should strengthen your memory because the physical features of the room become associated with the material you're trying to remember. Seeing these features again at test time can help trigger your memory of that material.

A classic, fascinating study supporting this recommendation was once conducted on a group of deep sea divers. Some divers learned a list of words on a beach, while the others learned the list underwater. They were later tested for their memory of the words. Half the divers who learned the words on the beach remained there to take the test; the other half were tested underwater. Half the divers who studied the words underwater took the test in the same place; the other half took the test on the beach. The results showed that the divers who took the test in the same place where they learned the list recalled 40% more of the items than the divers who did their learning and testing in different places (Godden & Baddeley, 1975). This study provides strong evidence that memory is strengthened when studying and testing takes place in the same location.

Other intriguing studies have shown that if students are exposed to a certain aroma while they're studying (e.g., the smell of chocolate) and they're later exposed to that same smell during a memory test for what they studied, they display better memory for the information they studied (Schab & Crowder, 2014). One possible, practical application of this finding to improve your memory during a test is to put on a particular cologne or perfume while studying, and put in on again on the day of the test. This may improve your memory for the information you studied by matching the scent of your study environment with the scent of your test environment. Although this strategy may seem silly, keep in mind that the area of the human brain where humans perceive smell has connections with the brain's memory centers (Jensen, 2005). These neurological connections probably explain why people often report that certain smells can trigger long-ago memories (e.g., the smell of a summer breeze triggering memories of summer games played during childhood).

Since smell is related to memory, you may be able to use smell as a retrieval cue to stimulate recall for information you've studied. In so doing, you may improve your performance on essay tests.

Box 9.1

Nutritional Strategies for Strengthening Academic Performance

Is there a "brain food" that can enhance our test performance? Can we "eat to learn" or "eat to remember"? Some animal studies suggest that memory can be improved by consumption of foods containing lecithin—a substance that helps the brain produce acetylcholine—a chemical that plays an important role in the formation of memories (Ueda, et al., 2011; Ulus & Wurtman, 1977). Fish contains high amounts of lecithin, which may explain why fish is sometimes referred to as "brain food."

Despite the results of some animal studies, not enough human research evidence is available to conclude that consuming certain foods will dramatically increase our ability to retain information or knowledge. However, the following nutritional strategies can improve mental performance on days when our knowledge is tested.

1. Eat breakfast on the day of the exam. Studies show that when students eat a nutritious breakfast on the day they are tested, they achieve higher test scores (Phillips, 2005; Schroll, 2006). Breakfast on the day of an exam should include grains, such as whole wheat toast, whole grain cereal, oatmeal, or bran, because those foods contain complex carbohydrates that deliver a steady stream of energy to the body throughout the day. These complex carbohydrates also help your brain produce a steady stream of serotonin—a brain chemical that reduces tension and anxiety.

No man can be wise on an empty stomach."
—*George Eliot, 19th-century English novelist*

2. Make the meal you eat before a test a light meal. The meal you consume nearest test time should not be a large one because it will elevate your blood sugar to a high level, causing large amounts of insulin must be released into the bloodstream to reduce the blood sugar level. This draws blood sugar away from the brain, causing mental fatigue.

3. If you need an energy boost prior to a test, eat a piece of fruit rather than a candy bar. Candy bars are processed sweets that infuse synthetic sugar into the bloodstream, which provides a short and sudden burst of energy. That's the good news; the bad news is that this short-term rush of blood sugar and sudden jolt of energy can also increase bodily tension followed by a sharp drop in energy and feelings of sluggishness (Haas, 1994; Thayer, 1997). The key is to find a food that elevates energy without elevating tension and sustains this energy level over an extended period of time. The best nutritional option for producing such a steady, sustained state of higher energy is *natural* sugar contained organically in a piece of fruit, not processed sugar artificially slipped into a candy bar.

4. Avoid consuming caffeine before a test. Although caffeine increases alertness, it's a stimulant that elevates bodily tension and nervousness. These are feelings you don't want to experience during a test, particularly if you're prone to test anxiety. Also, caffeine is a diuretic, which means it will increase your urge to urinate. You certainly want to avoid this urge during an exam—when you're confined to a classroom and can't afford to take time to tend to urological needs (or be distracted by them).

Consuming large doses of caffeine or other stimulants before exams is likely to increase your alertness, but it's also likely to increase your level of stress and test anxiety.

Strategies to Use *During* Tests

1. Before you receive a copy of the test, write down any hard-to-remember terms, formulas, and equations and any memory-retrieval cues you may have created as soon as you start the exam. This will help ensure you don't forget this important information when you start focusing your attention on the test itself.

2. First answer questions you know well and carry the most points. Before automatically attacking the first question that appears on test, take a moment to check out the overall layout of the test and note the questions that are worth the most points and the questions you're best prepared to answer. Tackle these questions first. Put a checkmark next to questions whose answers you're unsure of and come back to them later—after you've answered the questions you're sure of—to ensure you get these points added to your total test score before you run out of test time.

3. If you experience "memory block" for information you know, use the following strategies to unlock it.
   - Mentally put yourself back in the environment in which you studied. Recreate the situation by mentally picturing the place where you first heard or saw the information and where you studied it—including sights, sounds, smells, and time of day. This memory-improvement strategy is referred to as *guided retrieval*, and research supports its effectiveness for recalling information of any kind, including information recalled by eyewitnesses to a crime (Glenberg, 1997; Glenberg, et al., 1983).
   - Think of any idea or piece of information that relates to the information you can't remember. Studies show that when students forget information they studied, they're more likely to suddenly remember that information if they first recall a piece related to it in some way (Reed, 2013). This strategy works because related pieces of information are typically stored in the same area of the brain—as part of an interconnected neural network.
   - Take your mind off the question by turning to another question. This frees your subconscious to focus on the forgotten information, which can suddenly trigger your conscious memory of it. Moving on to other test questions also allows you to find information included in later test questions that may enable you to recall information related to the earlier question that you previously forgot.

- Before turning in your test, carefully review and double-check your answers. This is the critical last step in the test-taking process. Sometimes the performance pressure and anxiety associated with test taking can cause students to overlook details, misread instructions, unintentionally skip questions, or make absentminded mistakes. So take time to look over your answers and check for any mindless mistakes you may have made. Avoid the temptation to immediately cut out of class after answering the last test question because you're pooped out or stressed out. When you think about the amount of time and effort you put into preparing for the exam, it's foolish not to take a little more time to detect and correct any silly mistakes you made that could cost you points and lower your test score.

Think About It—Journal Entry 9.3

I'm most likely to experience memory block during exams in the following subjects:

_____

_____

_____

_____

_____

During tests, when I experience memory block, I usually . . .

_____

_____

_____

_____

_____

Strategies for Answering Multiple-Choice Test Questions

You're likely to encounter multiple-choice questions on college tests (particularly in large classes), on certification or licensing exams for particular professions (e.g., nursing and teaching), as well as on admissions tests for graduate school (e.g., master's and doctoral degree programs) and professional school (e.g., law school and medical school). Since you're likely to take multiple-choice tests frequently in college and beyond, this section of the text is devoted to a detailed discussion of strategies for taking such tests. These strategies are also applicable to *true–false* questions, which are really essentially multiple-choice questions with two choices: true or false.

1. **Read the question and think of the answer in your head before looking at the possible answers.** If the answer you thought of is in the list of possible answers, it is likely that is the correct answer. However, if you see an answer that is similar but you feel is more correct, select that answer. Thinking of the answer in your head allows you to recall what you studied before recognizing it.

2. **Read all choices listed and use a *process-of-elimination* approach.** Search for the correct answer by first eliminating choices that are clearly wrong; continue to do so until you're left with one choice that represents the best option. Keep in mind that the correct answer is often the one that has the highest probability or likelihood of being true; it doesn't have to be absolutely true—just truer than all the other choices listed.

A process-of-elimination approach is an effective test-taking strategy to use when answering difficult multiple-choice questions.

3. **For a choice to be correct, the *entire statement* must be true.** If any part of the statement is inaccurate or false, eliminate it because it's an incorrect answer.

4. **Use *test-wise* strategies when you cannot narrow down your choice to one answer.** Your first strategy on any multiple-choice question should be to choose an answer based on your knowledge of the material, not by guessing the correct answer based on how the question is worded. However, if you've relied on your knowledge, used the process-of-elimination strategy to eliminate clearly wrong choices, and you're still left with two or more answers that appear to be correct, then you should turn to being *test wise*—use the wording or placement of the test question itself to increase your chances of selecting the correct answer (Flippo & Caverly, 2009). Here are three test-wise strategies you can use for multiple-choice questions when more than one choice appears to be correct:

   - **Pick the answer that contains qualifying words.** Correct answers are more likely to contain modifying words such as "usually," "probably," "often," "likely," "sometimes," "perhaps," or "may." Knowledge often doesn't come neatly packaged as absolute or unqualified truths, so choices are more likely to be false if they make broad generalizations or contain words such as "always," "every," "never," "only," "must," and "completely."
   - **Pick the longest answer.** True statements often require more words to make them true.

- Pick a middle answer rather than the first or last answer. If you've narrowed down the correct answer to either "a" or "c," go with "c." Similarly, if you've narrowed your choices to "b" or "d," your best bet may be to go with "b." Studies show that instructors have a tendency to place the correct answer in the middle, rather than as the first or last choice (Miller, Linn, & Gronlund, 2012)—perhaps because they think the correct answer will be too obvious or stand out if it's placed at the top or bottom of the list.

5. **Check to be sure that your answers are aligned with the right questions.** When looking over your test before turning it in, search carefully for questions you may have skipped and intended to go back to later. Sometimes you may skip a test question on a multiple-choice test and forget to skip the number of that question on the answer form. This will throw off all your other answers by one space or line and result in a disastrous "domino effect" of wrong answers that can do major damage to your total test score. To prevent this from happening, check the alignment of all your answers to be sure there are no blank spaces on your column of answers and that your order of answers line up with the order or test questions.

6. **Don't feel that you must remain locked into your first answer.** When reviewing your answers on multiple-choice and true–false tests, don't be afraid to change an answer after you've given it more thought. Don't buy into the common belief that your first answer is always your best answer. There have been numerous studies on the topic of changing answers on multiple-choice and true–false tests, dating all the way back to 1928 (Kuhn, 1988). These studies consistently show that most changed test answers go from being incorrect to correct, resulting in improved test scores (Bauer, Kopp, & Fischer, 2007; Prinsell, Ramsey, & Ramsey, 1994). In one study of more than 1,500 students' midterm exams in an introductory psychology course, it was discovered that when students changed answers, 75% of the time they changed from an incorrect to correct answer (Kruger, Wirtz, & Miller, 2005). These results probably reflect the fact that students often catch mistakes when reading the question again or when they find some information later in the test that causes them to reconsider (and correct) their first answer to an earlier test question.

   If you have good reason to think an answer change should be made, don't be afraid to make it. The only exception to this general rule is when you find yourself changing many of your original answers; this may indicate that you were not well prepared for the exam and are just doing a lot of guessing and second-guessing.

Be sure you don't overthink the question and talk yourself into changing a correct answer. Sometimes "go with your gut" is the best decision if you are not sure. Don't change an answer if you are not sure the new answer is correct.

 ## Think About It—Journal Entry 9.4

On multiple-choice exams, do you ever change your original choice?

If you do make changes, what's your usual reason for doing so?

_____

_____

_____

_____

Strategies for Answering Essay Questions

Along with multiple-choice questions, essay questions are among the most common types of test questions on college exams. The following strategies are recommended for strengthening your performance on essay questions.

1. Look for "mental action" verbs in the question that point to the type of thinking your instructor expects you to demonstrate in your answer. **Box 9.2** contains a list of thinking verbs you're likely to see in essay questions and the type of mental action typically called for by each of these verbs. As you read this list, place a check mark next to the verbs that represent a type of thinking you've rarely or never been asked to do in the past.

Box 9.2

Mental Action Verbs Commonly Found in Essay-Test Questions

Analyze. Break the topic down into its key parts and evaluate the parts in terms of their accuracy, strengths and weaknesses.

Compare. Identify the similarities and differences between major concepts.

Contrast. Identify the differences between ideas, particularly sharp differences and clashing viewpoints.

Describe. Provide details (e.g., who, what, where, and when).

Discuss. Analyze (break apart) and evaluate the parts (e.g., strengths and weaknesses).

Document. Support your judgment and conclusions with scholarly references or research evidence.

Explain. Provide reasons that answer the questions "why?" and "how?"

> I keep six honest serving men. They taught me all I knew. Their names are what and why and how and when and where and who."
> —*Rudyard Kipling,* "The Elephant's Child," The Just-So Stories

Illustrate. Supply concrete examples or specific instances.

Interpret. Draw your own conclusion and explain why you came to that conclusion.

Support. Back up your ideas with logical reasoning, persuasive arguments, or statistical evidence.

Think About It—Journal Entry 9.5

Which of the mental actions listed in **Box 9.2** was most often required on your high school writing assignments?

_____

_____

_____

_____

Which was least often (or never) required?

_____

_____

_____

_____

_____

2. **Make an outline of your key ideas before you start writing sentences.** First, do a quick "information dump" by jotting down the main points you plan to make in your essay answer in outline form. Outlines are effective for several reasons:

   - **An outline ensures you don't forget to include your most powerful points.** The points listed in your outline serve as memory-retrieval cues that help you remember the "big picture" before getting lost in all the details.

   - **An outline earns you points by improving your answer's organizational quality.** In addition to reminding you of the points you need to make, an outline gives you a plan for ordering your ideas in a sequence that flows smoothly from beginning to middle to end. One factor instructors consider when awarding points for an essay answers is how well that answer is organized. An outline will make your answer's organization clearer and more coherent to the reader, which will increase the amount of points you're awarded.

   - **An outline helps reduce test anxiety.** By organizing your points ahead of time, you can focus on expressing (writing) those points without the added stress of figuring out _what_ you're going to say at the same time you're trying to figure out _how_ to say it.

   - **An outline can add points to answers you don't have time to complete.** If you run out of test time before writing out your full answer to an essay question, an outline shows your instructor what you planned to include in your written answer. The outline itself is likely to earn you some points because it demonstrates your knowledge of the major points called for by the question.

Exhibit 1

Identical twins
Adoption
Parents/family tree

6/6

1. There are several different studies that scientists conduct, but one study that they conduct is to find out how genetics can influence human behavior in <u>identical twins</u>. Since they are identical, they will most likely end up very similar in behavior because of their identical genetic makeup. Although environment has some impact, genetics are still a huge factor and they will, more likely than not, behave similarly. Another type of study is with <u>parents and their family trees</u>. Looking at a subject's family tree will explain why a certain person is bipolar or depressed. It is most likely caused by a gene in the family tree, even if it was last seen decades ago. Lastly, another study is with adopted children. If an <u>adopted child</u> acts a certain way that is unique to that child, and researchers find the parents' family tree, they will most likely see similar behavior in the parents and siblings as well.

No freewill
No afterlife

6/6

2. The monistic view of the mind-brain relationship is so strongly opposed and criticized because there is a belief or assumption that <u>free will</u> is taken away from people. For example, if a person commits a horrendous crime, it can be argued "monistically" that the chemicals in the brain were the reason, and that a person cannot think for themselves to act otherwise. This view limits responsibility.

Another reason that this view is opposed is because it has been said that <u>there is no afterlife</u>. If the mind and brain are one and the same, and there is <u>NO</u> difference, then once the brain is dead and is no longer functioning, so is the mind. Thus, it cannot continue to live beyond what we know today as life. <u>And</u> this goes against many religions, which is why this reason, in particular, is heavily opposed.

> **A college sophomore's answers to short essay questions that demonstrate effective use of bulleted lists or short outlines (in the side margin) to ensure recall of key points.**

3. **Get directly to the point on each question.** Avoid elaborate introductions that take up your test time (and your instructor's grading time) but don't earn you any points. An answer that begins with the statement "This is an interesting question that we had a great discussion on in class . . ." is pointless because it doesn't add points to your test score. Timed essay tests often leave you pressed for time; don't waste that time on flowery introductions that contribute nothing to your test grade.

One effective way to get directly to the point on essay questions is to include part of the question in the first sentence of your answer. For example, suppose the test question asks you to, "Argue for or against capital punishment by explaining how it will or will not reduce the nation's homicide rate." Your first sentence could be, "Capital punishment will not reduce the homicide rate for the following reasons . . ." Thus, your first sentence becomes your thesis statement—it points you directly to the major points you're going to make in your answer and earns immediate points for your answer.

4. **Answer essay questions with as much detail as possible.** Don't assume that your instructor already knows what you're talking about or will be bored by details. Instead, take the approach that you're writing to someone who knows little or nothing about the subject—as if you're an expert teacher who is explaining it from scratch.

Note

As a general rule, it's better to over-explain than under-explain your answers to essay questions.

5. **Support your points with evidence—facts, statistics, quotes, or examples.** When you're answering essay questions, take on the mindset of a lawyer: make your case by presenting concrete evidence (exhibit A, exhibit B, etc.).

6. **Leave space between your answers to each essay question.** This strategy will enable you to easily add information to your original answer if you recall something later in the test that you would like to include.

7. **Proofread your answers for spelling and grammar.** Before turning in your test, proofread what you've written and correct any spelling or grammatical errors you find. Catching and correcting clerical errors will improve your test score. Even if your instructor doesn't explicitly state that grammar and spelling count toward your grade, these mechanical mistakes are still likely to influence your professor's overall evaluation of your written work.

8. **Neatness counts.** Many years of research indicate that neatly written essays are scored higher than sloppy ones, even if the answers are essentially the same (Huck & Bounds, 1972; Hughes, Keeling, & Tuck, 1983; Pai, et al., 2010). These findings aren't surprising when you consider that grading essay answers is a time-consuming, labor-intensive task that requires your instructor to plod through multiple answers written by students with multiple styles of handwriting—ranging from crystal clear to quasi-cryptic. If you make your instructor's job a little easier by writing as clearly as possible and cleaning up any sloppy markings before turning in your test, you're likely to earn more points for your answers.

Strategies for Online Tests

More instructors are using technology to enhance their courses. It is very possible that you could have to take an online test even when you are not taking an online course. When taking a test online, you should always read the instructions carefully. Below are some things you should consider when taking online tests.

1. **Online tests are often timed.** Because you are taking these tests outside of class, you are able to use your notes and books. For this reason, many instructors will place a time limit on the test. If you do not complete the test in time, it will shut off when your time is up and you won't be able to do the rest of the test. Be sure to study for online timed tests. You will not have enough time to look up all of the answers, and if you don't study, you won't do well.

2. **Backtracking might be prohibited.** Sometimes you have to answer a question before you can move on to the next question, and once you move on, you cannot go back and change an answer. If this is a timed test, be sure to use your time wisely and don't spend too much time on any one question.

If you have not taken an online test before, be sure to ask your instructor what to expect. Online tests can be created just like an in-class test. Don't assume that online tests will be made up of only multiple-choice and true–false questions.

Be sure you do not wait until the last minute to take your online test. Because you are dealing with technology something can (and often will) go wrong. Be prepared for something to go wrong (e.g., you lose your internet connection in the middle of the test) by giving yourself enough time to deal with any problems that might arise during the test.

When taking online tests, be sure you are using a reliable computer and you are free from anything that could take your focus away from the test (e.g., cell phone, children, etc.). If something does go wrong during the test, be sure to contact your instructor immediately.

Post-Test Strategies: What to Do *After* Receiving Your Test Results

Successful test performance involves both forethought (preparation before the test) and afterthought (reflection after the test). Often, when students get a test back, they check to see what grade they got, then stuff it in a binder or toss it into the nearest wastebasket. Don't fall prey to this unproductive habit; instead, use your test results as feedback to improve your future performance. Reflect on your results and ask yourself: How can I learn from this? How can I put it to use to correct my mistakes and repeat my successes? Remember: A test score isn't an end result; it may tell you where you are now, but it doesn't tell you where you'll end up. Use your results as a means to another end—a higher score on the next test.

> "When you make a mistake, there are only three things you should do about it: admit it; learn from it; and don't repeat it."
>
> —Paul "Bear" Bryant, legendary college football coach

 Think About It—Journal Entry 9.6

What do you usually do with tests and assignments after they're returned to you? Why?

_____

_____

_____

_____

_____

Note

If you do poorly on an exam, don't get bitter—get better. View your mistakes in terms of what they can do for *you, not* to *you. A poor test performance can be turned into a productive learning experience, particularly if it occurs early in the course when you're still learning the rules of the game. You can use your test results as a valuable source of feedback for improving your future performance and final course grade.*

In the movie and record industry, if the first cut isn't successful, additional "takes" ("take two," "take three," etc.) are made until it's done right. Successful students do the same thing: If they make a mistake on "take one," they stick with it and continue working to improve their performance on the next take.

In the movies, a clipboard is used to signal the next take (shooting) if the previous take was unsuccessful. Take the same approach to your test performances. If you make a mistake, consider it "take one," learn from it, and approach the next take with the mindset that you're going to improve your previous performance.

> "A man who has committed a mistake and doesn't correct it is committing another mistake."
>
> —Confucius, ancient Chinese philosopher and educator

Listed below are strategies you can use to transform your test results into performance-enhancing feedback.

1. **When you get a test back, determine where you gained points and lost points.** Pinpoint what went right so you do it again, and troubleshoot what went wrong so you don't make the same mistake again. On test questions where you lost points, use the strategies summarized in **Box 9.3** to pinpoint the source of the problem.

Box 9.3

Strategies for Pinpointing the Source of Lost Points on Tests

On test questions where you lost points, identify the stage in the learning process where the breakdown occurred by asking yourself the following questions.

- Did I have the information I needed to answer the question correctly? If you didn't have the information needed to answer the question, where should you have acquired it in the first place? Was it information presented in class that didn't get into your notes? If yes, consider adopting strategies for improving your classroom listening and note-taking (such as those found on **p. 120**). If the missing information was contained in your assigned reading, check whether you're using effective reading strategies (such as those listed on **pp. 153–154**).

- Did I have the information but didn't study it because I didn't think it was important? If you didn't expect the information to appear on the test, review the strategies for detecting the most important information delivered during class lectures and in reading assignments. (See strategies on **p. 162**.)

- Did I study it, but didn't retain it? Not remembering information you studied may mean one of three things:

  (a) You didn't learn it deeply and didn't lay down a strong enough memory trace in your brain for you to recall it at test time. This suggests you need to put in more study time or use a different study strategy to learn it more deeply. (See **p. 254** for specific **strategies**.)

  (b) You may have tried to cram in too much study time just before the exam and may have not given your brain time enough to "digest" (consolidate) the information and store it in long-term memory. The solution may be to distribute your study time more evenly in advance of the next exam and take advantage of the "part-to-whole" study method. (See **pp. 211–212**.)

  (c) You studied hard and didn't cram, but you may need to study smarter or more strategically. (See strategies on **p. 237**.)

- Did I study the material but didn't really understand it or learn it deeply? This suggests you may need to self-monitor your comprehension more carefully while studying to track whether you're truly understanding the material and moving beyond "shallow" or "surface" learning. (See **p. 218**.)

- Did I know the material but lost points due to careless test-taking mistakes? If this happened, the solution may simply be to take more time to review your test after completing it and check for absent-minded errors before turning it in. Or, your careless errors may have resulted from test anxiety that interfered with your concentration and memory. If you think this was the factor, consider using strategies for reducing test anxiety. (See **p. 240**.)

2. Get feedback from your instructor. Start by noting any written comments your instructor made on your exam; keep these comments in mind when you prepare for the next exam. You can seek additional feedback by making an appointment to speak with your instructor during office hours. Come to the appointment with a positive mindset about improving your next test performance, not complaining about your last test grade.

3. Seek feedback from professionals in your Learning Center or Academic Support Center. Tutors and other learning support professionals can also be excellent sources of feedback about adjustments you can make in your test preparation and test-taking strategies. Ask these professionals to take a look at your tests and seek their advice about how to improve your test performance.

4. Seek feedback from your classmates. Your peers can also be a valuable source of information on how to improve your performance. You can review your test with other students in class, particularly with students who did well. Their test answers can provide you with models of what type of work your instructor expects on exams. You might also consider asking successful students what they did to be successful, such as how they prepared for the test and what they did during the test.

    Teaming up after tests and assignments *early in the term* is especially effective because it enables you to get a better idea of what the instructor will expect from students throughout the remainder of the course. You can use this information as early feedback to diagnose your initial mistakes, improve your next performance, and raise your overall course grade—while there's still plenty of time in the term to do so. (See **Box 9.4** for a summary of the type of feedback you should seek from others to best strengthen your academic performance.)

Box 9.4

Key Features of Performance-Enhancing Feedback

When asking for feedback from others on your academic performance, seek feedback that has the following performance-improvement features:

- Effective feedback is *specific*. Seek feedback that identifies precisely what you should do to improve your performance and how you should go about doing it. After a test, seek feedback that provides you with more than information about what your grade is, or why you lost points. Seek specific information about what particular adjustments you can make to improve your next performance.

- Effective feedback is *prompt*. After receiving your grade on a test or assignment, *immediately* review your performance and seek feedback as soon as possible. This is the time when you're likely most motivated to find out what you got right and wrong, and it's also the time when you're most likely to retain the feedback you receive.

- Performance-enhancing feedback is *proactive*. Seek feedback *early* in the learning process. Be sure to ask for feedback at the start of the term. This will leave you with plenty of time and opportunity to use the feedback throughout the term to accumulate points and earn a higher final grade.

Think About It—Journal Entry 9.7

How would you rate your general level of test anxiety during tests? (Circle one.) Explain.

high   moderate   low

What types of tests or subjects tend to produce the most test stress or anxiety for you?

Why?

Strategies for Reducing Test Anxiety

High levels of anxiety can interfere with the ability to recall information that's been studied and increases the risk of making careless concentration-related errors on tests—such as, overlooking key words in test questions (Fernández-Castillo & Caurcel, 2014; Tobias, 1993). Studies also show that students who experience high levels of test anxiety are more likely to use ineffective "surface"-level study practices that rely on memorization, rather than more effective "deep-learning" strategies that involve seeking meaning and understanding (Biggs & Tang, 2007; Ramsden, 2003). The strategies listed below can help you recognize and minimize test anxiety.

1. **Understand what test anxiety is and what it's not.** Don't confuse anxiety with stress. Stress is a physical reaction that prepares your body for action by arousing and energizing it; this heightened level of arousal and energy can actually strengthen your performance. In fact, to be totally stress-free during an exam may mean that you're too laid back and could care less about how well you're doing. Peak levels of performance—whether academic or athletic—are not achieved by completely eliminating stress. Research shows that experiencing a *moderate* level of stress (neither too high nor too low) during exams and other performance-testing situations serves to maximize alertness, concentration, and memory (Sapolsky, 2004). The key is to keep stress at a manageable

level so you can capitalize on its capacity to get you pumped up or psyched up, but prevent it from reaching a level where you become stressed out or psyched out.

If you often experience the following physical and psychological symptoms during tests, it probably means your stress level is too high and may be accurately called *test anxiety*.

- You feel bodily symptoms of tension during the test, such as pounding heartbeat, rapid pulse, muscle tension, sweating, or a queasy stomach.
- You have difficulty concentrating or maintaining your focus of attention while answering test questions.
- Negative thoughts and feelings rush through your head, such as fear of failure or self-putdowns (e.g., "I always mess up on exams.")
- You rush through the test just to get it over with and get rid of the uncomfortable feeling you're experiencing.
- Even though you studied and know the material, you go blank during the test and forget much of what you studied. However, after turning in the test and leaving the test situation, you're often able to remember the information you were unable to recall during the exam.

2. **Use effective test preparation strategies prior to the test.** Test-anxiety research indicates that college students who prepare well for tests and use effective study strategies prior to tests—such as those discussed in Chapter 6—experience less test anxiety during tests (Zeidner, 1995; Zohar, 1998). Studies also show that there is a strong relationship between test anxiety and procrastination—that is, students who put off studying to the very last minute are more likely to report higher levels of test anxiety (Carden, Bryant, & Moss, 2004). The high level of pretest tension caused by last minute rushing to prepare for an exam often carries over to the test itself, resulting in higher levels of tension during the exam. Furthermore, late night cramming deprives the brain of stress-relieving dream (REM) sleep (Voelker, 2004), causing the sleep-deprived student to experience higher levels of anxiety the following day—the day of the test.

3. **Stay focused on the test in front of you, not the students around you.** Don't spend valuable test time looking at what others are doing and wondering whether they're doing better than you are. If you came to the test well prepared and still find the test difficult, it's very likely that other students are finding it difficult too. If you happen to notice that other students are finishing before you do, don't assume they breezed through the test or that they're smarter than you. Their faster finish may simply reflect the fact that they didn't know many of the answers and decided to give up and get out, rather than prolong the agony.

4. **During the test, concentrate on the here and now.** Devote your attention fully to answering the test question that you're currently working on; don't spend time thinking (and worrying) about the test's outcome or what your grade will be.

5. **Focus on the answers you're getting right and the points you're earning, rather than worrying about what you're getting wrong and how many points you're losing.** Our thoughts can influence our emotions (Ellis, 2004), and positive emotions—such as those associated with optimism and a sense of accomplishment—can improve mental performance by enhancing the brain's ability to process, store, and retrieve information (Fredrickson & Branigan, 2005). One way to maintain a positive mindset is to keep in mind that college

> " If you focus on growth . . . on making progress instead of proving yourself, you are less likely to get depressed because you won't see setbacks and failures as reflecting your own self worth." And you are less likely to stay depressed, because feeling bad makes you want to work harder and keep striving."
>
> *—Heidi Grant Halvorson, psychologist and author of Succeed: How We Can Reach Our Goals*

tests are often designed to be more difficult than high school tests, so it's less likely that students will get 90% to 100% of the total points. You can still achieve a good grade on a college test without having to achieve a near-perfect test score.

6. **Don't forget that it's just a test, not a measure of your intelligence, academic ability, or self-worth.** No single test can measure your true intellectual capacity or academic talent. In fact, the test grade you earn may not be a true indicator of how much you've actually learned. A low test grade also doesn't mean you're not capable of doing better work or destined to end up with a poor grade in the course—particularly if you adopt a "growth mindset" that views mistakes as learning opportunities (see **p. 237**) and uses test results as feedback for improving future performance (see **p. 237**).

7. **If you continue to experience test anxiety after trying to overcome it on your own, seek assistance from a professional in your Learning (Academic Support) Center or Personal Counseling Office.** You can try to overcome test anxiety (or any other personal issue) through the use of self-help strategies. However, if the problem persists after you've done your best to overcome it, there's no need to keep struggling on your own; instead, it's probably time to seek help from others. This doesn't mean you're weak or incompetent; it means you have the emotional intelligence and resourcefulness to realize your limitations and capitalize on the support networks available to you.

Chapter Summary and Highlights

Effective performance on college tests involves strategies used in advance of the test, during the test, and after test results are returned. Good test performance starts with good test preparation and awareness of the type of test questions you will be expected to answer (e.g., multiple-choice or essay). Test questions can be classified into two major categories, depending on the type of memory required to answer them: (1) *recognition* questions and (2) *recall* questions. Each of these types of questions tests your knowledge and memory in a different way.

Recognition test questions ask you to select or choose the correct answer from choices provided for you. Falling into this category are multiple-choice, true–false, and matching questions. These test questions don't require you to supply or produce the correct answer on your own; instead, you recognize or pick out the correct answer. Since recognition test questions ask you to recognize or select the correct answer from among answers provided for you, reviewing your class notes and textbook highlights may be an effective study strategy for multiple-choice and true–false test questions because it matches the type of mental activity you'll be asked to perform on the exam—which is to read test questions and look for the correct answer.

Recall test questions, on the other hand, require you to retrieve information you've studied and reproduce it on your own. This means you have to recall (re-call or "call back") the information you studied and supply it yourself. Recall test questions include essay and short answer questions; these questions don't involve answer recognition, but answer *production*—you produce the answer in writing. Studying for these types of test questions require *retrieval*—such as reciting the information without looking at it.

Effective test performance not only involves effective test-preparation strategies, but also effective test-taking strategies. For multiple-choice tests, effective test-taking strategies include using a *process-of-elimination* approach to weed out incorrect answers before identifying the best option, and *test-wise* strategies that use the wording of test questions to increase the likelihood of choosing the correct answer (e.g., choosing the longest answer and eliminating answers that contain absolute truths or broad generalizations).

Lastly, effective test performance involves carefully reviewing test results and using them as feedback to improve your future performance and final course grade. When test results are returned, determine where you earned and lost points. Pinpoint what went right so you continue doing it, and troubleshoot what went wrong so you prevent it from happening again.

Learning More through the World Wide Web: Internet-Based Resources

For additional information on strategic test-taking and managing test anxiety, see the following websites:

Test-Taking Strategies:
https://miamioh.edu/student-life/rinella-learning-center/academic-counseling/self-help/test-taking/index.html

https://www.stmarys-ca.edu/academics/academic-resources-support/student-academic-support-services/tutorial-academic-skills-8

Overcoming Test Anxiety:
http://www.studygs.net/tstprp8.htm

http://www.sic.edu/files/uploads/group/34/PDF/TestAnxiety.pdf

References

Bauer, D., Kopp, V., & Fischer, M. R. (2007). Answer changing in multiple choice assessment: change that answer when in doubt—and spread the word! *BMC Medical Education, 7*, 28–32.

Biggs, J., & Tang, C. (2007) *Teaching for quality learning at university* (3rd ed.) Buckingham: SRHE and Open University Press.

Carden, R., Bryant, C., & Moss, R. (2004). Locus of control, test anxiety, academic procrastination, and achievement among college students. *Psychological Reports, 95*(2) 581–582.

Carey, B. (2014). *How we learn*. London: Random House.

Ellis, A. (2004) Rational emotive behavior Therapy: It works for me—It can work for you. Amherst, NY: Prometheus Books.

Fernández-Castillo, A., & Caurcel, M. J. (2014). State test-anxiety, selective attention and concentration in university students. *International Journal of Psychology, 50*(4), 265–271.

Flippo, R. F., & Caverly, D. C. (2009). *Handbook of college reading and study strategy research* (2nd ed.). New York: Lawrence Erlbaum Associates.

Fredrickson, B. L., & Branigan, C. (2005). Positive emotions broaden the scope of attention and thought-action repertoires. *Cognition & Emotion, 19*, 313–332.

Glenberg, A, M. (1997). What memory is for. *Behavioral and Brain Sciences, 20*, 1–55.

Glenberg, A. M., Schroeder, J. L., & Robertson, D. A. (1998). Averting the gaze disengages the environment and facilitates remembering. *Memory & Cognition, 26*(4), 651–658.

Godden, D., & Baddeley, A. (1975). Context dependent memory in two natural environments. *British Journal of Psychology, 66*(3), 325–331.

Haas, R. (1994). *Eat smart, think smart*. New York: HarperCollins.

Huck, S., & Bounds, W. (1972). Essay grades: An interaction between graders' handwriting clarity and the neatness of examination papers. *American Educational Research Journal, 9*(2), 279–283.

Hughes, D. C., Keeling, B., & Tuck, B. F. (1983). Effects of achievement expectations and handwriting quality on scoring essays. *Journal of Educational Measurement, 20*(1), 65–70.

Jensen, E. (2005). *Teaching with the brain in mind* (2nd ed.). Alexandria, VA: Association for Supervision and Curriculum Development.

Kruger, J., Wirtz, D., & Miller, D. (2005). Counterfactual thinking and the first instinct fallacy. *Journal of Personality and Social Psychology, 88*, 725–735.

Kuhn, L. (1988). What should we tell students about answer changing? *Research Serving Teaching, 1*(8).

Miller, M. D., Linn, R. L., & Gronlund, N. E. (2012). *Measurement and assessment in teaching* (7th ed.). Englewood Cliffs, NJ: Pearson.

National Resource Center for the First-Year Experience and Students in Transition (2004). *The 2003 Your First College Year (YFCY) Survey*. Columbia, SC: Author.

Pai, M. R., Sanji, N., Pai, P. G. & Kotian, S. (2010). Comparative assessment in pharmacology multiple choice questions versus essay with focus on gender differences. *Journal of Clinical and Diagnostic Research* [serial online], *4*(3), 2515–2520.

Phillips, G. W. (2005). Does eating breakfast affect the performance of college students on biology exams? *Bioscene, 30*(4), 15–19.

Prinsell, C. P, Ramsey, P. H., & Ramsey, P. P. (1994). Score gains, attitudes, and behaviour changes due to answer-changing Instruction. *Journal of Educational Measurement, 31*, 327–337.

Ramsden, P. (2003). *Learning to teach in higher education* (2nd ed.). London: RoutledgeFalmer.

Rankin CH, Abrams T, Barry RJ, Bhatnagar S, Clayton DF, Colombo J, Coppola G, Geyer MA, Glanzman DL, Marsland S, McSweeney FK, Wilson DA, Wu CF, Thompson RF (2009) Habituation revisited: an updated and revised description of the behavioral characteristics of habituation. Neurobiol Learn Mem 92:135–138

Reed, S. K. (2013). *Cognition: Theory and applications* (3rd ed.). Belmont, CA: Wadsworth/Cengage.

Roediger, H., & Karpicke, J. (2006). The power of testing memory: Basic research and implications for educational practice. *Perspectives on Psychological Science, 1*(3), 181–210.

Sapolsky, R. (2004). *Why zebras don't get ulcers.* New York: W. H. Freeman.

Schab, F. R., & Crowder, R.G. (2014). *Memory for odors.* New York: Psychology Press.

Schroll, R. M. (2006). Effects of breakfast on memory retention of students at the college level. *Saint Martin's University Biology Journal, 1*, 35–50.

Smith, S., & Vela, E. (2001). Environmental context-dependent memory: A review and meta-analysis. *Psychonomic Bulletin & Review, 8*(2), 203–220.

Sprenger, M. (1999). *Learning and memory: The brain in action.* Alexandria, VA: Association for Supervision and Curriculum Development.

Thayer, R. E. (1997). *The origin of everyday moods: Managing energy, tension, and stress.* New York: Oxford University Press.

Tobias, S. (1993). *Overcoming math anxiety.* New York: W.W. Norton.

Tulving, E. (1983). *Elements of episodic memory.* Oxford: Clarendon Press/Oxford University Press.

Ueda, Y., Wang, M. F., Irei, A. V., Sarukura, N., Sakai, T., & Hsu, T. F. (2011). Effect of dietary lipids on longevity and memory in SAMP8 mice. *Journal of Nutritional Science Vitaminol, 57*(1), 36-41.

Ulus, I. H., Scally, M. C., & Wurtman, R. C. (1977). Choline potentiates the induction of adrenal tyrosine hydroxylase by reserpine, probably by enhancing the release of acetylcholine. Life Sci 21:145–148.

Voelker, R. (2004). Stress, sleep loss, and substance abuse create potent recipe for college depression. *Journal of the American Medical Association, 291*, 2177–2179.

Willingham, D. B. (2009). *Cognition: The thinking animal.* Upper Saddle River, NJ: Pearson.

Zeidner, M. (1995). Adaptive coping with test situations: A review of the literature. *Educational Psychologist, 30*(3), 123–133.

Zohar, D. (1998). An additive model of test anxiety: role of exam-specific expectations. *Journal of Educational Psychology, 90*, 330–340.

Chapter 9 Exercises

9.1 Quote Reflections

Review the sidebar quotes contained in this chapter and select two that were especially meaningful or inspirational to you.

For each quote, provide a three- to five-sentence explanation why you chose it.

9.2 Reality Bite

Bad Feedback: Shocking Midterm Grades

Fred has enjoyed his first weeks on campus. He has met lots of people and really likes being in college. He's also very pleased to discover that, unlike high school, his college schedule doesn't require him to be in class for five to six hours per day. That's the good news. The bad news is that unlike high school, where his grades were all As and Bs, Fred's first midterm grades in college are three Cs, one D, and one F. He's stunned and a bit depressed by his midterm grades because he thought he was doing well. Since he never received grades this low in high school, he's beginning to think that he's not college material and may flunk out.

Reflection Questions

1. What factors may have caused or contributed to Fred's bad start?

2. What are Fred's options at this point?

3. What do you recommend Fred do right now to get his grades up and avoid being placed on academic probation?

4. What might Fred do in the future to prevent this midterm setback from happening again?

9.3 Self–Assessment of Test-Taking Habits and Strategies

Rate yourself in terms of how frequently you use these test-taking strategies according to the following scale:
4 = always, 3 = sometimes, 2 = rarely, 1 = never

1. I take tests in the same seat I usually sit in to take class notes.	4	3	2	1
2. I answer easier test questions first.	4	3	2	1
3. I use a process-of-elimination approach on multiple-choice questions to eliminate choices until I find one that is correct or appears to be the most accurate option.	4	3	2	1
4. Before answering essay questions, I look for key action words indicating what type of thinking I should display in my answer (e.g., "analyze," "compare").	4	3	2	1
5. On essay questions, I outline or map out the major ideas I'll include in my answer before I start writing sentences.	4	3	2	1
6. I look for information included on the test that may help me answer difficult questions or that may help me remember information I've forgotten.	4	3	2	1
7. I leave extra space between my answers to essay questions in case I want to come back and add more information later.	4	3	2	1
8. I carefully review my work, double-checking for errors and skipped questions before turning in my tests.	4	3	2	1

Self-Assessment Reflections

Which of the above strategies do you already use?

Of the ones you don't use, which one are you *most* likely to implement and *least* likely to implement? Why?

9.4 Midterm Self-Evaluation

At this point in the term, you may be experiencing the "midterm crunch"—a wave of midterm exams and due dates for assignments. This is a good time to step back and assess your academic progress.

Using the form below, list the courses you're taking this term and the grades you are currently receiving in each of these courses. If you don't know what your grade is, take a few minutes to check your syllabus for your instructor's grading policy and add up your scores on completed tests and assignments; this should give you at least a rough idea of where you stand in your courses. If you're having difficulty determining your grade in a course, even after checking your course syllabus and returned tests or assignments, ask your instructor how you could estimate your current grade.

	Course No.	Course Title	Grade
1.			
2.			
3.			
4.			
5.			

Reflection Questions

1.   Were these the grades you *expected*? If not, were they better or worse than you anticipated?

2.   Were these the grades you were *hoping* for? Are you pleased or disappointed?

3.   Do you see any patterns in your performance that suggest what you're doing well and what you need to improve?

4.   If you had to pinpoint one action you could immediately take to improve your lowest course grades, what would it be?

9.5 Calculating Your Midterm Grade Point Average

Use the information below to calculate what your grade point average (GPA) would be if your current course grades turn out to be your final grades for the term.

How to Compute Your Grade Point Average (GPA)

Most colleges and universities use a grading scale ranging from 0 to 4 to calculate a student's grade point average (GPA) or QPA (quality point average). Some schools use a grading system that involves only letters (A, B, etc.), while other institutions use letters as well as pluses and minuses (A-, B+, etc.). Check you college catalog or student handbook to determine what grading system is used at your campus.

The typical point value (points earned) by different letter grades are listed below.

Grade = Point Value

A = 4.0
A- = 3.7
B+ = 3.3
B = 3.0
B- = 2.7
C+ = 2.3
C = 2.0
C- = 1.7
D+ = 1.3
D = 1.0
D- = .7
F = 0

1. **Calculate the grade points you're earning in each of your courses this term by multiplying the course's number of units (credits) by the point value of the grade you're now earning in the course.** For instance, if you have a grade of B in a three-unit course, that course is earning you 9 grade points; if you have a grade of A in a two-unit course, that course is earning you 8 grade points.

2. **Calculate your grade point average by using the following formula:**

$$\text{GRADE POINT AVERAGE (GPA)} = \frac{\text{Total Number of Grade Points for all Courses}}{\text{Divided by Total Number of Course Units}}$$

For instance, see the fictitious example below:

Course	Units	×	Grade	=	Grade Points
Roots of Rock 'n' Roll	3	×	C (2)	=	6
Daydreaming Analysis	3	×	A (4)	=	12
Surfing Strategies	1	×	A (4)	=	4
Wilderness Survival	4	×	B (3)	=	12
Sitcom Analysis	2	×	D (1)	=	2
Love and Romance	3	×	A (4)	=	12
	16				48

$$\text{GPA} = \frac{48}{16} = 3.0$$

Reflection Questions

1. What is your GPA at this point in the term?

2. At the start of this term, was this the GPA you expected to attain? If there is a gap between the GPA you expected to achieve and the GPA you now have, what do you think accounts for this discrepancy?

3. Do you think your actual GPA at the end of the term will be higher or lower than it is now? Why?

Note: It's very typical for GPAs to be lower in college than they were in high school, particularly during the first year of college. Here are the results of one study that compared students' high school GPAs with their GPAs after their first year of college:

- A total of 29% of beginning college students had GPAs of 3.75 or higher in high school, but only 17% had GPAs that high at the end of their first year of college.

- A total of 46% had high school GPAs between 3.25 and 3.74, but only 32% had GPAs that high after the first year of college (National Resource Center for the First-Year Experience and Students in Transition, 2004).

Chapter 9 Reflection

What are some ways that you currently prepare for tests that do not seem to be working? Why do you think these methods of preparing for tests do not work?

List and explain three ways you can change your current methods of preparing for tests that you believe will help you perform better on tests.

1.

2.

3.

What are two things you can do during the test that will help you perform better?

1.

2.

What are two things you can do after you get your test back that can help you perform better on future tests?

1.

2.